The Red Dream

The Red Dream

The Chinese Communist Party and the Financial Deterioration of China

Carl E. Walter

WILEY

This edition first published 2022

Registered Offices
John Wiley & Sons, Inc., 111 River Street, Hoboken, NJ 07030, USA
John Wiley & Sons Singapore Pte. Ltd, 1 Fusionopolis Walk, #06-01 Solaris South Tower, Singapore 138628

Editorial Office
1 Fusionopolis Walk, #06-01 Solaris South Tower, Singapore 138628

For details of our global editorial offices, customer services, and more information about Wiley products visit us at www.wiley.com.

Wiley also publishes its books in a variety of electronic formats and by print-on-demand. Some content that appears in standard print versions of this book may not be available in other formats.

Library of Congress Cataloging-in-Publication Data is Available:

ISBN 9781119896159 (Hardback)
ISBN 9781119896166 (ePDF)
ISBN 9781119896173 (epub)

Cover Design: Wiley
Cover Image: © Nerthuz/Getty Images:

SKY10035374_071922

For Lesley Yu Yicen

Contents

Preface

It's been a decade since I sat in Beijing spending a couple of summers thinking and writing about China's financial system. In those days Fraser Howie (my co-author on other Wiley books), who had started working at real jobs in Singapore, and I would laugh when we dug up bits and pieces of the story that were new to us. But access to a good library was one thing I lacked in Beijing and I was interested in understanding how the country's fiscal system interacts with its banks. A stint at Stanford in 2013 solved that problem. What I found changed my thinking about China and led eventually to the writing of this book during another stint at Stanford in 2021. So here goes another attempt to influence the way we look at China's history with the emphasis on financial history.

My reading in 2013 led to the conclusion that the basic source of extreme leverage in China's banks, enterprises, and the state itself is found in the fiscal arrangements of its self-reliant local governments. Self-reliance and inadequate budgetary income have driven inefficient capital investment especially in an overgrown real estate sector and its millions of empty and unfinished apartments. There is a shadow fiscal system at the local levels that is so deeply imbedded in how the party operates locally that even the most determined fiscal reforms have ultimately been rejected by its "immune" system. In short, local debt, the obverse side of which is bank and enterprise lending, cannot be explained only by reference to the last decade of overflowing liquidity or poor management or the party's interference; it has always been a major feature of China's fiscal system.

The second observation is that the party, which can do whatever it wants, has failed to adjust its aspirations to the level of fiscal revenues that the official system can generate. The party recognizes no constraints; the pull of the China Dream may be too strong. But there are constraints in the real world. Each year the party presents a new central and local budget for the coming year to the National People's Congress. But after approval, there is no one who holds the party at any level accountable for borrowing excessively outside of this budget not simply to meet a budget gap, but to build unplanned infrastructure and buildings. Who said every provincial capital could have a 100-story building or two? And who is going to fund such lending or live in the buildings and use the infrastructure when the population in 2100 is the same as it was in 1976?

Looking into the fiscal system reminded me that China, as a modern country, is at best 20 years old. It has come a very long way in two decades, but it remains an unfinished project much influenced by history. It would be fair to say that in 1979 China had no fiscal system. During the Republican Era in the 1930s work had begun to establish one but was interrupted by events. In any event, Nanking's reach did not extend far beyond the city's walls. After the revolution Soviet advisors gave it a try as part of their effort to establish a planned economy. That didn't work for reasons that are well documented. From 1957 to the start of the reform era at best Beijing depended on negotiations with provincial governments and state enterprises for whatever fiscal revenues it could generate. Any semblance of a technical fiscal system was purely propaganda for outsiders.

Looking at this brief history, what stands out is the self-reliance of local governments at all levels. Prior to the revolution it was said that regional governments were run by warlords, so it is not surprising that a look at China's fiscal system today reveals the existence of a shadow fiscal system. Local governments and their party secretaries then, as now, are responsible for what happens in their jurisdictions. With little in the way of revenue trickling down from higher administrative levels, they must fend for themselves. And it has always been this way.

This is where banks come in. During the 1980s local officials generated what Beijing called "extrabudgetary" or "extrasystem" revenues by pilfering bank branches and state enterprises, all of which were "owned" locally. The scale of such income in some years exceeded official revenues, sometimes by a multiple. In 1994 Beijing was able to pass a Budget Law that for the first time specified types of taxes and what government level collected which tax. In the face of opposition by the richer provinces, Beijing committed the "original sin," promising the majority poor provinces central government fiscal transfers to make up for shortfalls and, as a result, prohibited them from fiscal borrowing; there would be no need. Ever since, and especially in recent years, Beijing has had to borrow to make good on this promise, and the banks bought the government bonds.

The Budget Law also walled off state enterprises, at least directly, from local raids on their bank accounts. At the same time, two important things happened as part of the economic reform effort. First, Beijing devolved capital investment in new enterprises and infrastructure out of the national budget and into the hands of state enterprises and local governments. This offered locals a new way to access banks since the bulk of such investment was officially designated as "self-raised" funds. The second event was the privatization from 1997 of people's homes and the development of a huge new industry—real estate—that now generates nearly one-third of the country's GDP. Developers cannot build new homes without land and land was something local governments had in spades. Experimentation created a process allowing the sale, not of land itself—that belongs to the Emperor—but of "land use rights," a new and huge source of revenue for those localities with the best locations.

But with these new revenues also came the obligation to prepare the land for development. If the land was in the city center, then the local government had to resettle residents; remove buildings; and install power, water and sewers. If it was agricultural land, it was the same story, perhaps even more expensive. Over the first few years of this activity, arable land in China was reduced nearly 6 percent. All this cost significant amounts of money, more than offsetting revenues from sales of land rights. It was raised by securitizing bank loans into long maturity trust plans, then selling the plans to banks and rich individuals.

On an ongoing basis, the land business was a money loser; expenses have always exceeded revenues. As a result local governments got caught up in a constant fundraising process that can only be partially offset by sales. They must sell more land to meet earlier debt obligations. Real estate became a Ponzi scheme and this explains why there are 64 million unoccupied apartments, ghost towns and, not to forget, the bullet train network. Looking only at self-raised funds for capital investment prior to the post-2008 decade suggests that local debt equals somewhere around 25–40 percent of total banking loans or 40–60 percent of the all important bank funding source, corporate and household deposits.

This leads to the conclusion that the fundamental reason for China's excessive leverage in its banks and enterprises today is found in the decentralized fiscal arrangements of self-reliant local governments. The second point is that the party has failed to adjust its aspirations to the level of fiscal revenues the official system can generate or hold its local party officials to their official budgets. With this background it is not surprising that China's state banks have grown like ". . . trees reaching for Heaven." Today the four largest are Globally Systemically Important Banks (GSIB) whose health impacts the world economy. The system's total assets are 3.5 times the country's GDP. They have grown to this scale organically and not through acquisitions and mergers as has JPMorgan Chase, their only rival in size. Their funding and scale of lending has been the result of China's policy of "opening up." The country's entry to the World Trade Organization (WTO) in 2001 resulted in the creation of a middle class to rival that of the United States. And, as the world knows, Chinese, faced with few investment alternatives or a sound social security system, save their money in banks, state banks. This is the party's deliberate policy.

Chinese state banks have grown at a compound rate of 17 percent a year since 2008, yet they maintain strong performance metrics, including sustained low non-performing asset levels. The answer to such success is found in the shadow banking system that has grown up along with them. Products include wealth management, trust plans, asset-based securities, debt-equity swaps and more, all designed to enable the state banks to sculpt their balance sheets. Flexible accounting also adds its own support. How can these four banks create such huge piles of financial assets at such a rate in an economy that in 2008 totaled US$4.4 trillion as against that of the US at US$15 trillion? They lent to local governments, real estate, the railways and to the public, the only sectors that have true scale. And they lent with long maturities; the loans stacked up.

If one existed, an official consolidated balance sheet for the Chinese government sector would show the impact of the party's economic and financial decisions. Fortunately a rough, but instructive one can be developed from official sources and compared with work done earlier by Chinese analysts. The result shows China's state with total consolidated assets of only 952 billion *yuan* in 1978 and 123 trillion in 2008; not much really changed during those two decades. But by 2018 the balance sheet had exploded to almost 400 trillion *yuan*, quadrupling in just a decade. It is not surprising that in 2018 financial assets including foreign reserves made up two-thirds of total assets—investment takes time after all—and 89 percent of total liabilities and equity. One would think a de-leveraging campaign could be quite successful looking at these numbers!

But with that number of liabilities the equity account owned by the party (no need to talk about a state here) has been crushed. In 1978 the party's stake in the state sector was nearly 90 percent; in 2018 it was 5 percent with minority shares of the same level—household and some foreign investment in A- and H-shares. Reviewing these assets the question must be asked, can the party meet its obligations to the household sector, which holds currency, deposits and equity in the state totaling 87 trillion? The answer is barely.

These results can be supported by calculating the costs associated with financial crises in China and the United States. There are two sets of crises that may work. The first is the US savings and loan crisis of 1980–1994, a crisis termed a "debacle" by the Federal Deposit Reserve Corporation. This is compared to China's bank restructuring effort of 1997–2005, an effort that was spectacularly successful. The second set relates to the global financial crisis of 2009. The costs to the United States of resolving this crisis are compared to China's response. For the two US crises, the Congressional Office of the Budget has calculated official cost figures and presented them to Congress. For China I have done cost calculations based on estimates derived from official data and shown in Chapter 4. For the first set of crises, the costs to total assets and recovery rates in the two countries are fairly comparable, but for China the cost to GDP of recapitalizing its banks was quite high, while for the United States it was only 4.3 percent. The cost to the United States of the cleanup after the mortgage crisis was nearly US$500 billion, constituting 33 percent of assets involved, but again only 3.4 percent of GDP. The recovery rate was similar to the savings and loan (S&L) crisis.

But China's strategy of preventing a financial crisis *in advance* by providing financial support to its major state banks and enabling almost continuous recapitalization has cost a fortune if compared to the original level of banking assets in 2009. From the start of the deleveraging campaign in 2016–2020, costs have amounted to 17 percent of total banking assets. The value of this pay-as-you-go support simply added up reaches nearly US$5 trillion or 42 percent of 2015's GDP. No estimate is possible for recoveries that would reduce the number. In both crises the costs to China have been similar. Where has this money gone?

The answer is that the financial system has absorbed shadow banking risk in all its nooks and crannies while bureaucrats at all levels push risk aside to get on with their jobs. No one knows or possibly can know just how much risk is out there. The regulators and some officials in Beijing from 2016 are making a stab at deleveraging, but this seems a distant second in importance to the volatile program to create "common prosperity" through a takeover of the private sector.

Unlike the earlier bank restructuring costs, this time China cannot inflate the costs away: they are too big. The other way out is a sustained deleveraging effort in combination with the bureaucracy and party backing away from the private sector. The growth stimulated there might then make it possible over time for deleveraging to take effect. But small Chinese banks on the periphery have already begun to fail, as has a major core part of the banking system, China Huarong. And the true costs of the party's deliberate bankruptcy of China Evergrande and China's real estate sector as a whole have yet to be exposed in the local government, banking, and trust systems, but they are there. And what of the collateral underlying the people's mortgages? Banks will be forced to ask for more as property values decline. In Japan the bursting of a massive real estate bubble seriously exacerbated a banking crisis in the 1980s. An old regulatory paradigm had first to be demolished by near-continuous bank failures before the Japanese government could fully understand the nature of the crisis and take substantive actions to end it. Earlier action might have stabilized the banking system and perhaps even alleviated the pains of the deflation that followed. China's political and economic system is very different from Japan's, but there are also some important similarities. And the obstacles thrown up by old thinking may prevent the country's leaders from seeing the extent of the financial crisis they have created.

I'm hoping that *The Red Dream*, like *Red Capitalism* a decade ago, will be seen as a constructive comment that sparks a conversation about how China has arrived today as the world's second largest economy and what the cost of this has been. There are many people and institutions I must thank who have helped me in the research that has gone into this book. First of all, I must thank the Shorenstein Asia Pacific Area Research Center (APARC) at Stanford's Freeman Spogli Institute for International Affairs. I have been fortunate to spend two stints at APARC, and without them this book would not have been possible. For this I must thank the sponsorship of Professors Jean Oi and Andy Walder, who have always found interest in my point of view. Also at Stanford I must thank Zhaohui Xue, the East Asia Library's Chinese studies librarian and the rest of the staff at the library there who always made me feel welcome. Stanford's East Asian Library is a real open-stack treasure of real and not digital materials. Speaking of Stanford, I'd also like to thank the wonderful staff at APARC as well as those at the Braun Music Center where I was inspired on a daily basis by the students I heard practicing. Stanford turned the writing of this book into a truly enjoyable experience.

Thanks go to Fraser for providing extensive comments on versions of several chapters and for help on charts; I wish he'd been along for the full ride. Thanks also go to Christine Wong, *the* expert on China's fiscal system, who looked at that chapter of the book. Christine was so generous with her time and shared many of her papers. I met Carsten Holz at Stanford in 2013. His 2001 paper on Chinese state bankruptcy inspired me to follow up. Carsten also read and commented on an early version of what became Chapter 6. I must truly thank Andy Walder, who commented extensively on all chapters; his comments enabled me to make real improvements and additions to my original plan. In 2013 I participated in a conference in Hong Kong where I met Don Chew, the publisher of the *Journal of Applied Corporate Finance*, a publication with a long pedigree in the financial world. Since then, Don has asked me to provide articles and I have gladly done so; it has been a wonderful cooperation because he is a great editor. Larry Goodman, president of the Center for Financial Stability, has always been interested in the things I am interested in and his support has always been positive. Thanks also go to Andy Andreasen and Josh Cheng, who have helped me think about things Chinese such as yellow millet (sic), to Andrew Zhang, who explained the Balloon Theory to me, and to Wren Hsu Ponder, who came up with the data I needed when I needed it. It was also great to catch up with Richard McGregor in Australia to go over the famous Boao Forum of 2009; I'm glad he was there.

I also need to thank all of the folks at Wiley who have so kindly published the last three of the books I have written (or co-written). This time in particular I would like to thank Syd Ganaden, Purvi Patel, Sharmila Srinivasan, Missy Garnett and Tami Trask for copyediting, and the people who do the cover artwork. It's always been easy working with Wiley and I certainly appreciate their support.

Special thanks go to my brother-in-law, Lloyd Yu, who allowed me to stay at his home during both of my stints at Stanford. Although I tried to balance my presence with restaurant meals, trips to BevMo and, when wanted, cleaning up the kitchen, little can compensate for a stranger, especially a brother-in-law! in the household. Lloyd's cooking and his magical backyard are nonpareil. Thanks also go to my Number 1 daughter Dorothy and her husband Roman Hasenbeck for putting me up after Lloyd put his house on the market. Both are great hosts and cooks and their cat, Fritz, a terrific, if trying, service animal! And what can I say about my wife, to whom I have dedicated the book? Lesley, my lifelong sweetheart, allowed me to disappear from our home in New York for several months while I worked on finishing this book at Stanford. It is impossible for me to even begin to thank her enough for her support and understanding.

I have traipsed across several research specialties in writing this book and am quite aware that I have made many errors of data interpretation and judgment. But these are mine and I look forward to receiving corrections.

Carl E. Walter
Stanford
March 2022

List of Abbreviations

ABS   asset-backed security
AIC   asset investment company
AMC   asset management company
BOJ   Bank of Japan
CBIRC   China Banking and Insurance Regulatory Commission
CDB   China Development Bank
CSRC   China Securities Regulatory Commission
CGB   China government bond
CIC   China Investment Corporation
COB   Congressional Office of the Budget
FDIC   Federal Deposit Insurance Corporation
FHA   Federal Housing Administration
FSLIC   Federal Savings and Loan Insurance Corporation
GSIB   Global Systemically Important Bank
IMF   International Monetary Fund
JGB   Japanese government bond
LGFP   local government financing platform
MOF   Ministry of Finance

NAO   National Audit Office
NPC   National People's Congress
NPL   nonperforming loan
PBOC   People's Bank of China
RTC   Resolution Trust Corporation
SAFE   State Administration for Foreign Exchange
SASAC   State Administration of State-owned Assets Commission
SOE   state-owned enterprise
SPV   special-purpose vehicle
WMP   wealth management product
WTO   World Trade Organization

Chapter 1

From Turning Point to Turning Point

Now people suddenly think we are lovable!

—*Senior official, Boao Forum, April 2009*

Beijing: huge black Yukons, Suburbans, and Navigators swept by at 160 kilometers an hour on the airport expressway rushing to receive two American presidents. Making a dark wall, they thundered down the fast lane locking in two lanes of Chinese commuters. It seemed awe-inspiring. The next day, August 8, 2008, at 8 o'clock in the morning the two presidents celebrated the opening of the new US Embassy. The time was meant to be auspicious. In the evening, seated in the Bird's Nest with a roaring and heavily sweating crowd, they joined in the fantastic opening ceremony of the Beijing Summer Olympics. Two American presidents, father and son, both with China in their personal histories. Everyone was comparing the Olympics with the 1964

Tokyo Olympics that ushered Japan back into the fraternity of nations. Would 2008 mark China's big coming out party too? The welcoming of two US presidents, a new US Embassy, the large foreign population of students and expats with families, new international schools, and countless foreign tourists—the list goes on. All evidence on the ground suggested that China's WTO boom had launched it into the "normal country" orbit.

An Abrupt About-Face

But the rumblings in the background were growing louder. The US financial system appeared to be in a slow-motion collapse since early 2007. It grew slowly in intensity in early 2008 and then exploded right after the Beijing Olympics when the US government took possession of the two national mortgage banks, Fannie Mae and Freddie Mac. Things moved quickly then. Bank of America bought Merrill Lynch! How could this happen? Merrill had been the first investment bank Beijing chose to underwrite its historic first US dollar bond. Merrill had even structured and underwritten China's first-ever IPO of a state enterprise, Shanghai Petrochemical. Then Lehman Brothers filed for bankruptcy. The Chinese could not believe the US government would allow a blue chip bank, as they considered Lehman, to go under. Then it was Morgan Stanley's turn to face a liquidity crisis. Morgan Stanley! The Chinese owned 9.9 percent of Morgan and their concerns grew exponentially. The unthinkable happened next: after a run on money market funds the net asset value of one fund closed under one dollar; this was theoretically impossible. The carnage rolled on with Wachovia and Washington Mutual both bankrupted. And it was not just the United States: Canada, England, Switzerland, Australia, and Japan all under pressure and all putting in place measures to ensure market liquidity; all this just in September, right after the Olympics!

So Chinese Communist Party members, assuming they still believed in Marxism, had good reason to think that the crisis of capitalism had arrived and that the US government was powerless to do anything about it. In December the government nationalized General Motors and Chrysler, complete financial chaos. Beijing did not sit still. Without consultation it introduced a four trillion *yuan* (US$590 billion) stimulus package in late 2008. This was the largest such stimulus the world had ever seen, amounting to nearly 13 percent of the country's GDP. After a sharp downturn in 2008 the economy began to grow, by 8.7 percent in 2009 and 10.4 percent in 2010, making China the first to emerge from the impact of the crisis.

By February 2009, the tone in Beijing was very different when a US secretary of state arrived, downplaying human rights and asking China to keep buying US Treasury bonds. Her words must not have been convincing, since China's premier in early March publicly demanded that the US government guarantee its own debt; Wall Street's lessons hadn't entirely sunk in apparently.[1] In March, Wang Qishan met with Hank Paulson, Secretary of the US Treasury, and bluntly commented, "You were my teacher, but now here I am in my teacher's domain, and look at your system, Hank. We aren't sure we should be learning from you anymore."[2] That comment without a doubt reflected the general tone among China's top officials.

A "triumphant" Boao Forum, China's Davos for Asia, supplied proof of this conclusion in early April. China's premier took the lead laying out what he called the roadmap for Asia's future development; the United States was not included. The head of China's sovereign wealth fund, as was his character, was not nearly so diplomatic. Describing his past difficulties accessing investments in Europe due to protectionism, he said, "I want to thank those in the past year who were particularly protectionist regarding China. Take Europe as an example; officials there before I even arrived wanted me to accept that any investment would not exceed 10 percent or would be without voting rights. I said, 'No,' I cannot accept this' . . . So this year [2009] I would like to especially thank these protectionists who would not let me invest a cent last year . . . Now people suddenly think we are lovable!"[3] So it's not just Xi Jinping and his Wolf Warriors that changed the tone of relations with the United States and the western world; it had changed well before 2012.

And what an abrupt about-face! Just two years previously these same people were cheering the salvation of China's banking system accomplished with the guidance of Wall Street and the money of the people they now disrespected. In fact, the primary reason China was surviving the crisis at all well was because of the just-completed recapitalization of its major banks. Of course, in March 2009, when their annual results were announced, their booming profitability was made much of in *People's Daily*, the party newspaper.

How, then, should one view the Olympics brought to such a triumphant close barely six months previously? Was it Beijing's effort to show that China had joined the world as a member? Or were the two US presidents who attended simply bearing tribute and paying their respect to the new leading country that had just emerged into full light? Thanks to the spiraling financial crisis, for the Chinese the Olympics became a statement of the country's superiority. September 2008, topped by Lehman Brothers' collapse, changed how the Chinese leadership saw everything; the new US Embassy, the visits by two US presidents, one sitting? All changed. September 2008 ushered in the era of the China Dream.

It seems, however, that party officials may have forgotten the basic elements of dialectical materialism, the *yin* and *yang* and not only of Chinese history, but of Western history as well. They now seem overwhelmed by the vision that in less than a decade, not even 10 years, China had gone from stagflation to achieving superiority to America; if Big Brother, the Soviet Union, could fall in a day, why not the United States? And Wall Street fed this notion with research showing the Chinese economy growing larger than that of the United States by 2030—always on the sell side, Wall Street. In the background, however, the Chinese system cried out for attention. As many local officials and state enterprise *laozong* (老总: bosses) routinely said, "The system doesn't work (or, maybe, it's non-responsive: 体制不灵)." This book is about showing why those people felt that way.

The Golden Age: A Short Story

As a short aside, it may provide some perspective on current events to be briefly reminded of the past four decades of Chinese history. Each and every decade marked the end of one policy approach and the start of another often radically different approach, all with the aim of what? Modernizing China? Enriching the populace? Strengthening the basis of party rule? The objective has always been couched in nationalistic terms that obscured the real intent: saving the party. This objective is based on the simple equation: no party = no country. The sudden changes in political and economic approach should put an end to any idea that Chinese technocrats have known exactly what to do from the start and that China's rise has been linear; no need to mention here the years from 1949 to 1978.

The years 1978 and 1979 marked a real turning point for China as it broke away from the previous 30 years of political and economic experimentation (to put it lightly). In 1978 Hua Guofeng, Mao Zedong's anointed successor ("You take care of things, I'll not worry"), wisely stepped aside to let Deng Xiaoping take the reins. There was a nation-wide exhalation; society tangibly relaxed as politics also stepped aside. The big red billboards with "Quotations of Ma Zedong" began to be torn down—they were solid brick. The first foreign show on TV was a 15-minute tour of Disneyland. And the first Western TV show, *The Man from Atlantis*. It hardly needs be said, this marked a 180-degree turnaround in party policy.

What followed in the 1980s, a slight tinkering with the old, planned approach, proved economically and politically disastrous despite good intentions. The decade ran out chased by a political uprising that nearly toppled the regime. Tinkering did not pan out. Deng's "Southern Tour" in early 1992 saved the day and marked the second major turning point. By casually remarking to a reporter (a reporter!) that anything, even stock markets, was permissible, he set the country on a course that has seemed to be a breakthrough for China (see Figure 1.1). Deng in a few words ushered in the age of stock and debt capital markets combined with near hyperinflation. This was a total break with what had gone before; after all, the Soviet Union itself had disappeared a month before Deng's "Southern Excursion." But this anything-goes attitude left the country in stagflation at the end of the decade and facing the 1997 Asian Financial Crisis. If in 2001 the premier had not been able to seal China's entry into the WTO, would there have been a boom decade? But he did and this together with a thorough restructuring of the financial system was thought to mark China's entry into the global economy.

The world, never mind China itself, had never seen such a boom as China's. Gone were the bikes clogging the streets, now choked with cars. Gone too was the old "iron rice bowl" economy. By the eve of the 2008 summer Olympics, 300 million people established China's first middle

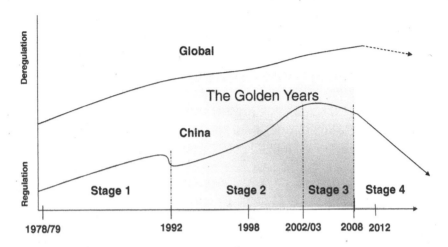

Figure 1.1 The breakthrough years, 1992–2008.

class. The coastal cities were gleaming and mobile technology was creating new worlds; the party had stepped back to let it happen. These years truly were an "Age of Openness,"[4] a Golden Age the likes of which China, at least parts of it, had not witnessed since the interwar era. Then came September 2008 and 2012. The innocuous sounding China Dream once again turned the country around 180 degrees. "Bombard the Headquarters!" became "The Headquarters bombards *you*!"[5] It is simply that the Emperor doesn't like the China that he sees. There followed a retreat behind closed doors after the outbreak of Covid-19 in late 2019: entire cities locked down, the international borders effectively closed, and they have remained so for going on three years.

Talk about whiplash—has a generation of people anywhere been put through an experience like this by their government, every decade marking a sharp shift in policies and political power? How can anyone talk of a consistent, coherent approach to economic and social development when reflecting on these 10-year sudden shifts in policy? And what about the costs involved? Across the Straits at the same time, 20 million Chinese developed a brand-new democracy with world-beating companies, including the largest branded athletic shoemaker company in the world—Poe Chen—Taiwan Semiconductor, and Foxconn. Compared to this one province, can China's government still be called effective? Now in the search for "common prosperity" they are going to go through it all again: Will the goal really be China, the new Hermit Kingdom?

Underlying Conditions

It would be nothing new to say that China's challenges today are rooted in a past that is reflected in its overstrained fiscal system. Officials running local governments are driven by a traditional fiscal incentive structure and political pressure that compel them to chase economic growth and social stability, but without the necessary resources—namely, capital. Beijing, the Imperial government, has deliberately shortchanged revenues in local budgets, but at the same time has increased expenditure responsibilities. In response, local officials across the country have created a powerful shadow fiscal system. A report by the National Audit Bureau in 2011 noted that as of 1979 no local government at any level had incurred debt. By 1985, there were 78 percent of provincial governments, 15 percent of city governments, and 13 percent of county governments borrowing outside of their budgets. By 1996, these figures were, respectively, 100 percent, 90 percent, and 87 percent.[6]

The fundamental reason for China's excessive leverage in its banks and enterprises today is found in the decentralized fiscal arrangements of highly self-reliant local governments. This system is deeply imbedded, so even the most determined fiscal reforms have ultimately been rejected by its "immune" system. Local debt, the obverse side of which is bank and enterprise lending, cannot be explained only by reference to the last decade of overflowing liquidity.

China's strong regionalism is a consequence of the country's historical development and, therefore, it has grown organically. At the time of the revolution China was an underdeveloped agricultural country with a thin modern rim. The central government in Nanking collected little fiscal revenue from the interior rural sector, and it had little influence over semi-autonomous provincial and local interests.[7] What money it could collect went to the military. In other words, Nanking was unable to channel a material share of national income in ways that would have moved the Chinese economy out of its stagnant state. In truth, there was no formal budget at all.

Central governments have always depended on local officials to generate revenues, always keeping something for themselves; it was a negotiated outcome. A start toward a formal budget was made during the 1930s but came to a halt with the Japanese invasion.[8] The post-revolution effort of Soviet experts collapsed in the face of Mao's political movements. During the 1958–1976 period of the so-called Great Leap Forward/Cultural Revolution such technical things as budgets and banks were subsumed to the politics that raged: too "expert" and not "red" enough. It was as if the civil war of the 1940s had never ended.

An eminent economist's description of China's economy as "cellular" is entirely correct even today, as local governments have remained ever more self-reliant.[9] The only connection among local governments is "up" through Beijing and not across, and regional protectionism has always been strong. This localism can be seen on China's streets: Beijing has Hyundai cabs, Tianjin its Datsuns, Shanghai its Volkswagens and Buicks, Chongqing its Fords, Chengdu its Volvos; each is related to the particular city's auto plant. The continued top-down nature of the state and the trickle-down nature of budgetary revenues, against the weight of unfunded local budgetary obligations, create the conditions that preserve regional protectionism and, ultimately, lead to the system's overall financial leverage.

Table 1.1　Distribution of budgeted revenues and expenditures by government level, 1992–2013.

% of official budget total	1992	1998	2002	2006	2010	2013
Revenues						
Central	34.0	49.5	55.0	52.8	51.1	46.6
Province	11.0	10.5	11.7	12.1	10.6	10.7
Prefecture/City	29.0	19.7	16.3	16.5	15.8	16.2
County	16.0	20.3	17.1	18.6	22.5	26.5
Expenditures						
Central	22.0	28.9	30.7	24.7	17.8	14.6
Province	13.0	18.8	19.6	18.3	17.1	16.1
Prefecture/City	34.0	24.1	28.6	22.5	22.5	22.9
County	16.0	28.2	22.0	34.4	42.6	46.3

SOURCE: Wong (2021).

Table 1.1 shows the "incentive structure" faced by local governments. As an example, local governments at the county level in 2013 received only 26.5 percent of budgetary revenues but were responsible for social services equal to 46.3 percent of official budgeted expenses. In contrast, the central government received almost half of all revenues, but was responsible for only 14.6 percent of expenditures. The bulk of those revenues Beijing apparently spent on transfers to poor provinces.

Jumping ahead a bit, this fiscal gap explains why there are 64 million[10] empty apartments scattered across the country's landscape; every capital-hungry government has eagerly cut its own deal with developers. But even such income from sales of land rights is offset against the expenses required to put power, water, sewers, roads, and the costs to move existing populations. The result is a rolling process that generates economic activity, but not profit for local governments. The end result is that real estate at the local level becomes a huge Ponzi scheme.

The cure for this, and other economic problems, cannot be found by simply rectifying the banking system or the state enterprises; this has been done already. It is found in setting political aspirations for economic development in line with the capacity of the fiscal system to generate revenue and then ensuring that there is accountability at all levels of the government. The inefficiencies and political difficulties involved in managing today's negotiated system explain why party bosses, bankers, bankruptcy clean-up specialists, and enterprise managers complain. These people are in the very bowels of the Chinese state, and they know the reality.*

The focus of this book, then, is the financial consequences of China's overextended fiscal system on the "state" itself. To do so, it is not enough to examine one by one the banks or state enterprises, or local government debt, or household savings. Instead *all* these aspects making up the

---

*Just to be clear, this book does not mean "state" in the Chinese sense of 国家, which suggests "country." Nor does it refer simply to the "government," in Chinese 政府. To be more precise, this book looks only at the "state-owned (国有)" sector for lack of a better phrase for "state sector." This definition includes everything the government, that is the party, owns in the economy, banks, enterprises, agencies, research institutes, the military, police, and armed forces.

state must be looked at as a whole. A balance sheet containing all these parts of the Chinese state is the key to seeing the overall picture of how the party has directed the country's financial resources. It also permits comparisons with other countries, including how the United States has managed financial crises and Japan to see whether there are lessons that may open the way forward. The book looks only at the "state sector" because this is where the party channels the bulk of China's capital resources; there is little need to explore the private sector, which finances itself and knows the value of money.[11]

The *Yin* and the *Yang* of the China Dream

Local governments have created a strong shadow fiscal system far beyond that of the Ministry of Finance. Money can be found in many places; state enterprises have been reliable targets, if not for money, then for project finance—for example, steel companies building urban bridges. When Beijing put a halt to this in 1994, planned capital investment projects and fees on the population took their place. When reforms made private real estate ownership possible after 1997, local governments sold land use rights to property developers. This was the most economically dynamic of all for some but not all localities: location, location, location! Capital investment and the preparation of land both require financing from banks, so there was plenty of opportunity for local governments to take their share, a share that in many years added up to far more than official revenues. The boundaries of the shadow fiscal system plus those of the official fiscal system are based on official data and are presented in Chapter 2.

This "extrabudgetary" system exists because the central government itself is always in need of more funds. So when shadow funds reach a certain scale, Beijing will seize them as a part of the official budgetary process. And regardless of Beijing's efforts, banks and enterprises continue to be the foundation of the shadow system. Figure 1.2 shows that the local government *maximum* "take," or share, from capital investment activity in 2005 had grown to equal 40 percent of total bank loans, equivalent to around 60 percent of bank deposits.[12] At this level, local skimming would be crowding out funding for regular lending of all kinds!

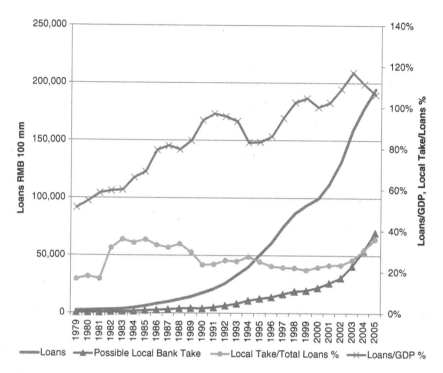

Figure 1.2 The "take" from capital investment alone to total loans, 1979–2005.
SOURCES: *China Fiscal Almanac, China Banking Yearbook*, author's calculation.

This funding is completely outside the official budgetary needs of the financial system! The result is inefficient investment, greater enterprise leverage combined with an irremediable layer of loans on bank balance sheets. And this was before the money from the stimulus policies from late 2008 poured in.

Whatever the official stated source of funding for capital investment or those monies dubbed "Other fees," the ultimate source must inevitably be a bank and its deposits. This money once lent out was not going to be paid back by local officials. It went to fill the fiscal expenditure gap for social services and not to investments that might yield a return.[13] The "ghost towns" and 100-story buildings in provincial capitals had to wait until the financial crisis and its massive stimulus got underway.

The gap between the official and shadow fiscal system contributes materially to the pressure that has been building within the banking system since 2008. Figure 1.3 shows how total banking assets exploded

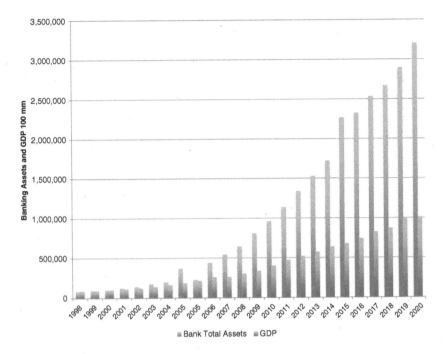

Figure 1.3   Trends in banking assets and GDP, 1999–2020.
SOURCE: China Banking Almanac.

after the outbreak of the global financial crisis. These assets are compared
to GDP, and for all years, even the years of bank restructuring, they
exceeded the latter by material amounts. At the end of 2008 bank assets
exceeded GDP by a ratio of five to three; by 2020 the figure was three
to one. Is it any wonder that China grew out of the crisis? Along the way
China's state banks topped the *Fortune* Global 500 and accounted for
four of the 30-member category of Globally Systemically Important
Banks (GSIB) subject to the Basel Committee on Financial Supervision's
(Basel) regulatory framework and oversight.

In just 20 years Chinese bank assets grew 25 times, but their performance metrics still appeared excellent. In contrast, US banking assets
during the same period of 2000–2020 remained at around one time
GDP. Chinese bank balance sheets owed their phenomenal growth in
part to the funds that local governments scraped together. Whether
rolled over and held until convenient to dispose of, these loans hung
around. This state-driven growth and the measures used to manage it

have had a major and negative impact on banks as institutions as discussed in Chapters 4 and 5. The impact on state enterprises is discussed in Chapter 7.

Chapter 3 shows what enabled China's banks to grow so rapidly and to lend as much as they did. Figure 1.3 is only one half of the story, and it is the easy half: lending is easy; getting it back can be hard. The important question about banks is not about how big their loan portfolios are. It should be, how do Chinese banks finance their lending operations and where do they find that financing? Every *fen* they make as a loan has to be funded with money, mostly someone else's money. Aside from their initial IPOs, even the big state banks have not been allowed to raise money internationally: Beijing was not going to permit another fiasco like Guangdong International Trust and Investment! So what China's banks did have, whether in accumulated equity capital (their "own" money) or in deposits or in subordinated bonds, nearly always came from domestic sources.

Fortunately China entered the WTO in 2001. This had the effect in a very few short years of very dramatically increasing China's economic growth and, therefore, corporate and household savings. The vast bulk of these savings stay in banks as deposits, because the party does not permit the creation of true investment products that are not beneficial to the party itself: deposits are beneficial. Stock markets serve "troubled" state enterprises, and securities funds mainly contain their shares and are a sponge for government and bank bonds. Wealth management products (WMP) have played a huge role in helping banks improve their balance sheets; giving depositors a slightly better return than bank deposits is a distant second place. When fintech companies developed scale over the past decade, they were ultimately closed or their operations restructured. Added to this is a rickety social security system that encourages an aging population to be super-savers, so it is no wonder that the party can make use of the massive savings deposits overwhelmingly in its own banks.

An "Authoritative Person" was quoted in *People's Daily* in 2016 as saying, ". . . trees cannot grow to heaven."[14] In China, banks are trees and they have grown very close to heaven indeed, as Figure 1.4 shows. China's large state banks and many of its medium and even small city banks are professionally audited and listed in Hong Kong and Shanghai. The four state banks are Globally Systemically Important Banks (GSIB)

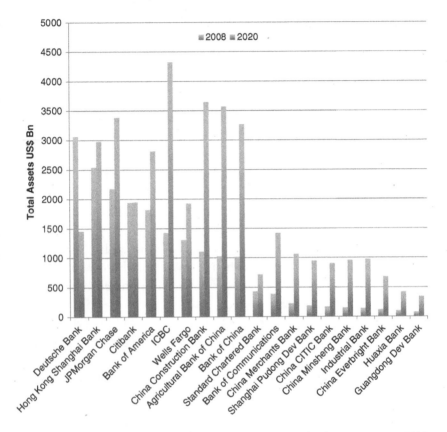

Figure 1.4   Total assets of selected Chinese and foreign banks, 2008 versus 2020.
SOURCE: *The Banker* and *Forbes*.

subject to the Basel layer of regulations. As noted earlier, over the 20 years reviewed in this book their assets grew 25 times. The Chinese state banks have grown organically. By comparison JPMorgan Chase, the only bank of similar size in the world, grew three times and largely from acquisitions.

Local governments have their Shadow Fiscal System; the banks in China with the assistance of regulators (and the instructions of the party) have their Shadow Banking System as laid out in Chapter 4. Trust plans, asset-backed securities, WMPs, structured entities, and debt for equity swaps have all been added to a mix designed to strengthen state banks. To these have been added a number of helpful institutions: central and local asset management companies, asset exchanges, structured entities and online auctions. In a few short years these all became parts of an extremely complicated financial ecosystem that is best understood in the light of bank balance-sheet pressures from financing investment-led GDP growth.

China's shadow banking products have contributed to the removal from bank balance sheets of problematic assets with official values of 20–30 percent of total bank assets. This by itself has almost been enough to allow banks to present strong financial metrics to the world. Astounding figures, but comparable to the levels of bad assets reached in the 1990s. And these problematic assets have not gone away, as the experience of China Huarong in 2021 has shown; they fill bad banks and other nooks and crannies of the state system to bursting.

But shuffling bad assets off to someone else's balance sheet, assuming the receiving entity even has one, is not enough. Banks also make the best use of flexible accounting principles, and this is not necessarily a criticism of bank auditors. Accounting principles are founded on the idea that the quality of an asset is based on the nature of its risk. Some assets, for example, lending to other banks, are less risky than lending to enterprises, largely due to the supposed heavy regulatory oversight of banks. Loans to local governments can be made less risky simply by replacing them with debt securities, the assumption being that such securities can easily be sold into the market. In that case, banks may suffer only a pricing loss, not a loss of principal. In China there is no trading in the debt markets, but the principles are applied all the same.

The problem is that in China, accounting principles that were developed internationally to suit those conditions have been applied equally to a situation that is entirely different. It is like saying A, but not mentioning that A depends on B.

Table 1.2 illustrates this point by showing the effect of replacing loans to local governments with bonds. Bonds as a rule carry a 20 percent risk weighting in internationally accepted bank risk calculations, while loans are 100 percent. The weighting relates to how much bank capital must be assigned to a given asset. So bonds take up only one-fifth as much capital as loans: 100 *yuan* of bonds requires only 20 *yuan* of capital to cover its risk. What happens next is obvious. Over the 2013–2019 period, local debt (Column C) was transformed into bonds as shown in Column E. The total value of capital freed up by this transformation is shown in

Table 1.2 Local government bonds: more risk, less risk weight.

100 mms	Local Govt Bonds Held by All Entities	Local Govt Bonds Held by Banks/ Total Local Debt	Total Local Debt	Net Local Debt Risk Weight 100%	Bank Held Bonds Risk Weight 20%	Total Risk Weight Removed	Net Risk Weighted Local Debt
	A	B	C	D	E	F	G
				C – A	A × .20	A – E	C – F
2013	8,498	6.3%	135,515	127,017	1,700	6,798	128,717
2014	11,472	7.4%	154,074	142,602	2,294	9,178	144,896
2015	44,557	30.2%	147,568	103,011	8,911	35,646	111,922
2016	93,631	61.0%	153,558	59,927	18,726	74,905	78,653
2017	127,556	77.3%	165,100	37,544	25,511	102,045	63,055
2018	153,272	92.3%	166,100	12,828	30,654	122,618	43,482
2019	211,183	86.3%	228,219	17,036	42,237	168,946	59,273

SOURCE: China Bond, PBOC; author's calculations.

Column F, and the value of local risk left on bank balance sheets is shown in Column G. So, for example, in 2019 total local debt on bank balance sheets was 22.8 trillion *yuan*. After these loans were refinanced with bonds, bank risk became 4.2 trillion *yuan*. The difference is 16.8 trillion *yuan* of capital freed up for new lending (Column F). This is the power of accounting. The only problem with this calculation, the B of the metaphor, is that the Chinese debt capital market is moribund: it does not trade.[15] If it does not trade, then these bonds are nothing but disguised loans, and bank risk weights should be calculated as such.

There are other examples in Chapter 5; equity investments (risk weight 400 percent) may by the terms of a contract be characterized as a loan (100 percent) until maturity, when they again become equity, so accounting risk is again minimized. Then there are the off-balance-sheet locations to park risky or bad assets. And all of this, in the end, is subject to management and auditor's judgment. Regulators, investors, and depositors must be presented with a picture of solid banks that "fairly presents" the risk they contain. But financial history shows that this is not always the case, even in developed markets.

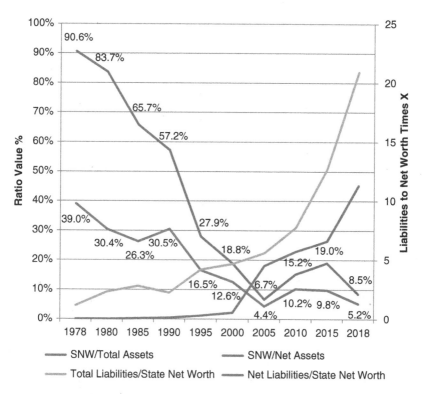

Figure 1.5 State net worth to total state assets and liabilities, 1978–2018.
NOTE: State Net Worth post-1995 does not include Minority Interest.
SOURCE: 1978–1997, Holz (2001); 1998–2018, author's calculations.

Just how much debt China has taken on in the past decade has been a common topic among analysts. Chapter 6 brings together the financial data of the state sector, its banks, enterprises and governments, in a rough consolidated balance sheet (a full balance sheet and details on its creation are in Appendix 1). The phenomenal growth of the state's balance sheet particularly over the past 10 years has rapidly raised China's economic profile. But the volume of capital injected into the country's economy—US\$41 trillion in a US\$10–15 trillion economy—could hardly be put to use in so short a time. Assets that produce a return take time to create, and financial assets including foreign reserves yield little. As a result, the very volume of liabilities has crushed the state's own net worth beneath them as Figure 1.5 illustrates. The figure presents the results of two

Table 1.3 Household claims versus state assets, 2018.

100 mm	2018	Discounted Values	Discount Rate	Plus Net Current Assets
Household deposits	724,439			
Estimated currency held	57,102			
Savings bonds	7,218			
A share investments	85,204			
Total Household claims	**873,963**	**873,963**		**762,128**
Foreign exchange reserves	212,557	212,557		212,557
SOE fixed assets	393,808	393,808		393,808
SOE investments	106,685	53,343	50%	53,343
Bank loans to SOEs	427,150	256,290	60%	256,290
Net current assets				764,128
Selected State Assets	**1,140,200**	**915,998**		**1,680,126**

SOURCE: See balance sheet in Appendix 1.

calculations of net worth, one market based and the other accounting based; the liabilities reflect the two different approaches. No matter how net worth is calculated the trend over 40 years has been to shrink to single digits. This suggests that the party should have felt constrained by its capital spending in the past decade, but its actions show that it has not been.

It is even questionable whether state assets are of sufficient value to make the deposit and other investment obligations of households whole (see Table 1.3). In fact, the massive deposits of households were always less similar to a liability than to equity. Calculations made this way support the fact that the Chinese people are, in fact and not simply party rhetoric, truly the effective owners of the Chinese socialist state and all its assets, including foreign exchange reserves, and that the party itself is bankrupt. Of course, there is no one outside the party who will assert their ownership right.

To support these conclusions about the party's financial management, Chapter 7 presents comparisons of how Beijing and Washington have managed respective financial crises. The two crisis sets are the US savings and loan crisis of 1980–1994 and the Chinese bank restructuring of 1997–2007. The second set includes the US mortgage crisis and what now seems to be a rolling debt crisis in China in which Beijing is trying to pay in advance the costs of maintaining strong state banks in an environment of declining economic growth. The costs associated with the restructuring of Beijing's state banks was significant, nearly 44 percent of the country's GDP; the process simply took too long. This figure alone should underline the fact that in the 1990s and the years up to 2008 China's leadership was set on joining the existing international order embodied in the World Trade Agreement. In contrast, the cost of the S&L crisis was just a bit over 4 percent of US GDP. There are other cost comparisons a well.

In the second set of crises the difference is far starker. The Congressional Budget Office estimated the mortgage crisis to have cost nearly US$500 billion, again only 3 percent of GDP, but 33 percent of total assets involved. The impact on society and politics was far more important than the money lost. In contrast, China is seeking to maintain social stability by buying economic growth through massive lending by the state banks. As a result, Beijing has set in motion a shadow banking system that preserves the integrity of the major banks while saturating society with questionable investment products. The costs associated with this policy are as large as the banks have become. In China the impact will be a financial one followed by a societal and political one, the reverse of the US experience.

Where will China go with all its debt? Inflating it away as was done with the costs to the bank restructuring is no longer possible; the problem is too big. The Japanese experience may provide the best answer if not to a way forward then to the consequences of delayed response. The two countries are different in political and economic systems and the organization of their state sectors, yet there are many similarities. Japan's deflationary period was catalyzed by a banking crisis exacerbated by the collapse of a massive real estate bubble. Could the Imperial Palace in Tokyo really be worth all the real estate in California? And why did it take the Japanese government eight years to fully address the banking crisis? The principal problem was that the eyes of Japanese regulators and politicians were blinded by their long and successful experience with an existing regulatory paradigm. China shares this problem and its piecemeal approach to resolving increasingly major financial collapses today may prove insufficient in the future.

Convergence

China and the United States have weaved back and forth in a dance over these past 40 years; parallel movement and mutually supporting periods have been brief. Now, at the start of the third decade of the twenty-first century, China's financial system appears to be facing the same problems the US financial system did at the end of the first decade. Has so-called "state-capitalism" and the party really managed an outcome better than plain old capitalism? In the United States, banks were subject to political importuning for "low-cost mortgages for all" and responded by creating complex financial products that led to a global crisis. In response, China's government encouraged its own banks to drive economic growth and maintain employment with massive lending to real estate, bullet trains and personal mortgages.

While international banks with the support of the Federal Reserve restored their balance sheets, Beijing obliged Chinese banks to continue to make excessive loans for a decade. Along the way these banks continued to present strong regulatory metrics to the world. To achieve this, regulators were complicit in the creation of China's own "exotic" financial products. While the products are simpler than those created in the United States, over the decade they have led to the creation of a complex financial ecosystem in which bad loans have been spun off to myriad "investing" entities throughout the economy. Far smaller entities have also copied the big banks and, if they could, issued their own products. The near saturation of the system may now have been reached. This can be seen in the defaults of smaller city banks and, most obviously, in the default and bankruptcy of China Huarong, the result less of corruption than of simple overstuffing with bad assets. Now, Beijing has deliberately collapsed China's real estate developers. There has been much sound and noise, but nothing about which banks are holding what kind of debt obligations and how their problems are being resolved. And since real estate means local governments, their difficulties have hardly been touched on.

None of these shadow banking products has a real, market-based valuation.
How much and what value these things may have no one knows (except
that they are overvalued) and the party today is little interested in finding
out. China's financial situation is like a map that reads in fine print, "Not
to scale," except that the map covers not just China's domestic market;
unlike a decade ago, China's financial health directly affects international
markets and developed economies. Can it be that China's political leaders, in an effort to avoid the fault lines of the US economy, have
succeeded in doing just the opposite and because of the complexity they
have allowed to evolve are unable to see it? Is the "Authoritative Person"
(of whom more later) the only one who can see that China's banks may
be about to ". . . toss the people's savings into the soup"?

Notes

1. *New York Times*, p. A1, March 14, 2009.
2. Henry M. Paulson, Jr., *Dealing with China* (New York: Hachette Books, 2015), p. 240.
3. CIC's Lou Jiwei, "Last Year in Europe I Didn't Invest a Cent (中投楼继伟: 我去年在欧洲没有投一分钱)," Boao Forum, April 17, 2008, http://www.sina .com.cn 2009年04月18日 16:06; Richard McGregor, *The Party*, p. xi.
4. Frank Dikotter, *The Age of Openness* (Berkeley: the University of California Press, 2008).
5. "Bombard the Headquarters" was the *People's Daily* headline that launched the Cultural Revolution and was also the title of Richard McGregor's article in *The Wire*, "Bombard the headquarters: Xi Jinping's crackdown keeps growing," September 29, 2021.
6. National Audit Office, 2011 #35; 审计署, 2011年35号:全国地方政府性债务审计结果, http://www.audit.gov.cn/in192130/n1992150/n1992500/275 2208.html.
7. Albert Feuerwerker, "The Chinese Economy, 1912–1949" (Ann Arbor: Michigan Papers in China Studies, No. 1, 1968), pp. 47 ff.
8. Ibid., pp. 51 ff.
9. Audrey Donnithorne, "China's Cellular Economy," *China Quarterly*, no. 52 (October–December 1972), pp. 605–615.
10. Yoko Kubota and Liyan Qi, "Empty Buildings in China's Provincial Cities Testify to Evergrande Debacle," *Wall Street Journal*, October 4, 2021, https://www.wsj .com/articles/evergrande-china-real-estate-debacles-empty-buildings-cities-beijing.

11. See Lardy's book solidly making this point. Nicholas R. Lardy, *Markets before Mao: the Rise of Private Business in China* (Washington DC: Petersen Institute for International Economics, 2014).

12. Loans are funded by deposits and regulators set a maximum level of deposits that can be used to support lending, say 60 percent. This means that the remaining 40 percent are unused and should be factored into the overall cost of the loan itself. Thus a $60 loan will occupy nearly $100 of deposits.

13. Official data on how extra budgetary funds are used can be found, for example, in 财政部国库司遍, 2009地方财政统计资料 (2009 statistical materials of local finance)(2011, 经济科学出版社, 北京), pp. 409–412.

14. *Renmin ribao* (People's Daily), September 9, 2016, p. 1.

15. See Chapter 4 in Carl Walter and Fraser Howie, *Red Capitalism*, 2nd ed. (Singapore: John Wiley & Sons, 2010), for a demonstration of this.

Chapter 2

The Shadow Fiscal System

Local Governments, National Budgets

Who wants to be the mayor who reports that he didn't achieve
8 percent GDP growth this year?

—*Unnamed local government official*[1]

The city's streets were plastered with signs and self-standing boards advertising brands of cigarettes and bottles of Chinese "wine." The annual Wine and Spirits Conference (烟酒会: sic!) had just concluded. All of China's producers and sellers had gathered in one spot to brag and celebrate and drink and smoke. The conference had been held in a brand-new exhibition hall in the just-built part of town that had been carved out of the old town. The hall from a distance looked like a paper parasol opened on top of a building; designed by

Japanese architects the complex was beautiful. In the background was a park and what was to be a large 100-story skyscraper that was still under construction. Where did the money come from for all this?

Finding some of that money is the objective of this chapter, which describes how local governments developed an alternate fiscal universe. In this universe, up to the financial crisis in 2008, they generated funding resources far in excess of the expenditures specified in their officially approved budgets. But if they were too successful, Beijing, with the same sort of fiscal insufficiencies, snatched away and even canceled altogether these lucrative resources in order to increase official revenue. This cycle of underfunding, finding new money and having it taken away, strengthened already-strong local self-reliance that the decade since 2008 has done nothing to change.

Local officials have created a shadow fiscal system in which financial institutions and state enterprises have been leveraged both directly and indirectly to make up for the formal system's "insufficiency." Disguised inside bank and state enterprise balance sheets is a struggle between central and local governments for control of China's limited capital. The strength of this alternate fiscal system and the party's instinctive reliance on local governments, and not private enterprise, to drive economic growth are the strongest forces leading to massive distortions in bank balance sheets and soaring off-balance-sheet assets, as will be discussed in Chapter 4. It has also meant the failure of enterprise reform. State enterprises, both local and the local subsidiaries of central enterprises, have never become fully independent operating entities. Rather, they have remained firmly embedded financially with local governments, and this distorts their balance sheets and impacts their performance metrics.

China's "Centralized" State and Localized Financing

A common saying heard everywhere among officials and staff of the Chinese government and its SOEs in the 1990s and beyond was that "the system doesn't work (or, maybe, it's nonresponsive: 体制不灵). Everyone knew, or at least said, that it didn't work. There was even a ministry-level entity created in the 1980s to study solutions: the State

Commission for the Restructuring for the Reform of the Economic System (体改委; SCRES). This Commission and the party itself succeeded in tearing apart most of the old Soviet bureaucratic structure by the late 1990s; even the industrial ministries were demolished with the Ministry of Railways the last to go. In their place rose the world's finest supply chains and infrastructure and a handful of powerful private fintech companies. During that phase of reform and even now, little thought was given to local governments. They were treated as mirrors of Beijing but were given no independent resources to fulfill their social obligations and develop their economies. This is the fiscal system's biggest problem.[2]

Chinese administrative structure and bureaucratic culture are irreducible. The names of its departments change, but Beijing remains the heart of the country's governing structure and the source of its fiscal difficulties. Beijing can say NO, but its Yes does not always translate to Yes at local levels. The reasons are rooted in China's long history. For most of the post-1949 period (and all of it before, back 500 years to the Ming Dynasty) the state was built on five administrative levels (since 2011, four). At its base today are nearly 40,000 towns and most of the populace. These were subordinated to 2,851 counties and 334 cities and rural prefectures that, in turn, were governed by 22 provinces, five autonomous zones, and four provincial-level cities: Beijing, Tianjin, Shanghai, and Chongqing (and maybe Suzhou). Administrative relationships are always vertical: interactions start at the center and proceed to the base. Within this hierarchy relationships exist only between each two levels, and in all cases the superior level rules. So, the central government deals only with the provincial-level governments, the provincial with the city/prefectural level, and so on. The Emperor is always on top and resources always trickle down and it's a long way down.

During the first decade of the post-1978 reform era it is fair to say that there was no national fiscal system. Local governments continued, as they had done during the Cultural Revolution period and before, to extract revenues from what was at hand, the population and state-owned enterprises (SOEs), mostly the latter.[3] These efforts were not new and they were hardly a secret to party leaders in Beijing, most of whom had earlier in their careers rotated through provincial governments. Called Extrabudgetary Funds (EBF; 预算外资金) and Extrasystem Funds (ESF;

体制外资金), these monies grew over the 1980s to equal and then exceed by multiples formal budgetary revenues.[4]

EBFs had three main components: first, directly collected surcharges from, for example, utilities; and second, miscellaneous fees such as school tuition. The third component accounted for the lion's share: "borrowing" from state enterprises in their jurisdictions. The specific target was the so-called "enterprise self-owned fund." This consisted of retained profit, depreciation, and major repair funds.[5] In short, local governments appropriated enterprise capital resources. Since city and county governments were their main "owners," appropriating was easy. The party, after all, can do anything. Moreover, in the 1980s there was no distinction between central and local state enterprises, so local governments could find plenty of financing. The SOEs, in turn, replaced them with short-term loans from banks.

This kind of "borrowing" was never repaid, since local governments used the funds primarily to finance health, education, and social security, as well as similar consumption items. Social goods do not directly generate returns that could be used to repay SOE "loans." If there was any repayment, it was likely to be money borrowed from other SOEs in what would become local Ponzi schemes. In other words, once such money was spent, it was spent. As for the banks, these sorts of credits were rolled over on their books and at some point in the future written off. Banks and enterprises were inseparable and fundamental "pillars" of government.

In addition to EBFs, there was another revenue stream, Extrasystem Funds. These are called *extrasystem* because they were gathered without Beijing's authorization so there were no formal regulations defining their collection or use. This made these monies very attractive. There is, therefore, little official data on ESFs, but at least two major components can be identified, the largest being termed *fund raising*, or *self-raised funds* (自筹资金). All such funds can only refer to money ultimately sourced from banks or other financial entities or through enterprises. The scale of these funds is shown in Tables 2.1 and 2.2.

Table 2.1 shows the size of EBFs and ESFs compared to official local budgetary revenue until 1993, when Beijing, as part of its tax and enterprise reform packages, fenced off SOEs from grasping local hands.

Table 2.1 Extrabudgetary and bank-sourced funding, 1979–1993.

RMB 100 mns	Official Local Budgetary Revenue	Total EBF + ESF	Total EBF+ESF as % of Local Budget	Extrabudgetary Funds		Extrasystem Funds	
				Local Extrabudgetary Funds (EBF)	Of which SOE Self-Owned Funds (EBF)	Local Agency Self-Raised Funds (ESF)	Of which Self-Raised Funds Residual (ESF)
		A + C		A	B	C	D
1979	1,146	453	40%	453	344	0	0
1980	1,160	557	48%	557	442	0	0
1981	1,176	601	51%	601	475	0	48
1982	1,212	1,151	95%	803	652	348	68
1983	1,367	1,442	105%	968	804	474	78
1984	1,643	1,822	111%	1,188	991	633	106
1985	2,005	2,492	124%	1,530	1,253	962	170
1986	2,122	3,030	143%	1,737	1,400	1,293	209
1987	2,199	3,529	160%	2,029	1,626	1,501	277
1988	2,357	4,514	192%	2,361	1,873	2,153	349
1989	2,665	4,764	179%	2,639	2,084	2,153	300
1990	2,937	4,737	161%	2,709	2,071	2,028	343
1991	3,149	5,769	183%	3,243	2,478	2,526	487
1992	3,483	7,561	217%	3,855	2,879	3,706	792
1993	4,349	9,705	223%	1,433	0	8,272	1,555

SOURCES: *China Statistical Yearbook* for EBF and self-raised funds; *China Banking Almanac*, for self-raised funds residual; for example, see the *Almanac* for 2013, p. 531, and Jia Kang (1998), p. 50.

For example, by 1992 local governments had generated funds that were roughly 220 percent of their official budgets. In the table, enterprise capital funds (B) are broken out of the total extrabudgetary fund (A) number to show their scale. Local agency self-raised funds (C) are sourced largely from banks, but also include all types of fees charged largely to the populace. The Self-raised Funds Residual (D) figure is discussed in a following paragraph. As the table shows, by 1987 these funding sources began to exceed formal local fiscal revenues. The jump in self-raised funds in 1993 came as local governments acted in advance of the new 1994 Budget Law (more later). Even after 1993, when Beijing removed enterprise capital from local reach, the reality of self-raised funds remained. Given the way they are calculated, these figures indicate a sort of maximum amount of capital possible for local governments to access.

Table 2.2 is taken directly in the same format from the *China Statistical Yearbook* and shows funding sources for capital investment. In the table, the item called "self-raised funds" consistently makes up about half of all state-approved capital investment. In this context, it means the amount of funding Beijing expects local governments to arrange. This unfunded gap in investment projects was deliberate. It compelled local governments to seek out financing sources in their own jurisdictions. And as arrangers they had direct access to this capital and, of course, not all of it was used for the designated projects. They could also arrange for their state enterprises to, for example, build a bridge or construct a building using enterprise funds.

Then there is the what this analysis calls the self-raised funds residual (其他费用; "Other") that appears in banking almanacs and provides an idea of how much local government might have retained for their own use.[6] The figure is the result of taking the total investment budget and subtracting from it the value of completed investment in buildings and equipment, leaving a remainder that, on average, is around 10–15 percent of the total planned investment. This is likely to be a lowball estimate since local governments also took advantage of the opportunities construction presented by using their own construction companies and suppliers.

There are two important points to be made here. First, Beijing's deliberate underfunding of local budgets and investment projects

Table 2.2 Financing sources for total state-approved capital investment, 1985–1990.

RMB Bns	Budget	Domestic Loans	Foreign Direct Investment	Self-raised	Other	Total Investment	% Self-Raised
1985	40,780	51,027	9,148	153,364	NA	254,319	60%
1986	44,063	63,831	13,216	148,851	32,000	301,961	49%
1987	47,554	83,594	17,737	174,518	40,883	364,286	48%
1988	41,001	92,668	25,899	290,087	NA	449,655	65%
1989	34,162	71,636	27,415	235,550	45,009	413,772	57%
1990	38,765	87,088	27,826	232,949	58,301	444,929	52%

SOURCE: *China Statistical Yearbook* 1991.

compels local governments to seek out other sources of capital. It also strengthens local self-reliance. Second, where else could they find such money but in the banks? Local governments preyed on bank funds both directly and indirectly through enterprises during the 1980s. This reliance increased as fiscal reforms progressively sought to increase the independent operation of state enterprises. But at local levels, the separation of banks and enterprises from the state has always proved difficult: the party can always do anything.

Aspirational Central Finances, Fiscal Collapse and the 1994 Budget Law

While local governments lived well in the 1980s, the central government was increasingly impoverished; tinkering with the arrangements of a planned economy had eliminated the enterprises' planned surpluses that Beijing had lived on before. After the events of 1989, the party even feared the possibility of state collapse, a fear publicly discussed by Chinese scholars.[7] This did not happen, of course, and Beijing emerged even stronger as it asserted control over the country's financial system beginning in 1993. A new budget law was passed in 1994 giving the central government control over revenue collection, Beijing took over the two stock exchanges, plus the nascent fixed-income market, and the big four state banks. By the end of the 1990s, the central government seemed to have control of the country's financial resources well in hand.

This degree of centralization, as uneven as it was, was unprecedented in China's history. Before 1949, China did not have the technological wherewithal to establish a modern financial or fiscal system. After the revolution, Soviet advisors, armed with the ideology of a centrally planned economy, were able to change very little. They had tried to put in place a fiscal system that treated the entire country as if it were a single, centrally managed industrial enterprise. And in China they faced a situation that perfectly suited their ideas—a fiscal history that also ignored geographies. The façade, and not just the façade of the Soviet system, was dispatched with when Mao Zedong threw the country into 20 years of political turmoil in 1957. But life goes on, and local governments—and, to some extent, Beijing—continued to finance themselves in a traditional fashion, mobilizing funds within their own geographic areas, keeping what they needed, and passing up as little as possible.

The failure of reform in the 1980s meant Beijing faced not just a major political crisis, but also a fiscal one: the country was bankrupt (see Figure 2.1). By 1990 the central government could no longer pay for even its most indispensable budgetary items. Three years later, the deficit had grown to the point where 43 percent was financed by domestic loans, 34 percent by foreign borrowing and 23 percent unfunded, that is, self-raised extrabudgetary funds if they could be found.[8] If it was not to collapse, the central government had to assert central control over the fiscal system.

Despite the desperate financial situation, change proved to be politically difficult. Not only were the voices of the party's left wing calling for a halt to reforms altogether, but the wealthier provinces also raised objections, not wanting to give up any of their "own" resources to support poorer parts of the country. This selfishness has yet to change even today. As the dispute evolved, it became obvious that the rich were a minority—there were many poor provinces—and the leftists' proposed solutions led only back to where the country had already been. Finally, technocrats in Beijing were able to team up with the poor parts of the country to push through the extremely important Budget Law of 1994. The key takeaway is that to get there required a huge crisis, that of Tianenmen Square on June 4, to break up political logjams.

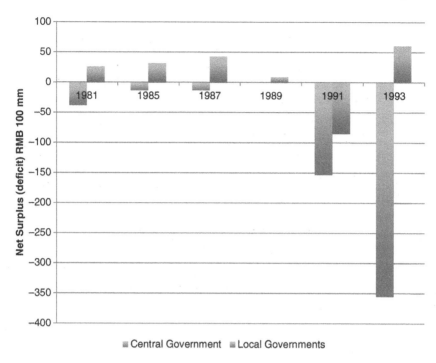

Figure 2.1   Central and local net budget surplus (deficit), 1981–1994.
SOURCE: *China Statistical Yearbook*; excludes extrabudgetary revenues.

With the new Budget Law, Beijing achieved for the first time a specific tax code that was imposed on local governments. This eliminated contentious annual negotiations over lump-sum payments. Taxes were divided into three categories: belonging to Beijing, or to the provinces, or shared. Second, the central party no longer trusted local governments to work in the national interest. This absence of trust is demonstrated in the establishment of central tax offices at the provincial level. These offices collected not just central taxes, but also all so-called "shared" taxes. Beijing claimed these would be transferred back after they had been "safely" collected. Third, Beijing established the principle that state enterprises were independent of government. In doing so, Beijing hoped to improve their profitability, thereby increasing tax payments and profits.[9] This expectation did not work out, however.

Nonetheless, this was a great victory for the central government. But in China especially, there is no victory without compromise. To win the support of the poor provinces, Beijing promised to top up their annual budgetary shortfalls with fiscal transfers from central revenues. In other words, Beijing, believing that the new Law would generate significantly greater revenues, promised to make payments out of its own revenues to balance local budgets. In truth, the new arrangements did succeed in restoring growth to revenues until the outbreak of the global financial crisis when a large and still growing deficit emerged (see Figure 2.2).

So poor provinces got a top up for their budgets, but nothing is free; the law forbade them from borrowing or enacting their own taxes. As Beijing's logic went, there would be no need because (1) the rich provinces were rich and did not need to enact taxes; and (2) the poor provinces would have their full budgeted revenues, so they also had no need to borrow or enact taxes. Of course, the law could hold only if hard budgets[10] were enforced on everyone, which was a future goal (still far in the future). As a part of this effort, Beijing also placed existing extrabudgetary funds into a managed account as part of the formal budgetary

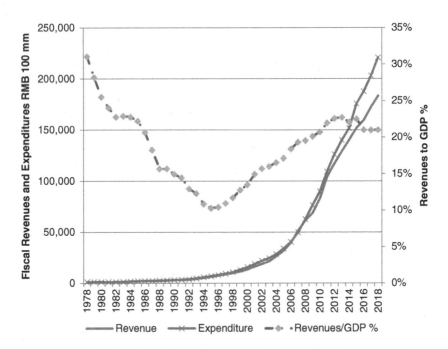

Figure 2.2   Official final budgetary revenues and expenditures, 1979–2018.
SOURCE: China Finance Almanac.

process. This explains why the Ministry of Finance provides data for this revenue source.

But these new arrangements would work only if they generated sufficient fiscal revenues to cover all the promises made, and this became hard to realize. Revenues did increase, but so did expenditures, and politicians are never happy to live within limits. Nor did the party want to enforce hard budgets on any party committee. While local governments were forbidden by law to borrow, Beijing continued to allow them to do so in traditional ways. As Figure 2.2 shows, the new Budget Law increased central revenues significantly, as Beijing had hoped. This was the public part of the picture: fiscal revenues to GDP steadily increased, everyone was satisfied, but then there were the transfers.

Digging a bit deeper, however, showed that on a net basis, provincial transfers materially weakened Beijing's own finances.[11] Beijing was compelled to issue more and more bonds to finance its own budgetary needs.

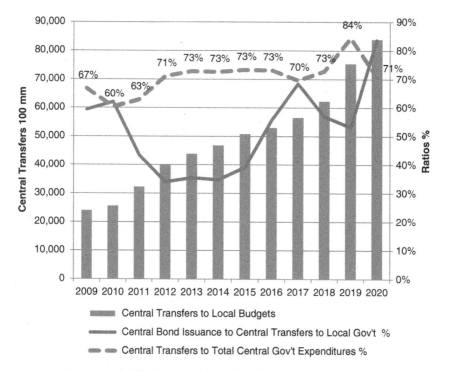

Figure 2.3   Central debt issuance to total local fiscal transfers.
SOURCE: *China Finance Almanac, China Statistical Yearbook*, author's calculations.

In the 1990s central government debt levels remained modest, but the gap as compared to GDP after transfers became a real weakness in the years following the global financial crisis. Figure 2.3 shows the ratio of central government new bond issuance per year to total budgeted provincial fiscal transfers. Since 2014 Beijing has had to issue increasing amounts of debt to pay the provinces; the amount in 2020 was heading toward a 1:1 ratio of central debt to provincial transfers. The figure also shows the ratio of local transfers to total central government expenditures. This ratio hovered around 70 percent until increasing for the years 2017 to 2019 to over 80 percent. These figures suggest that Beijing is helping the weak provinces stay current on their debt load, but such largesse cannot last forever.

To conclude, the Budget Law must be seen as a failure, not because it didn't raise enough revenues, but because it failed to address the division of governmental functions and *expenditure* responsibilities among the five (now four) local administrative levels.[12] Beijing assigned obligations, but did not assign the authority or the revenues required to fulfill them. This double whammy further strengthened local governments' self-reliance and their search for revenue would inevitably lead them back to their traditional partners—the banks and enterprises. Even with

Table 2.3 Distribution of budgetary revenues and expenses by level of government, 1992–2013.

as % of official budget total	1992	1998	2002	2006	2010	2013
Revenues						
Central	34.0	49.5	55.0	52.8	51.1	46.6
Province	11.0	10.5	11.7	12.1	10.6	10.7
Prefecture/City	29.0	19.7	16.3	16.5	15.8	16.2
County	16.0	20.3	17.1	18.6	22.5	26.5
Expenditures						
Central	22.0	28.9	30.7	24.7	17.8	14.6
Province	13.0	18.8	19.6	18.3	17.1	16.1
Prefecture/City	34.0	24.1	28.6	22.5	22.5	22.9
County	16.0	28.2	22.0	34.4	42.6	46.3

SOURCE: Christine Wong (2021).

the largesse of stimulus lending following the crisis, local governments continued to add to overall state leverage outside the formal fiscal system and they somehow forced Beijing to increase transfers adding even more.

Table 2.3 details the heart of the problem and explains why local governments continue to scramble for financing and why Chinese bank and enterprise balance sheets expand. As an example, in 2002 counties received only 17 percent of budgetary revenues, but those counties were responsible for 22 percent of expenditures. This gap widened through 2013 when it was 26 to 46 percent. And transfers trickle down slowly through the provincial bureaucracy with each level reserving a portion for its own needs. Beijing, for its part, increased transfers, but at the same time also retained more revenue for itself and to accommodate larger transfers.

A final comment emerges from this discussion. Taking China's financial system as it presents itself to the outside world, to look at its budgets, regulations, and the statistics coming out of the Ministry of Finance, the central bank and other agencies (as this book does) is only one part of the story. The picture such official data paints is aspirational. Even more important, the central government and party leadership do not care if the picture represents an ideal; the trend and control of resources are the only things they believe are important. All the good work to develop a real fiscal system done by the IMF and World Bank during the precrisis years of reform, when the party had stepped back, is useless when there is no state and only the party as is the case today. Meanwhile, at local levels, leaders must manage the populace and build roads. To do so they must generate financing outside of formal budgets. This is the entrenched reality of China's financial system, and any expectation of change would be misleading.

The Continual Local Scramble for Funds

Even as the Budget Law was being debated, local governments had begun scrambling for new funding sources and maxing out old ones. Small fees levied on many things became an identifiable type of Extrasystem Funding (termed ESF 1; see Table 2.4). Beijing sought to limit this activity many times to little effect until, in 2004, new party

Table 2.4 Extrabudgetary revenues and bank-sourced funding, 1994–2007.

RMB 100 mms	Official Local Budgetary Revenue	Total EBF + ESF + Land Fees A+B+C+D	Total EBF+ESFs as % of Local Budget	Local Extrabudgetary Funds (EBF) A	Local Agency Self-Raised Funds (ESF)	Of which Self-Raised Funds Residual (ESF) B	Extrasystem Funds 1 (ESF 1) C	Land Use Rights Fees Gross D
1994	2,312	5,825	252%	1,863	10,927	1,928	568	1,466
1995	2,986	6,567	220%	2,416	12,605	2,584	756	811
1996	3,847	8,397	218%	3,893	13,922	2,878	967	659
1997	4,424	7,956	180%	2,826	16,594	3,080	1,167	882
1998	4,984	9,246	186%	3,082	18,966	4,004	1,251	909
1999	5,595	9,732	174%	3,385	19,630	4,006	1,277	1,064
2000	6,406	10,304	161%	3,826	22,151	4,596	1,286	596
2001	7,803	12,312	158%	4,300	26,120	5,425	1,291	1,296
2002	8,515	15,266	179%	4,479	30,682	7,037	1,333	2,417
2003	9,850	20,795	211%	4,567	41,015	9,438	1,370	5,421
2004	11,893	23,687	199%	4,699	54,236	11,147	1,429	6,412
2005	15,101	25,396	168%	5,544	70,139	13,968	0	5,884
2006	18,304	32,144	176%	6,408	90,360	17,658	0	8,078
2007	23,573	41,268	175%	6,820	116,770	22,231	0	12,217

SOURCE: *China Finance Almanac, China Statistical Yearbook, China Banking Almanac.*

leadership abolished all agricultural taxes, including these ad hoc fees. This made Hu Jintao, China's now distant leader from 2002–2012, an unforgettable hero to China's farmers.

Although farmers' fees and state enterprise money were no longer touchable, it appears to have been business as usual otherwise. Table 2.4 shows the various components of extrabudgetary funds (EBF) and extra-system funds (ESF) during the years following enactment of the Budget Law. From the very day of the Budget Law's passage, local governments were assembling finances that were more than double their formal budget. The capital came largely from the "self-raised" category, that is, bank loans and funding related to capital investment.[13] These funds, as well as a part of extrasystem funds (ESF 1), burgeoned when China joined the World Trade Organization in 2001, driving a near-decade-long economic boom that made China what it is today.

The pressure to raise funds led to the creation of bankable, or at least locally bankable, borrowers, the now well-known Local Government Financing Platform (LGFP).[14] By the late 1990s Beijing's restructuring of the financial system was hastened by the 1997 Asian Financial Crisis and the bankruptcy of Guangdong International Trust and Investment Co. (GITIC). GITIC's demise led to the elimination of similar international trust and investment companies that had become major financing arrangers for provinces up and down the Eastern China seaboard. At the same time party secretaries began to have an understanding of the experiment with incorporating state enterprises and listing their shares. The language (up until 1992 the very word *capital* (资本) was too politically fraught to touch) and financial techniques were quickly being adopted across eastern China. In 1997 large cities began bundling up whatever profitable assets they had and listing the agglomeration in Hong Kong; these were called Red Chips of which Beijing Enterprise was the first. This was the wrong idea, that is, it didn't work since most cities had no profitable enterprises to speak of no matter how packaged and the rage for this soon passed but the concept remained. Why, then, not incorporate utility or transport assets as a real state enterprise and just borrow from banks legitimately? No need to go through all the work involved in a public listing. This was the right idea and the "local government financing platform (LGFP)" was born.

In short, the very idea that local governments did not engage in deficit financing by directly and/or indirectly borrowing from banks is not believable; it was customary given Chinese fiscal tradition. During the 1990s and first decade of this century the Ministry of Finance, working with the IMF and World Bank, made many improvements to the foundation put in place by the 1994 Budget Law. Even so, by 2007, just before the global financial crisis broke out "self-raised" loans accounted for 45 percent of total bank lending.

The reason local governments have easy access to banks can be seen in trends in the national budget. From the late 1980s the policy to replace budgetary grants with bank loans meant that capital investment, as a category of the national budget, would decline.[15] Similarly the raging inflation of the 1990s gradually depressed budgetary capital expenditures. Given the effort to develop a market-based economy, this trend also makes sense; state enterprises pursuing a commercial mandate should finance their own capital investments, either from banks or from issuing bonds and equity. The fiscal reform of 2004, in fact, announced that the market would be the source of capital investment funding; budgetary funds as capital investment grants as an independent expenditure category dropped out of China's budget entirely in 2007.[16] The banks or capital markets were now to provide this funding and local governments were the undoubted beneficiaries.

Then There Was the Land but It Is Not Free, 1999–2007

In 1997 governments across China began selling staff the apartments that had originally been provided as part of their benefits. A secondary market rapidly developed; new buildings went up and before too many years there was a real estate boom. Who owned the land? The state and its agents owned the land, including counties, towns, and cities. Well, they controlled, not actually "owned," the land within their administrative jurisdictions. And, of course, the need to locate new sources of revenue made local governments at all levels vulnerable to those with capital, domestic or foreign. This situation was ripe for the rise of real estate developers, who would acquire leaseholds (land use rights) to build apartment complexes and even new cities. Chinese needed new residences; their cities were entirely dilapidated, even Shanghai. With the real estate boom, governments in good locations could build new homes for their citizens and, even more important, they would no longer be poor. That, anyway, is the common understanding.

Figure 2.4 tells this story and shows that proceeds from the sale of land use rights quickly approached the value of locally generated tax revenues and by themselves became equal to nearly half local officially budgeted revenues. In fact, from 2000 to 2010, revenues grew 10 times, but from then on, during the postfinancial crisis decade, they grew exponentially. Is it any wonder that corruption was rife and that Evergrande and others prospered?

There was never any doubt that land in socialist (or Imperial) China was owned by the state (or the Emperor). But what is the value of land use rights in China? The early cases in the 1980s raised the issue for the

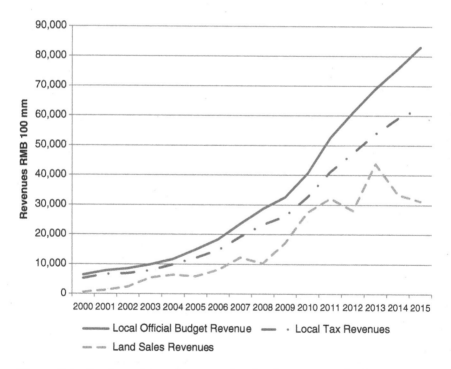

Figure 2.4   Land use rights sales revenues to local government budgets.
SOURCE: 2017 *China Fiscal Development Report*, pp. 259–295.

first time when foreign companies came to set up joint ventures. Their factories needed land to build on, but local governments had never confronted this problem before. There were no price indices, no regulatory guidelines to base decisions on, so it simply came down to negotiations. In the wake of June 4, the country began to actively welcome joint ventures and set up Special Economic Zones to house them. This raised the problem of land value to the national level for the first time in the history of the People's Republic. Then major SOEs began listing overseas and domestically. When their operations were incorporated into legal entities and audited based on international standards, the land they sat on had to be valued. Did the state own this land or did the SOE? The answer is that it depended. For the years up to 1998, such negotiations generated the series of revenues shown in Table 2.4.

Leasing avoided the entire ideological issue. As for valuation, it was easy for joint ventures (JV): the government set the price as high as the foreign investor could stand. For IPO auditing purposes when incorporating SOEs, the rent could be high or low, whatever was necessary to

Table 2.5 Land sale gross revenues to local budgetary revenues (%), 2000–2015.

%	Beijing	Shanghai	Jiangsu	Zhejiang	Anhui	Fujian	Guangdong	Chongqing
2000	21	7	18	34	6	14	7	11
2001	26	14	38	49	14	16	13	9
2002	25	18	71	82	34	36	11	24
2003	55	33	120	166	79	55	16	55
2004	85	44	69	108	84	61	17	77
2005	11	27	76	76	65	56	20	63
2006	17	24	72	78	73	96	28	77
2007	25	18	67	102	91	102	41	81
2008	37	24	48	53	63	28	20	49
2009	34	38	81	119	71	71	37	59
2010	56	31	94	140	95	99	30	77
2011	52	28	89	96	84	75	25	65
2012	20	16	66	59	70	58	24	70
2013	49	27	93	100	109	75	46	102
2014	50	32	61	57	82	46	38	69
2015	44	29	58	41	62	47	32	67

SOURCE: 2017 *China Fiscal Development Report*, pp. 259–295.

produce a profitable listing candidate. SOEs, by the way, had never paid a cent (or *fen*) for their land, and a high valuation boosted equity capital. In short, land-use rights have whatever value the local government says they have. In the 1990s these "sales" were all based on one-off agreements that soon became big "market-based" auctions, but auctions can be arranged.

By trial and error, an auction process leading to a more systematic valuation was worked out. It is not surprising that real estate salespeople in the United States are quite right when they emphasize "location, location, location." Table 2.5 shows eight provinces, or provincial-level cities, achieving land rights gross revenues in excess of 10 percent of budgetary revenues for the years 2000–2015. For example, Zhejiang Province, neighboring Shanghai, and perhaps the richest province in China, had little trouble achieving proceeds greater than its budgetary revenues. Nearly all these provinces have eastern seaboard locations and are the richest of the rich and so, of course, they got richer. The other 23 (excluding Hong Kong, Macau, and Taiwan) are poor and their land does not attract competitive bidding, but that doesn't mean there are no sales. The sale of "land" didn't help the poor local government unless, due to the luck of location, a major developer like Evergrande showed up, as the example of Lu'an shows.[17] These kinds of local governments are extremely vulnerable when the billionaire appears.

So what is the value of land in China? Can Beijing claim a value for land as an asset on its government balance sheet and, if so, how would it be calculated? This is an important issue when it comes to compiling a state balance sheet. The position taken in this analysis is that land is not being sold outright in China and never has been. There is no national or even municipal market that might provide some basis for an average per-hectare value. Therefore, the balance sheet discussed in Chapters 6 and 7 excludes consideration of land as an asset: where has it been valued and by which state agency? Including a number there is purely guesstimation, done to boost state net worth.

The process behind selling land use rights, however, isn't as easy for local governments as "borrowing" money from SOEs. The local government had to "own" the land in the first place, but land, unless it was agricultural, isn't empty; an SOE could be occupying it, for example. Nor did a plot typically have any of the required infrastructure needed before developers could go to work. So there were significant costs involved before rights could be sold. Who would pay to tear down old factory buildings, build roads, and put in place the power and sewage? In fact, if an SOE owned the old buildings, they would have to be bought out—even more expensive and time consuming, and how would existing residents or farmers on the land be compensated?

Farmers and urban residents—the People!—presented large issues for local governments in both the moral and political senses. They couldn't just chase them away, although this happened frequently to those who refused to move. Local governments would have to compensate them and move them somewhere where they could be housed. Then there was the question of jobs; the new location needed to be, but often wasn't, close to their places of work. So monetizing land was not straightforward. The local government would have to do some work, but they did not shirk. This explains why Figure 2.5 is completely misleading since it shows only the revenue side of the land sale business and not the associated costs or their timing.

Cost figures were unavailable until the MOF began publishing them in 2010.[18] This coincided with the time that Beijing seized control of this local money-spinner and brought the revenues from the sale of land use rights into the formal budgetary process as a fund that required (Beijing's) oversight. Table 2.6 shows the annual costs incurred by local governments, as well as *final* budget figures as of given fiscal year ends. In 2010 and 2011 the final costs were almost double the budgeted costs, reflecting, perhaps, a last great push in land acquisition before the transition to greater accountability. Thereafter they fell in line, as this activity was presumably overseen by Beijing but, as events have shown, the real estate sector during these years was out of control.

Considered as an ongoing process, local governments lacked the money to pay the initial land acquisition cost or preparatory expenses prior to the actual sale of land use rights. This was not necessarily a major problem; Figure 2.5 illustrates two simple ways that governments used to raise funds. Each province and some cities owned a trust company and most large cities had a city commercial bank. The trust creates an equity trust, which is sold through local banks to both retail and institutional investors. Or the bank makes a loan and places it in the off-balance-sheet wealth management product asset pool. The cash raised in these ways is

Table 2.6 Local government land development costs, budgeted and final budget, 2010–2014.

RMN 100 mm	2010 Budget	2010 Final	2011 Budget	2011 Final	2012 Budget	2012 Final	2013 Budget	2013 Final	2014 Budget	2014 Final
Land appropriation, demolition, and relocation	5,265	10,207	6,775	14,359	11,755	13,829	12,964	20,918	17,371	20,282
Land development	1,464	2,480	1,799	5,325	2,862	5,116	4,885	8,350	6,610	8,952
Urban construction	3,585	7,621	3,849	5,565	6,062	3,049	2,951	3,775	3,955	4,076
Rural infrastructure construction	473	1,077	875	760	632	486	695	517	999	459
Subsidy to farmers	228	457	602	690	313	521	605	852	857	857
Land sales business expenses	95	134	127	217	154	181	186	239	225	222
Low-rent housing expenses	209	422	873	520	472	356	343	392	476	368
Expenses for other land-use rights	1,128	4,225	3,360	3,616	4,087	3,126	3,031	3,223	4,014	3,485
Total	12,447	26,623	18,260	31,052	26,337	26,664	25,660	38,266	34,507	38,701

SOURCE: 2017 *China Fiscal Development Report*, pp. 259–295.

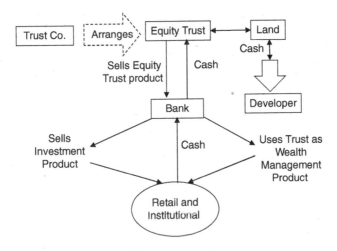

Figure 2.5 Trust company–arranged financing for land acquisition and predevelopment.

used to cover the cost of building a raw land reserve and, later on, to cover the costs associated with predevelopment. It would be difficult to describe the many ways local governments could generate funding for this business. Moral hazard is the asset the Chinese state relies on to do its business.

With the cost numbers in hand, a rough estimate of the so-called "actual" profitability of land leases can be made. This is calculated by netting out the costs of the previous year (the first year; land has to be prepared before rights can be sold) with the revenues from the current year sales of land-use rights. This shows that net profit is hard to find. In the case of the years 2011–2014, as shown in Table 2.7, there were no earnings, only losses as land prep expenses exceeded sales revenues. In other words, local governments must have borrowed to finance the acquisition costs of land for their land reserves.[19] Then they borrowed for all the other expenses shown in Table 2.6. In just these four years, gross borrowings nationally came to nearly two trillion *yuan* (US$231 billion). Of course, some of these loans might have been repaid, but it is far more likely that they were rolled forward or maybe even replaced by bonds. These borrowing figures are consistent with the bank loan estimates shown in Table 2.4. In short, in this land-rights business, local governments were borrowing *de facto* long-term funds to finance short-term needs.

Table 2.7 Net local revenues from land use right sales, 2011–2014.

RMB 100 mm	Final Expenses— Previous Year	Final Sales Revenue— Current Year	Revenues less Expenditures	Est. Bank and Other Financing
2011	26,622	18,261	−8,361	8,351
2012	31,052	25,305	−5,747	5,747
2013	26,664	25,598	−1,066	1,066
2014	38,266	34,342	−3,924	3,924
				19,088

SOURCE: *China Finance Almanac*; author's calculation.

Certainly, the net expenditures (or losses) shown in Table 2.7 do not tell the story in any way that might be called accurate, nor are the expenses. The important point to make is that all this activity *did not create capital assets* for the state. Local governments were not the builders on the land once the leases had been sold and the buildings that rose up were also not theirs. Developers did this work and financed themselves, although, of course, the construction companies, suppliers, and even banks were likely extensions of local governments. But if projects were not completed due to insufficient funding, as was the case with Evergrande and other developers recently, then these concrete shells would likely become direct assets of local governments. Who else was going to be responsible for finishing the buildings and making the original buyers whole? If the developer had no access to capital, so much less did the local government itself. To finish up failed projects, where was a local government to get funding? Even if a project were completed and sold, this would not mean that their expenses would be entirely covered. It is easy to imagine how these monies, never properly accounted for, could get lost in the jumble of urban renewal, but this, after all, has been the entire point of China's fiscal system.

Paving the Country Over

Stepping back from these accounting details, what matters for the party is the process itself; keeping accurate annual revenue and expense budgets are of little importance. Keeping people employed, providing new homes, urban renewal with new party headquarters—these are the things a party official points to when people from Beijing come down to inspect. The deliberate collapse of an Evergrande, from a local government's viewpoint, is simply an opportunity. As long as the process, resources, money all flow, then anything is possible. This is the party's work style, but what to do with the 64 million empty apartments that dot the Chinese landscape? Some of these may be second homes bought on the belief real estate values would always go up, but many are unfinished shells. Any trip by high-speed rail across today's China shows numberless unfinished 30-story apartment complexes dotting the horizon.

Still, the extent of urbanization that has taken place over the past 20 years is little short of incredible. Urbanization plus auctions eventually mean the use of agricultural land: there was only so much to be had from state enterprises. From the very start it was all about generating cash flow, and farmers were not going to stand in the way. The central government was, of course, doing the same thing in Beijing, a city that in the 1980s fit mostly inside what would become the Second Ring Road, built on the old city walls. By 2010 the city and district governments had filled the entire area inside the mountains on three sides and was starting to build a new city to the south. All this had been farmland. Bureaucracy and regulations were, of course, gradually created to manage the process nationally, including a Land Management Bureau and a Ministry of Land and Natural Resources, and together they produced a mountain of rules and regulations. These are all meant, however, to facilitate (and profit from) the process, not stop it. Over the nine years to 2008, as shown in Figure 2.6, China's total arable land was reduced by nearly 6 percent: the party was, in actual fact, paving over the countryside. In the years following 2008, the figure for arable land became fuzzy, added to by something called "recovered" land so comparable data does not go forward.

The Vulnerability of Local Governments, Banks, and Enterprises

The gap in China's fiscal system renders local governments vulnerable to whoever has capital, including central SOEs, foreign and private companies, and even rich domestic and foreign individuals. Local governments

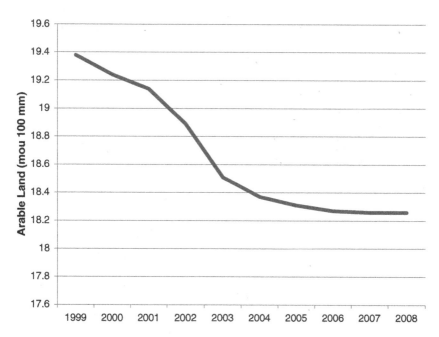

Figure 2.6 China total arable land, 1999–2008 (mou 100 mm).
SOURCES: China Ministry of Land and Natural Resources, 2006, 2011.

will do everything possible to attract such targets to invest in their jurisdictions. Of course, they cannot cross whatever "Red Line" may be set by Beijing, but these, after all, have a situational meaning. The evolution of China's real estate market is one example of this. Real estate development causes a great deal of activity, adds to local employment and GDP, and may even provide better housing for local citizens. It has not just been housing; cities have wholly recreated themselves, bulldozing their old cores, built glass towers and, if possible, 100-story skyscrapers and opera houses. The ease of building huge land banks in these conditions led to Evergrande's excessive leverage. It had the money, it controlled a bank, and it seemed that it visited everywhere looking for a place to plop down buildings. Local governments must have loved that company and they may love it again when they take over its projects (of course with Beijing's aid). This is a part of the story not being told. Overleveraged developers cannot exist without weak (and greedy) local governments.

But it is not only developers that have overleveraged balance sheets; so do state enterprises and banks, but for different reasons. Rich companies take advantage of weak local governments, but local governments have their own strengths. As this chapter has shown, political power enables them to strike deals with state enterprises and banks in their jurisdictions; the party, after all, is the ultimate "owner" of everything and, consequently, the ultimate dealmaker. In some sense, it can do whatever it wants. A symbiotic relationship between capital and political power exists at China's local levels, which also exists in Beijing. And such monies as local governments acquire in the process are not typically repaid. The result is that bank and enterprise balance sheets expand as loans are rolled over with longer and longer maturities. How such loans arc handled is a matter of the future when conditions will change. The problem with state banks and enterprises isn't that they are badly managed; it is that they are not independent of the political system itself. No amount of specialist tinkering and management MBAs is going to alter this fact.

Looking back, Dai Xianglong, a former head of the PBOC, noted that bank non-performing assets had added up to 20 percent of total loans in 1994, 22 percent at the end of 1995 and 25 percent at the end of 1997. By early 2012, Dai admitted to 35 percent, equal to 40 percent of China's GDP at the time.[20] It is not as if the party, or at least some technocrats in it, were not aware of the potential consequences of the system's nature.

How much capital did the party's extravagance waste over the years from 1990–2007? Table 2.8 adds up the total *public* costs of recapitalization and bad loan disposal for the 1997–2007 state bank restructuring (not including the MOF's promised support of Agricultural Bank). These restructuring charges came to 4.5 trillion *yuan* (about US$540 billion), by one calculation 44 percent of China's GDP in 1997. But this is only one way to put things together, and the actual costs are likely to have been much more. This episode is treated in greater detail in Chapter 7.

Implications

This is a picture of the costs incurred by China's fiscal system prior to the outbreak of the global financial crisis. The way the fiscal system is structured incents China's local governments, regardless of law or regulations,

Table 2.8   The cost of state bank restructuring, 1998–2007.

RMB Bn	Amount	Purpose	Recap	Source	Disposal	Note
1997	16	Closure of trusts, urban and rural co-ops	–		16	
1998	270	Initial bank recap	270	Bonds issued to MOF	–	
1999	40	Capitalization of Asset Management Companies (AMCs)	40	Bonds issued to MOF	–	
1999	858	AMCs issues bonds to respective banks	–	Bonds issued to banks	858	100% face value
2000	634	PBOC loans to AMCs for CCB/BOC bad loan acquisition	–	Loan from PBOC	634	100% face value
2002	10	Closure of 11 bankrupt securities firms			10	
2003	93	Capital writeoff at CCB/BOC	–		93	
2003	373	US$45 billion recap of CCB/BOC	373	Foreign reserves	–	
2004	279	PBOC auction of CCB, BOC, NPLs	–	Other entities buy at discount	279	100% face value
2005	122	PBOC second-round loans to AMCs	–		122	100% face value
2005	1	Capitalize Investor Protection Fund	–		1	
2005	620	PBOC finances ICBC bad loan disposal	–	PBOC loan	620	100% face value
2005	246	MOF IOU to ABC	-		246	
2006	118	US$15 bn to recap ICBC	118	Foreign reserves	–	
2007	139	US$19 bn for ABC recap	139	Foreign reserves	–	
2007	665	MOF IOU to ABC	–	MOF IOU	665	
Total	**4,484**	**US$382 bn**	**940**		**3,544**	
US$ Totals	**$541**		**$113**		**$428**	

SOURCE: Walter and Howie, *Red Capitalism*, pp. 54 ff.

to borrow, and they have always borrowed and they have borrowed a lot even before 2008. They borrow from those with the money, the local banks and enterprises. Indeed, where else should the party borrow but from its own banks, particularly in the years when there was no real private sector. When foreign or private companies offered, they got financing from them as well. When trust companies existed, they arranged funds through them. What did Beijing expect; local governments are responsible for covering social needs, maintaining social stability, and even raising the bulk of capital investment funds. It was their job to use whatever funds they could find; it was all the party's money after all.

All this collective deal making, however, would not work if Beijing succeeded in transitioning the financial system to a commercial basis. If this transition were to fail, then the snowball of bad debt would roll again. It did fail. Figure 2.7 shows the scale of *self-raised funds only* as a percent of total loans over the course of the reform era to 2005. During this period local government self-raised funds varied between 25 and 40 percent of total bank lending. At 40 percent such borrowing would require over 60 percent of bank deposits if loan-to-deposit requirements were 60 percent. To be clear, self-raised funds refers to the capital local governments might be able to use as part of their own efforts (Column B in Table 2.4). Nor are whatever funds generated directly from the sale of land use rights included in this figure. This figure shows the scale of only this one local funding source that leads to the bad debt that China's fiscal and financial system would generate in *normal* times. Unfortunately, banks did not transition to a commercial basis and command lending returned in force, so there was much more.

Stepping back again, a clear picture of China's fiscal system emerges, one that is far larger than that shown in official almanacs or ministerial reports to annual National Peoples' Congress. Figure 2.2, in an earlier section, draws the official picture. It shows that the 1994 Budget Law had a strong, positive impact on China's fiscal revenues and expenditures with revenues increasing to 25 percent of GDP in 2018. This is a strong number; the similar number for the United States is around 20 percent, including both central and local government revenues. The impact of the global financial crisis, unfortunately, halted this progress as revenues tailed off and expenditures increased, creating a large budgetary deficit. Bank lending to government in all its forms has filled this gap. Since 2010 both central and local governments, directly and via state agencies and enterprises, have been borrowing in domestic and international bond markets with abandon. Local governments are taking every *fen*

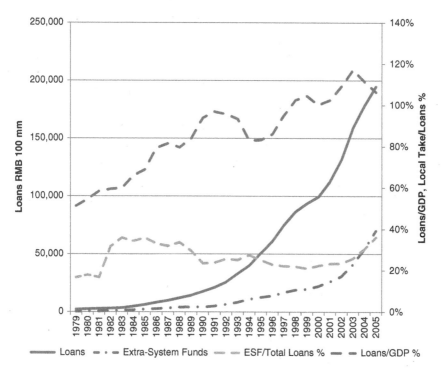

Figure 2.7   Extrasystem funds (ESFs) to total loans, 1979–2005.
SOURCED: *China Banking Almanac, China Finance Almanac,* and *China Statistical Yearbook.*

thrown at them to stimulate the economy, while Beijing squeezes the banks for more.

Figure 2.8 considers all sources of local extrabudgetary and extrasystem revenues and treats them as if they were in fact actual fiscal revenues, and why not? Beijing's deliberate actions have precluded them from raising funds to meet their obligations; a shadow fiscal system should be brought into the light. The total of official budgetary plus extrabudgetary revenues, therefore, illustrates a maximum level of fiscal revenues generated by local and central governments. At 50 percent of GDP in 2009, it is a maximum number because local governments do not necessarily have access to all such funds. But even at China's lowest economic point in the years 1989–1995 these figures have far exceeded official revenues. This may explain part of the reason that the party at all levels has been so successful in building a "New China" on its old foundations. This is the second observation.

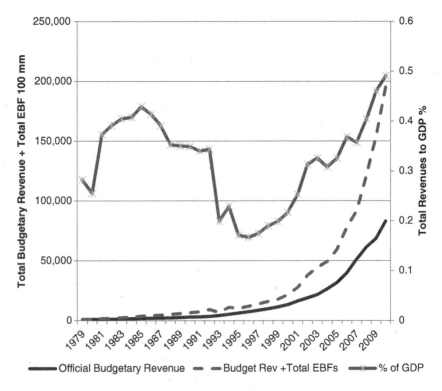

Figure 2.8   Comparative fiscal revenues of China, 1979–2009.
Sources: *China Finance Almanac, China Statistical Yearbook*, author's calculations.

The important point is that the fiscal system and its associated extrabudgetary financing mark out the boundaries of the party's ability to generate income. The political and fiscal strength of local governments calls into question the meaning of Beijing's leadership. Beijing can and has often changed the policies around how local governments can raise funds, but as the old adage says, "The Emperor has a policy, the locals have a counterpolicy (上面有政策下面有对策)." The very scale of extrabudgetary revenues reflects the long-term decline in Beijing's ability to redistribute funding equitably across China's geography; the fiscal system tends toward self-financing, and this limits the central government's capacity. This is not only a characteristic of the past decade of financial stimulus but, as this chapter has shown, an historical fact. The success of the current policy goal of "common prosperity" depends on local governments' willingness and even ability to cooperate and not the will of an all-powerful center.

To question why China has the sort of fiscal system described here is to miss the point. It did not choose; it already had such a system. Audrey Donnithorne, the greatest of traditional China economists, called China's a "cellular" economy formed by local governments and given a centralized veneer.[21] To call this complex organization "unitary," as the party describes its own state, as did the Emperor, Mao Zedong or anyone else, is misleading. It suggests that all power *is* actually centralized in Beijing and that an equally centralized Communist Party is in control of the machine implementing its edicts in the localities. This has always been the ideal across most of Chinese history and, of course, Lenin's own dream of the state.

As today, throughout Imperial history the central government's principal objective had been simply to maintain the political and social status quo.[22] Its fiscal system was built on the assumption that the entire country could be broken down into similar pieces: agricultural plots that never change ownership. Then, as now, the authority behind the system was centralized in a capital city, but the burden for operating this theoretically monolithic system and handing over taxes was, then as now, the problem of local officials. How else could it be? The roots of this "cellular" economy go far back into Chinese history. So it is not surprising that actual fiscal practice after 1978 functioned as it always had. It was not a matter of choice; it was simply the way things were, something that had never been consistently and sustainably challenged.

After Deng's visit to Shenzhen, the passage of the 1994 Budget Law was a singular achievement against strong local pushback: no local official wanted clear tax-collection obligations. Later on, Beijing has constantly sought to pass a variety of taxes including, for example, gasoline taxes and real estate taxes that would have strengthened official budgetary income, but failed. The personal income tax is paid only in the breech, and even then mostly by foreign-invested companies. The Ministry of Finance and its international advisors have done significant work to develop a modern rule-based fiscal system. Their work may continue even now, although the roots of immutable tradition are once again pushing back hard against them.

There has been no mention of a nonstate sector. Private sector companies do play major roles in the scope of the state, but as facilitators. For example, if it is true that the real estate sector contributes 29 percent of

China's GDP,[23] then Evergrande has perhaps done more than any other single Chinese enterprise to drive economic growth over the past decade. Such private companies exist at the behest of the state. Growing large, their existence becomes vulnerable to the benevolence of the party's central leadership, and there is little that pliant local officials can do. The global crisis and the accession of a new government in 2012 has forced continued fiscal and financial reform to the bottom of the agenda.[24] With increasing fiscal deficits and highly self-reliant local governments always looking for funding China's banking system is in a difficult position. The following two chapters look into how the banks—the critical part of the *fiscal* system—have managed to present strong performance metrics in an environment they cannot control.

Notes

1. Christine Wong, "The Fiscal Stimulus Program and Public Governance Issues in China," *OECD Journal on Budgeting* 11, no. 3 (2011): 19, http://dx.doi.org/10.1787/budget-11-5kg3nhjqrjl.
2. Lou Jiwei, *Rethinking of inter-governmental fiscal relations in China* (中国政府间财政关系再思考) (Beijing: China Finance and Economics Press, 2013)p. 2 and Chapter 7.
3. See Jia Kang and Hu Hongyou for explanations of the informal fiscal system in the 1990s including data; 贾康, "中国政府收入来源及完善对策研究" (Revenue sources of the Chinese government and research on improving them), 经济研究, 1998第6期; and Hu Hongyou 户洪友, "非税财政收入研究"(Research on non-tax fiscal revenues), 经济探究, 1998第6期; the following article explains obstacles to the implementation of the 1994 Budget Law, Lu Wanbin, " 要提高财政的政治地位" (Raise high the political position of finance)in 张佐才, 主编, 财税改革从论 上券 (1997, 经济科学出版社:北京), pp. 363–370.
4. For a detailed treatment of this issue see Le-Yin Zhang, "Chinese Central-Provincial Fiscal Relationships, Budgetary Decline and the Impact of the 1994 Fiscal Reform: An Evaluation," *China Quarterly*, March 1, 1999, pp. 127 ff.
5. Zhang (1999), p. 123; Jia Kang (1998). These funds were so designated under the old Soviet accounting system that was discarded in 1993. It was replaced by accounting principles similar to international standards. See Walter and Howie, *Privatizing China* (Singapore: John Wiley & Sons, 2005), pp. 73 ff. for a discussion on Soviet accounting principles.

6. For example, see *China Banking Almanac* 2013, p. 531; also see Carsten Holz's discussion of "investment inefficiencies" in his "Economic reforms and state sector bankruptcy in China," *China Quarterly*, June 2001, pp. 361–362.

7. See Shaoguang Wang, "The Rise of the Regions: Fiscal Reform and the Decline of Central State Capacity in China," in Andrew G. Walder, ed., *The Waning of the Communist State* (Berkeley: University of California Press, 1995), p. 87.

8. Jae Ho Chung, "Beijing Confronting the Provinces," *China Information* 9, nos. 2/3 (Winter 1995): 13.

9. 楼继伟, 中国政府间财政关系再思考 (Rethinking intergovernmental fiscal relations in China), (北京, 中国财政经济出版社,2013), pp. 118 ff. Lou was chairman of the China Investment Corporation and was then appointed Minister of Finance in 2012. One of the original group of reformers, his strong personality won him no friends and he left in 2016 to head up the National Social Security Fund.

10. "Hard budgets" refers to those that must be kept subject to legal or other constraints, whereas "soft budgets" have no such constraints. See Jing Jin and Heng-fu Zou, "Soft-Budget Constraints on Local Government in China," *World Bank Papers*, http://www1.worldbank.org/publicsector/decentralization/cd/china.pdf.

11. Christine P. W. Wong, "Rebuilding Government for the 21st Century: Can China Incrementally Reform the Public Sector?," *China Quarterly*, no. 200 (December 2009): 943 ff.

12. Christine P. W. Wong, Christopher Heady, and Wing T. Woo, *Fiscal Management and Economic Reform in the People's Republic of China* (Hong Kong: Oxford University Press, 1995), pp. 115 ff.

13. Christine Wong, "China: Public Investment under Reform and Decentralization," *World Bank Country Case Study*, 2014, pp. 7 ff.

14. Henry Sanderson and Michael Forsythe, *China's Superbank* (Singapore, Bloomberg Press, 2013), pp. 1–4.

15. Wong, "Rebuilding Government for the 21st Century," pp. 929–952.

16. This decision declares the independence of enterprises from government announcing the principle henceforth would be, "Whoever invests, whoever decides, whoever benefits, that one accepts responsibility." State Council, 关于投资体制改革的决定 (2004) 20号 2004年7月16日, http://baike.baidu.com/item关于投资体制改革的决定/2268337.

17. Yoko Kubota and Liyan Qi, "Empty Buildings in China's Provincial Cities Testify to Evergrande Debacle," *Wall Street Journal*, October 4, 2021, https://www.wsj.com/articles/evergrande-china-real-estate-debt-debacle-empty-buildings-cities-beijing-11633374710.

18. 2017 *China Fiscal Development Report*, 赵学秀, 主编, 2017中国财政发展报告 (北京; 北京大学出版社, 2017), pp. 259–295.

19. 白留杰, 白炜, 负责编辑, *2009* 中国地方财政发展研究报告 (北京,经济科
     学出版社, 2009), pp. 17 ff.
20. Chen Yuantung, "Current Problems and Reforms of China's Financial System,"
     US–China Business Review 2, no. 1 (2001): 1.
21. Audrey Donnithorne, "China's Cellular Economy," *China Quarterly*, no. 52
     (October–December 1972), pp. 605–615.
22. For a fascinating deep dive into the background of China's fiscal system, see
     Ray Huang, *Taxation and Government Finance in Sixteenth Century Ming China*
     (London: Cambridge University Press, 1974); for the short course, see
     pp. 313 ff.
23. Kenneth Rogoff and Yuanchen Yang, "Has China's Housing Production
     Peaked?" *China and the World Economy* 21, no. 1 (2021): 1–31, https://scholar
     .harvard.edu/rogoff/publications/peak-china-housing.
24. Christine Wong, "Plus ça Change: Three Decades of Fiscal Policy and Central-
     Local Relations in China," *Working Paper* WP22CW1, National University of
     Singapore, Lincoln Land Institute, June 2021.

Chapter 3

China's Banks and the Deposit Bonanza

Trees cannot grow up to the heavens.

—*Authoritative Person,* Renmin ribao, *September 9, 2016*

A nyone who has entered a Chinese bank retail outlet knows the sort of service that can be expected: either the outlet is small and airless with strange machines, many customers, several seats and one or two bank staff behind 2-inch-thick bulletproof glass, or the outlet is a huge branch with 20-foot ceilings, marble floors, and a sitting area near a bank of service windows. Those places feel like morgues. Service is provided in turn based on a slip with a number on it, like customers at a busy butcher shop. It once took three hours to remit US dollars overseas from a hard-currency account; no one was sure how to do it. The objective seems to be to keep money *in* the account and not allow it to be taken out! This experience seems standard across all types of Chinese banks, making a visit to a banking outlet the headache of the day. With foreign banks limited to adding one or at most two branches a year and few offering retail services, the prospect of change is distant. But the deposits are there, oh yeah!

When China joined the World Trade Organization (WTO) in 2001, its banks were bankrupt and in the midst of major restructuring and re-capitalization efforts. How then in less than 10 years was Beijing able to use its banks to provide massive, almost continuous stimulus to the economy after the Lehman Brothers bankruptcy in the fall of 2008? What was "Authoritative Person" talking about in the fall of 2016 when he wrote, ". . . trees cannot grow to heaven"? The previous chapter identified the trait of self-reliance that was strengthened by a flaw in the fiscal system leading to the creation of a shadow fiscal system. This chapter looks behind the loans taken up by local governments to ask how the party's unprecedented splurge was funded. It also looks into the simultaneous development of a consumer economy driven by new technologies that offered new "fintech" products, such as P2P lending, wealth management products, *TaoBao* and its partner *Yu'e Bao*. Demand for these new products generated a cascade of technological development and drove the creation of new bank funding channels. Their success, however, impacted the growth of household deposits in the state banks and after a time most were stopped or seriously altered. This action reflects exactly what Jack Ma spoke about in Shanghai in October 2020: the new Chinese economy cannot be managed as if it were a train station, but it is.

China's State Banks and the "Tree" Model of Banking

What makes understanding the financial system so difficult is the character of a Chinese bank, especially the state banks. Although the word "bank" is the same and there have been before the revolution truly commercial banks in China, those today are not banks in the way we understand them. This is not a question of whether they are independent of the government or party; they are obviously not. But they are also not similar to their international peers from an organizational standpoint.

China's banks from their founding after 1949 took on the structure of a government that organized itself geographically but called itself centralized. Although certain functions were and continue to be centralized, such as the military and armed police, the rest is strongly decentralized and largely self-reliant, despite outside appearances. This is a consequence of history. The Great Leap Forward 1958–1961 and the Cultural Revolution 1965–1976 both severely degraded the power of the central government. In those times, there was only a single bank, the PBOC, and around 1970 its Beijing head office was merged with the MOF. The provincial branches continued to operate under the purview of local party committees.[1]

From 1979, Beijing began to reconstitute the central government and, over the 1980s, the PBOC resumed an independent existence, spinning off its banking operations. In short, the head offices of the major state banks as well as Bank of Communications in Shanghai were, in effect, later add-ons to a system of provincial banks that had long been in existence under the control of local party officials.

In 1997 as a start to the restructurings of the major banks, an attempt was made to centralize provincial operations under head offices controlled by Beijing.[2] Vice Premier Wen Jiabao led national meetings of provincial party secretaries to explain that from here on banks would operate under the leadership of a party committee with offices inside the central bank in Beijing. The committee members would include the party secretaries of the central bank, the Chinese Securities Regulatory Commission, the state and policy banks, Bank of Communications, and China Life Insurance. The local party officials were told to no longer be involved with or interfere in bank operations except as requested by Beijing.

To say the least, this was a massive institutional change and it could not have been an easy conversation, but with this step the banks could begin to operate as national institutions with the goal of an ultimate listing in Hong Kong. Even with this move toward centralization and 20 years of history, the reality today is that each bank has remained a conglomeration of powerful provincial branches and a head office with relatively limited power. The creation of the basis for a modern banking system came and went within the career of a single banker!

Any trend toward a financially powerful center changed with the 2008 four trillion *yuan* stimulus loans. The urgency of the policy forced funds down on local governments with little planning about which deserving projects should receive capital. Once again, local governments and bank branches were strengthened. Four years later, in 2012, the new leadership took power. From its very beginning it sought to extend its (that is, the party's) control over all state entities. The days of division of party and state were ending. For the banks and all state enterprises, this was symbolized by revisions of the Articles of Incorporation in 2018 of all publicly listed bank and state enterprises. The Articles were rewritten to explicitly include the existence and emphasize the authority of party committees.[3] In contrast, the shareholding experiment from the 1990s through the great central enterprise listings early this century deemphasized the role of the party and often the party membership of senior management (a given) was explicitly excluded in listing prospectuses. The focus then was on separation of party and state.

From that time forward, the corporate governance mechanisms of each state enterprise and bank became coterminous with the party committee, and the banks themselves have answered only to the organs of the Central Committee. This means that each bank is subject to the same political policies as the others and the party manages all as if they were a single organization. Chinese banks are like schoolboys in a playground; some are faster, some are slower, but they all jump to the teacher's whistle and they all do basically the same thing.

This topic is the most important part of Jack Ma's now famous comments made about China's financial system on October 24, 2020. He said,

> Today financial supervision all over the world is very difficult. Innovation comes from the market . . . and the challenge to regulation is getting bigger and bigger. In fact, "supervision (监, jian)" and "to be in charge (that is, control)" (管, guan) are two different things. "Supervision" means watching over your development and paying attention to how you develop. "Management" means intervening when there is a problem or a foreseeable problem . . . Good innovation does not fear "supervision," but it is afraid of yesterday's "management."

We can't use the ways to manage a railway station to manage an airport.We cannot use yesterday's ways to manage the future.[4]

Of course Ma was well aware of the coming cancellation of his US$36 billion IPO that had just been priced in Shanghai, a first in Chinese stock market history. In this comment he well described the party's style of leadership.

Consequently, when viewing today's Chinese banking system, it is important to realize that the party is "managing" all banks as if they were one bank; the different names being presented are merely a formality. But they are not one bank; banks are a conglomeration of units, in which local branches hold operational authority. Put another way, the party may believe it controls the banks, but it has only cut off bank head offices from their bodies as happened during earlier politically charged times.

Figure 3.1 shows total banking assets, total assets by bank class, and year-on-year growth rates of total assets. From 2008 to 2020 China's banking assets grew in value by an astounding US$42 trillion, or about 10 times 2008 GDP. Asset growth peaked in mid-2009 at 27 percent in response to the first stimulus package. In the following years, loans continued to fund growth at somewhat lower rates of just below 20 percent. The success of the deleveraging campaign of 2016–2019 is also clear as loan growth (and therefore leverage) slowed from 2016, but it soon resumed in 2018, well before the outbreak of Covid-19.There is always a reason for the party to hit the gas.

For China's banks as banking institutions, this decade has been an organizational disaster. It has meant complete defeat to the effort made in the years 1997–2010 to create sustainable *commercial* banks in an economy based on market valuation of risk and lending. All the experience with Wall Street bankers, public listings, bad loan writeoffs, professional auditors and international investors meant nothing as soon as the party issued marching orders in 2009. If anything, the centralization of the bank party committees from 1997 facilitated the ease with which this happened. The consequence is that, as a group, they join China Development Bank as Chinese policy banks, yet they must maintain a façade to comply with Hong Kong Listing Rules and Basel's regulations.

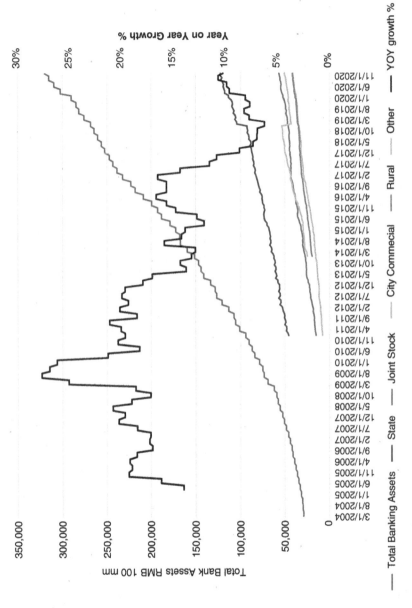

Figure 3.1 Trends in Chinese bank asset growth, 2004–2020.

Source: Wind.

Legend: —— Total Banking Assets —— State —— Joint Stock —— City Commecial —— Rural —— Other —— YOY growth %

Y-axes: Total Bank Assets RMB 100 mm; Year on Year Growth %

This is the new "new" Chinese banking model: the old Soviet-style command model, without a detailed credit plan but with audited balance sheets. Figure 3.2 shows the consequence of this reversion by comparing the total assets of China's principal banks with selected international peers for the years 2008 and 2020. In 2008, *after* the public offerings of CCB, ICBC, and BOC, China's state banks showed balance sheets much smaller than their global peers in line with the size of the economy then. This was to be expected after their restructurings and bad asset spinoffs. By 2020, in just over a decade, the picture has been completely reversed. International bank balance sheets have barely changed (except in the cases of Deutsche Bank and Wells Fargo, both of which experienced severe difficulties). The Chinese banks, on the other hand,

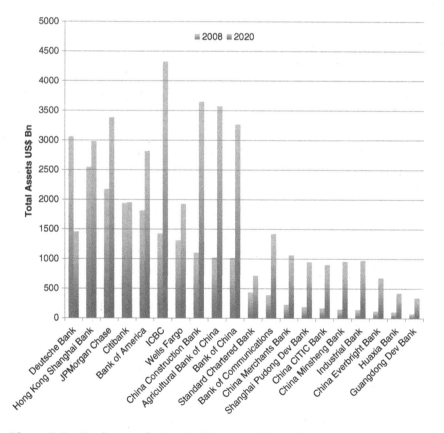

Figure 3.2   Total assets of selected Chinese and foreign banks, 2008 versus 2020.
SOURCE: *The Banker* and *Forbes*.

have become apparent world-beaters with balance sheets a multiple of their 2008 scale. Today China's banks sit on top of the *Fortune* Banking 500 and have become four of the 30 Global Systemically Important Banks (GSIBs).[5] They are what the Authoritative Person is calling "trees."

Bank market capitalization provides an even more meaningful way to compare banks that appear to be so different. Market capitalization is a simple calculation that takes the number of shares in a listed company, then multiplies them by the stock market value of a single share. The result is a metric for the value of a company and is commonly used in financial transactions. Merger and acquisition transactions routinely use this metric. This calculation is a fundamental measure of a company's value and will be used again later in Chapters 6 and 7. Figure 3.3 uses this metric to compare selected US and Chinese banks for the years 2008 and 2019. In 2008, after its recapitalization and listing, ICBC enjoyed the largest market cap of this group followed by China Construction Bank (CCB) and JPMorgan. In 2019, this picture was somewhat reversed with JPMorgan and Bank of America values increased by multiples. ICBC and CCB values grew as well, but not by as much. Among the rest of the group, China Merchants Bank's value increased the most. China Merchants, although much smaller in size (ICBC is more than four times larger), is commonly seen as the best bank in China, and its market value shows it. The figure suggests that stock market investors and analysts view US and Chinese banks the most favorably. For the party, what's not to like with such market-based performance?

Perhaps 2020 represented the peak year for the new, that is to say, old model. Cracks began to appear as a handful of city commercial banks collapsed and one, Baoshang Bank, was even closed and its licenses canceled, a first in Chinese financial history. Until the Hong Kong–listed China Huarong default in early 2021, such losses had taken place at the periphery of the financial system and were easily dealt with. This is no longer so in the case of China Huarong Asset Management, ICBC's shadow "bad" bank used in the latter's restructuring. Majority owned by the Ministry of Finance, Huarong was unable to file its annual report with the Hong Kong Exchange on time. Although the execution in 2020 of its former executive chairman indicated severe fraud had taken place, still one might have expected the MOF to at least make possible

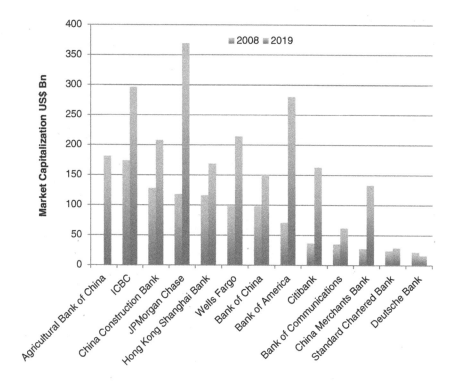

Figure 3.3 Market capitalizations of certain US and Chinese banks, 2008 and 2019.
Note: Agricultural Bank of China listed in 2010.
Source: Relbanks, https://www.relbanks.com/worlds-top-banks.

the completion of the annual report. This fact alone indicates both the depth of Huarong's problems and the ministry's technical illiquidity.

Huarong and its sister companies have long been the critical channels allowing banks to offload problem assets. Its default reveals the degree, not just of its corrupt management, but also of its overstuffed balance sheet and suggests the same situation for the other three, of which two are unlisted. The reverse side of this is the continued need of banks to rid themselves of bad assets. The banks, particularly the big state banks, enjoy very low non-performing asset ratios of between 1.5 and 1.8 percent. In other words, the Huarong case shows publicly the pressure felt by the banks to maintain acceptable audited metrics. There is no intention here to suggest that the bank auditors have been lax in their duties; they do their professional best. Nonetheless, non-performing loan ratios in the big banks and, apparently, the banking system as a whole have declined since the outbreak of the financial crisis. How China's banks have maintained such pristine, even strengthened, balance sheets while growing so quickly is the question raised here and the subject of Chapters 4 and 5. The *appearance* of high-quality lending is, however, the heart of the old "new" Chinese banking model.

Command Lending and Funding

The Chinese word for crisis (危机) signifies a crisis for some and for others, an opportunity; 2009 was truly a crisis for China. Thanks in large part to accession to the WTO in 2001 China had become an export-driven powerhouse, whereas a decade before the economy had been mired in stagflation. Even more significant, the private, not the state, sector now employed the majority of workers and drove economic growth. Consequently, the US mortgage crisis hit China in a very different way than the 1997 Asian Financial Crisis: suddenly nearly 40 million people were out of work and heading back to their home provinces. The Shenzhen-Guangzhou corridor, the home to the biggest chunk of exports in the country, became a ghost town.

It is little wonder that Beijing quickly unleashed a (supposedly) one-time, two-year four-trillion *yuan* (about US$600 billion) stimulus package in late 2008.[6] At the time, this amounted to 28 percent of China's GDP. The global recession persisted, however, so the one-time stimulus turned into a lending binge that became an economic model in its own right—namely, investment-driven GDP growth. And in retrospect, the bulk of that money went to real estate and bullet trains.

Local governments were the beneficiaries and, as has been shown, they were constantly searching for funds. Since the 1994 Budget Law, they had become responsible for 75 percent of total budgeted expenditures, but received just 47 percent of revenues. By this law, they had no authorized taxing authority. As usual, they filled this gap with bank loans using one pretext or another that, of course, were off budget. This (dis-) incentive structure continued into the precrisis years as was shown in Table 2.4 in Chapter 2.. Once a new funding source grew to size, however, the central government ring-fenced it as part of the formal budget or worse, eliminated it. For example, all fees levied on farmers were in a single Beijing stroke simply eliminated in 2000. This made Hu Jintao, the then Party Secretary, a god in rural areas. As another, the sale of land use rights was brought under central control in 2010.

Tightening central grip on local "small treasuries" (小金库) left the locals in difficult circumstances, especially since the land rights business turned out to be a GDP but not a money spinner. So when the stimulus was announced in late 2009, it was like throwing brush on a fire. Over the next few years, loans turned into a continuous river that ran far broader than the original package. As Table 3.1 shows, the initial package equaled 20 percent of total loans in 2009 and drove a 27 percent jump in lending in 2010. Things gradually settled down, but by then nearly all provincial capitals sported 100-story buildings (Guangzhou has two plus a world-class opera house), new airports, new city centers, Tang Dynasty water parks, and a high-speed rail system to every Podunk in the country including Bengbu.

Once the lending began, Beijing seemed to lose control. This was demonstrated by two audits. In the summer of 2010, hardly a year after

Table 3.1   On-balance-sheet local government–only borrowings, 2009–2017.

100 mms	General Borrowings	Special Project Borrowings	Total Local Loans	US$ Bns	Local Loans % GDP	Local Loans % Total Loans	Total Loan Net Increase YOY %
2009	NA	NA	78,000	1,149	23%	20%	NA
2010	NA	NA	107,000	1,621	27%	21%	27%
2011	NA	NA	NA	NA	NA	NA	14%
2012	NA	NA	121,153	1,945	23%	18%	16%
6/30/2013	NA	NA	135,515	2,239	24%	18%	14%
2014	94,272	59,802	154,074	2,482	24%	18%	13%
2015	92,639	54,949	147,568	2,272	22%	15%	15%
2016	98,313	55,245	153,598	2,293	21%	14%	13%
2017	103,632	61,468	165,100	2,538	20%	13%	12%
2018	NA	NA	166,100	2,534	20%	12%	13%
2019	NA	NA	228,219	3,270	23%	14%	12%

SOURCE: National Audit Office 2010–June 2013; *China Finance Almanac*, 2014–2019. Note that 2009–2013 may not be comparable to the later years and that these figures have not been verified by the Ministry of Finance.

the original stimulus announcement, Beijing sent out National Audit Bureau work teams to discover how much had been lent, which tells you something about the reliability of bank balance sheets. The 2010 work teams reported back, based on a limited scope, that the RMB 4 trillion stimulus had actually resulted in total loans outstanding of RMB 7.8 trillion (US$1.1 trillion), nearly double the original plan.[7] In 2013, Beijing again sent out another set of auditors. This audit was also limited in scope but showed outstanding local debt of RMB10.7 trillion (US$1.6 trillion) of loans, local government guaranteed loans, and other borrowings—some 24 percent of China's GDP.[8]

In 2014 Beijing sought to ring-fence local borrowing by establishing quotas and a budgetary approval process with final approval of the National People's Congress.[9] Official numbers provided by the Ministry of Finance for the following years show continued reliance on the debt machine while, as the world knows, China's GDP growth slowed into single digits. The MOF local debt data as shown in Table 3.1 was, however, "until a later date" self-reported by the local governments themselves. That later date has yet to be announced, so there is plenty of room to doubt the accuracy of local debt statistics.

In any event, whether for the reports of the work teams or these annual almanacs the purpose is not to measure an activity precisely, but to illustrate the problem. And the problem is that the true beneficiaries of the liquidity surge have been local governments. The real question such lending raises is not about the huge volume that has made China's banks world leaders, it is how did the banks fund such largess?

If the banks in the 1980s and 1990s also channeled money on command, then why were there no "trees"? During those decades, banking assets kept pace with GDP growth, never growing beyond GDP itself. It seems clear that the only difference between the old banking command model and the "new" one is funding. Without funding, a loan portfolio cannot increase and trees cannot grow to the sky. The only funding sources are deposits, bonds, and equity. In China's case it was corporate and household savings that were and are by far the most important contributors. Of the two, household deposits are the most important for two reasons: they are "stickier," and, as the example at the start of the chapter suggests, they can be made even more sticky. Household depositors take their money out less than enterprises, which need cash to fund operations, and the second reason is that there are more of them.

Figure 3.4 shows China's banking deposit growth since the start of the reform period. Both corporate and household savings grew in direct response to the huge societal changes created in the late 1990s as Beijing shifted away from the pure planned economy to a more market-driven one.[10] Traditional Soviet-style industrial ministries were closed as the focus of development turned to the enterprise, profitability, and capital raising through stock markets. SOEs themselves were restructured, leading to the loss of over 25 million jobs. Workers began to depend more on salary paid than on benefits provided. In rural areas the old barefoot doctor medical support service melted away as the cooperative farming model was done away with. Finally, the one-child policy resulted in less consumption and more saving for two reasons: cheaper to raise one child than two; and second, parents could expect less support in old age. By the turn of the century the old society and its social safety net were gone and what savings people had had been devalued by a huge inflationary spike. Given all this change and the growing uncertainties in the future, the Chinese people had little choice but to save heroically.

China's accession to the WTO in 2001 opened China's door wide to foreign investment. The pervasive belief among foreign governments and companies was that China was open to business, willing to abide by international rules, and clearly set on the road to some sort of capitalist-style market economy. Perhaps a more important factor was the assumption of power in 2002 by men with little support across the bureaucracies and military. This lack of support meant that the central government was even weaker vis-à-vis the provinces. Over the decade this group ruled, financial reform pushed forward, and the economy simply boomed. China was blasting into the modern age because it was no longer being managed, as Jack Ma has it, as a railway station. If China is a superpower today, it should thank Hu Jintao, the party secretary, and Wen Jiabao, the premier.

With WTO and a weak central government, hundreds of billions of direct investment dollars poured into local economies and government coffers. Local governments needed the jobs coming from such investment, and absent interference from Beijing bureaucracies they proceeded to cut Western companies terrific deals in terms of taxes and land costs, even building factories to measure. The joint venture disappeared as the Woofie ("wholly owned foreign enterprise") became the dominant form of foreign investment.

In addition to jobs, foreign direct investment and an export-heavy current account provided domestic liquidity from corporate savings. In the country's closed capital account, banks must sell to the central bank every US dollar brought in, with the exporting enterprise receiving renminbi (RMB) in return. The central bank balance sheet shows the resulting dollar as reserves on the asset side and local currency as a liability. Net exports and FDI became *the* chief drivers of liquidity in the Chinese economy and a prime, if indirect, driver in the growth of household deposits. In 2004, China began running a current account surplus (exports less imports) with the world that is commonly understood to have led to its huge foreign exchange reserves. But the other side of this is the huge amount of RMB released into the system. This RMB went first into corporate deposits, whether those of a foreign investor or a state enterprise or a private company. And part of this money was paid out in salaries to China's workers, who placed large parts into bank accounts.

During the early years of the century, the average wage in foreign invested companies began to increase strongly and consistently with wages doubling every five years.[11] Foreign paid wages also had the effect of pulling wages in the state sector up as well, so that for the years through 2015 *all wages* were doubling each five-year period. Private sector job creation and wage growth drove SOE wages, and all helped build China's huge middle class of over 300 million by 2020 and as a result, catalyzed the surge in household deposits.

Beginning in 2009 the measure of retail or household deposits to GDP after rising rapidly in the WTO years flattened out and began to trend down from 2013 as shown in Figure 3.4. There is a similar trend for total deposits. This trend explains the party's sensitivity to investment products that might attract deposits away from banks (see later sections). Deposits are the primary source of loans. As China's demography begins its inevitable decline in the very near future, household deposits will also decline and the party will be faced with a major constraint to its spending habits. This point will become more clear in Chapters 6 and 7.

The Chinese people are famous worldwide as savers, but not necessarily by choice. They do this because there are few attractive alternatives to bank deposits. Of the available alternatives some are seen as too risky, like the stock market, or are not yet well understood, like insurance products. The openings to the Hong Kong exchange or experiments, now ended, with P2P lending and wealth management products, show that Beijing prefers retail households to put their money in banks; more on this later. And, indeed, Figure 3.5 shows that the bulk of their money is mostly in low-yielding bank accounts that, with inflation, are in fact losing money. Wealth management products (WMPs) have been extremely popular since investors believed there was an implied government guarantee backing them. Insurance products, savings bonds, and mutual funds are less attractive given low yields, and trust plans and the bond market are mainly institutional and not open to retail.

Only the capitalization of the stock market can compare to household deposits and, as history has shown, can present large opportunities to "beat the bank." But China's stock market, despite its reputation, is dominated by institutional investors[12] and has been known to crash, so

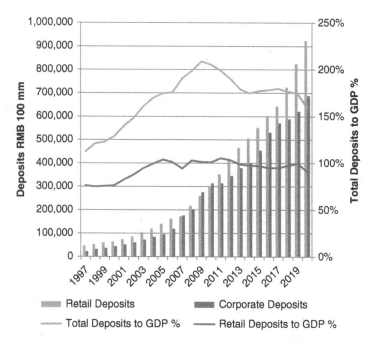

Figure 3.4 Trends in retail and corporate deposits, 1997–2020.
SOURCE: China Statistical Yearbook.

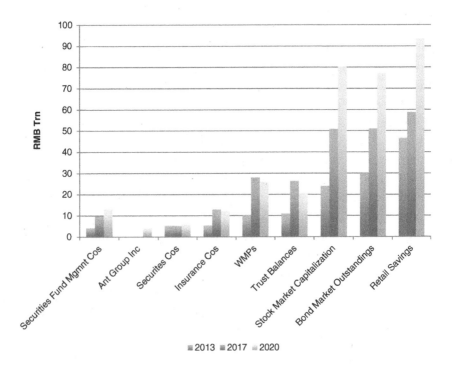

■ 2013 ■ 2017 ■ 2020

Figure 3.5 Selected investment products, 2013–2020.
SOURCES: PBOC, CBIRC, CSRC, China Bond, Chinese Banking Association, and Chinese Asset Management Association.

the safe money stays in the banks. Savings must be safe since the values contained in China's pension funds are murky at best. The result of all these factors is that the Chinese annual retail savings rate peaked at 25 percent in 2008 and has averaged over 20 percent of GDP in the following years. This rate is 15 percentage points higher than the global average[13] and more than any other factor explains why Chinese banks have been able to build such huge balance sheets.

Fintech and Other Challenges to Bank Deposits

Even after the change in party leadership in 2012 Beijing continued to experiment with different ways to put pressure on state banks to make them commercially competitive. The CBRC and PBOC acted as if the financial reform package created by the previous two generations of leaders would go forward as the new "400 reforms" policy position put forward by the party in 2012 suggested. In fact, there were liberalizations of the deposit and lending rates, and there was a slow but steady opening to foreign commercial banks. There was the big experiment liberalizing the capital account in 2015 and other less understood reforms that put pressure through the market on retail deposits nearly monopolized by the state banks earlier in the century. These included wealth management products, P2P lending, and licensing privately owned commercial banks. In all of this, the regulators were willing promoters.

As planned by the banking regulators, new financial reforms had the effect of diminishing the growth of state bank deposits. And new mobile-phone-based technologies empowered the retail public with more convenient and attractive product choices. With fewer deposits, how could the state banks step up when the party called on them to support the national economy? They began lobbying regulators for more regulatory oversight of the new products.

Local Bank Consolidation

An important part of restructuring the banking system was the consolidation of urban and rural deposit-taking entities into city and rural commercial banks. These small banks lacked any kind of technology and only a few became professionally audited and listed. But the populace sees them as being backed by the government, and so moral hazard had the effect of commoditizing all banks big or small. Deposit insurance also added protection up to a quarter-million *yuan*. Savers feel safe with putting their savings in banks. Even in the Baoshang Bank bankruptcy and closure, retail depositors were protected although larger depositors lost their funds. From a convenience standpoint, bank branches and sub-branches of the major state banks are liberally spread around in all cities, whereas the shareholding banks have branches only in the major cities. Of these, only China Merchants Bank has a strong retail operation. All have mobile and Internet banking.

The large increases in systemic risk came from the new city commercial banks. They became very competitive in raising deposits, as Figure 3.6 shows. This has implications for the relationship between the central government and the localities. In China everyone wants a bank

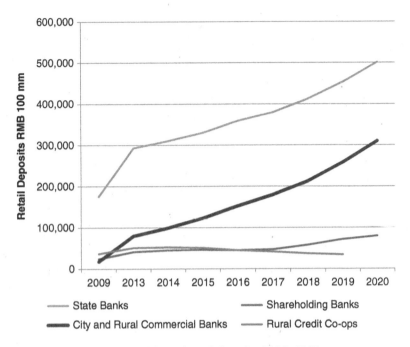

Figure 3.6   Institutional holders of retail deposits, 2009–2017.
SOURCE: China Banking Almanac.

because a banking license is a license to lend. All the huge corporate frauds over the past 20 plus years show this. Capital Steel in Beijing had Huaxia Bank, Baoshang Bank was one of many controlled by the Tomorrow Group, Shengjing Bank was controlled by Evergrande. Local governments are no different; with a bank and a trust company what can't be done out of Beijing's purview? In the highly liquid years following the financial crisis these city banks competed and were doing well, which means local governments had more capital to work with and the central government's big state banks had less. From this it would seem that central regulators favored intra-banking system competition.

Wealth Management Products

Wealth management products explain a large part of the success of the city banks in generating deposits. In 2010, the first year detailed information on WMPs in Wind Information was available, 146 city banks issued 56 percent of total WMPs by value, shareholding banks 22 percent and state banks 32 percent. In 2017, the year the CBRC issued new regulations, individuals accounted for 70 percent of outstanding WMPs. Big banks used the product defensively to hold on to depositors in an environment where deposit rates had been somewhat liberalized. At least, this was the original intention, but banks quickly saw that WMPs gave them greater flexibility to manage their balance sheets. Big banks dumped unwanted assets into off-balance-sheet asset pools, then repackaged them as WMPs and sold the product to retail investors. Shareholding banks worked with local government projects to arrange project financing and sold the resulting product to other institutions. City banks used WMPs to attract deposits that were used to fund city government projects. By 2017 the scale of this business had gotten out of hand, forcing the regulators to step in and begin to negotiate an end to this experiment. Negotiate because they didn't really know how much was out there and what the WMP asset pools contained: the banks themselves provided answers so that the situation remains opaque.

In their peak year of 2015 when they were being sold freely, WMPs represented 25 percent of total bank deposits (see Figure 3.7) with nearly 30 trillion *yuan* in value (more than US$4 trillion) as compared to total risk-weighted banking assets of the same year of 88.5 trillion! Following the release of draft regulations in 2017, the short-term principal guaranteed WMPs matured by year-end accounting for the rapid decline in outstandings. With WMPs in 2017 also equaling about 32 percent of GDP, it is easy to understand why regulators brought this to a halt. They did so not because of the risk involved—after all, the product was all off balance sheet and out of sight—but because of their impact on state bank deposits. Banks played accounting games with WMP maturities so as to maximize the audited size of their deposits at year end. This meant less real deposits were actually available during the year to lend to projects valued by Beijing. The city banks were, of course, using WMPs to fund local projects, as were the shareholding banks. This is exactly why China has generated so much redundancy across its national geography. The product needed redirection toward borrowers of national importance.

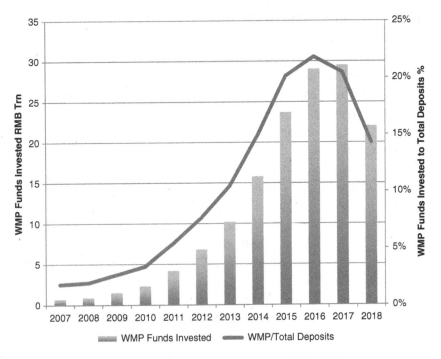

Figure 3.7   Trends in wealth management products, 2007–2018.
SOURCES: IMF, "Shadow Banking around the Globe," October 2014, p. 76, 2007–2012; *China Wealth Management Report*, 2013–2018.

Peer-to-Peer Lending

This directional issue also turned out to be the case for the peer-to-peer (P2P) investment product, a so-called "fintech" product." The affinity of Chinese for mobile phones combined with a traditional lending practice and supportive regulators explains the rapid take-off of P2P lending. The "hui (会)" is a traditional borrowing/lending practice in which a number of friends or relatives contribute money to the *hui* and can borrow from it by bidding the highest interest rate. Adding the mobile phone and online platforms simply scaled up a traditional micropractice to a national scale with the platforms substituting as borrowers. It is not surprising, then, that transactions took off fast in 2007 when the first P2P platform was set up and also not surprising that it was reined in 11 years later. During this time, P2P loans became a significant source of funding for small firms and consumers through as many as 6600 online platforms. In effect, every locality in China went online advertising higher interest rates to attract capital. Fraud was, of course, rampant.

By late 2017 new P2P loans had equaled over 5 percent of new bank loans! Figure 3.8 shows the volume of what were very short-term loans and the interest rates bid by existing platforms. The rates were higher than bank loan rates, but most borrowers were unable to access banks. The other alternative is private bankers in Wenzhou that charge even higher rates. Given the scale considering the amount of deposits that were diverted from bank balance sheets and the impact that had especially on state bank lending, this P2P activity in 2017 would have taken about 9 percent of related deposits.[14]

And it was easy. Platform organizers had only to establish a website (the platform) and advertise various projects and financial returns. The investor sends money to the platform, and its managers are basically free to use it however they like. From a banking viewpoint, the funds would have been remitted from the investor's bank account to the platform managers from which it is disbursed, likely to be a city bank, and from

Figure 3.8   P2P turnover, interest rate, and the Wenzhou rate, 2012–2021.
SOURCE: Wind.

there anywhere; a portion of the deposits would have been lost to the system.

Given the ease of establishment and national scale of online advertising, platforms were set up all over the country and in many cases became another source of local government funding. At the beginning, platform managers invested in single projects with a defined return. The transparency is what regulators had hoped for. Over a short time period others developed sophisticated frauds involving local bank wealth management products. Some research suggests that the failure or "run" on a platform is closely correlated to political leader transfers or national political events, that officials enabled platforms to continue despite illiquidity until such events were over.[15]

The regulator's experiment with P2P uncovered a huge market that state banks did not reach into. The larger issue was the sheer volume of bank deposits that were being diverted to areas that did not suit Beijing. By 2020 the last platform had been closed down. At the same time, regulators encouraged the major state banks to take over the market themselves by creating what is called "inclusive finance (普惠金融, *puhui jinrong*)." Also a fintech product, the large banks now compete to please regulators by making loans to theoretically screened microborrowers and enterprises with interest rates set by regulators. By June 2020 such loans equaled 24 percent of total new bank lending and were still growing aggressively.[16]

TaoBao, MyBank, and Yu'e Bao

Certain kinds of money market funds also became a serious challenge to the state banks and for the same reason. In late 2014 as part of the reform effort, the CBRC granted banking licenses to a small number of private investors, among which Alibaba Group received a banking license for MyBank. Alibaba shortly thereafter reorganized its back-office operations, mostly its mobile payment service, AliPay, into a new company, Ant Financial. As part of this, Ant created a money market fund called *Yu-e Bao* (or "Leftover Treasure") as a sort of simple sweep account for leftover change from customers buying on its website. In China such payments must be made in cash. Figure 3.9 illustrates the cash flows involved. Customers buying on Alibaba pay in cash transferred from bank deposits

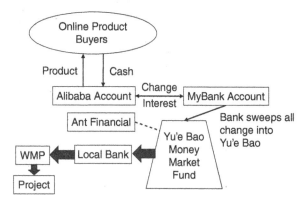

Figure 3.9   Cash flows into *Yu-e Bao* money market fund and beyond.

to MyBank. Over time transactions leave small change in the MyBank accounts. At the end of business day MyBank sweeps all such monies into the *Yu-e Bao* money market account. Of course, these accounts paid some interest.

Ant Financial, as the fund manager, used the funds to place deposits with contracted banks and then instructed that the deposits be used to acquire WMPs created by those banks. This enabled Ant to generate a higher return and a portion of the interest was then paid to MyBank depositors. This arrangement accomplished three things. First, it generated a high return that, over time, attracted much more money to MyBank and *Yu-e Bao* than just change from product sales. Second, the city banks were able to generate deposits and, third, they could use the deposits to support local projects. Here was a national Amazon-like company financing local governments.

In the end, this arrangement inevitably created a complex Ponzi scheme that stretched across the country. The money that savers placed in MyBank was simply short-term demand deposits and the deposits Ant made with its banking partners were short term, but local governments used the money for long-term purposes. Ant Financial had to carefully manage deposits into and withdrawals from the fund and to oversee local government actions. From a risk viewpoint, savers thought they were putting their funds in a bank deposit and ultimately in a high-paying money market fund, not a local WMP. Ant, for its part, was simply depositing funds in banks and buying WMPs. The local banks were taking not just a funding risk in the event Ant deposits were moved, they were also taking on off-balance-sheet credit risks if the project failed and could no longer pay interest on WMP loans. At that point the bank would be on the hook to purchasers of WMPs (see Chapter 4 for more detail) and so on back down the line to MyBank. Regardless, things exploded: in just over four years the number of users of *Yu-e Bao* grew to over 350 million, leaving over $210 billion equivalent in the fund as of FY2017. At that time *Yu-e Bao* accounted for nearly a quarter of all Chinese money market funds and was the largest such fund in the world. Then the regulatory pushback began. By third quarter 2018 the fund's assets under management had fallen to around 15 percent of all such funds.

The success of this "fintech" approach to apparently simple banking services had a significant negative impact on state bank deposit gathering and so was brought under regulatory control. It is reminiscent of US regulators allowing Merrill Lynch to offer the revolutionary Cash Management Account in 1977. This account offered customers a money market account with a brokerage account sweep function into a money market account, a debit card, and later checking. In China the broad acceptance of similar products by the Chinese public uncovered the real market for investment products. This market has always been there but cannot be developed for political reasons—to protect the state banks and behind them, the party.

Bank Capitalization

With the massive growth of deposits on the liability side of bank balance sheets, China's banks have had to grow their capital base. Following their initial listings, Chinese banks have been unable to issue more equity. Normally more owners' equity would be the answer. This is particularly so since, in China, most see equity as money that need not be repaid. The sole problem with equity is that since their original listings, the shares of the big state banks and nearly all others have traded below book value. Chinese regulations do not permit the sale of state assets, that is, shares that represent an asset, at below book value.[17] Debt on the other hand has to be repaid and, therefore, managed, especially foreign debt, but in recent years banks have not been allowed to go to the US dollar market for funding.

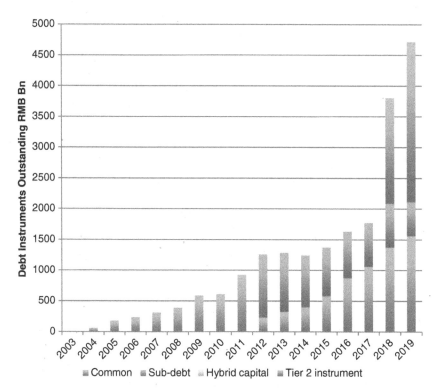

Figure 3.10   Bank debt instruments outstanding, 2003–2019.
NOTE: Reliable breakdown of bond categories not available before 2012.
SOURCE: China Bond.

In the early years following their public offerings and before the financial crisis, the big banks did proceed with share-rights offerings, but this soon revealed a problem with issuing bank equity. The government's shareholder, Central Huijin (see further discussion in Chapter 7), must come up with matched funds to prevent the dilution of the state's overall share. Central Huijin, for its part, is ultimately owned through China Investment Corporation by the Ministry of Finance, which, as Chapter 2 illustrated, is itself underfunded. So although the MOF would be happy with an enlarged dividend base, it can't afford to support one; consequently banks have switched to issuing subordinated debt (see Figure 3.10). An experiment with something called "hybrid capital" followed before the huge offerings of Tier 2 capital instruments and even the new logically necessary "perpetuals" that came out in 2019.[18] None of these require Central Huijin to put up any money, but all added to regulatory bank capital. Of course, such borrowings add to overall state leverage.

The sudden increase in issuance from 2018 is perhaps related to the government's requirement that the wealth management product be brought under control (see Chapter 4). To comply, banks would need to write-off material amounts of bad assets beginning in 2018. This in turn would reduce their capital adequacy ratios and therefore require additions to capital to offset losses.

Who invests in these bonds? Looking out over the Chinese financial landscape the question needs to be rephrased: Who has the funding to invest in these bonds? The answer is simple: funding can only come from the retail public and, as has been shown, their money is mainly found in banks. Retail investors hold only small amounts of savings bonds. In the case of the relatively small universe of bank bonds, mutual funds and insurance companies are also major investors; these, of course, represent retail funding. Table 3.2 provides a breakdown of investor holdings of bank bonds. And it is not surprising that banks themselves hold anywhere from 30–45 percent of their own bonds, making bond issuance a simple case of "You hold mine and I'll hold yours." The other major investor class has become mutual funds, which, since 2018, have stepped up to hold over 50 percent; these funds are also purchased by retail investors. The reality is that even though the bond market is second largest in

Table 3.2   Investor holdings of commercial bank bonds.

100 mm	2010	2011	2012	2013	2014	2015	2016	2017	2018	2019
Total Bank Bonds	6,095	9,248	12,653	12,938	12,535	13,811	16,370	17,753	38,063	46,964
State banks	1,564	1,732	2,734	3,110	4,072	5,385	7,021	8,270	14,105	15,730
Other banks	483	451	654	947						
Insurance Cos.	3,013	5,279	6,377	6,016	5,751	5,266	3,852	2,967	2,882	3,268
Funds	621	1,424	2,536	2,582	2,492	2,880	5,233	6,235	20,011	26,468
Other	414	362	352	283	220	280	264	281	1,066	1,498
State Bank Holding %	25.7%	18.7%	21.6%	24.0%	32.5%	39.0%	42.6%	46.6%	37.1%	33.5%

the world, it does not have the demand to absorb bank issues, so banks inevitably must buy each other's own bonds.

Implications

The importance of deposits to state banks and beyond them, to the party's capacity to direct financial resources, deters the creation of alternative ways for the retail market to channel its money. When the earlier reformist administration launched these new products, the funds they attracted did not go where Beijing wished. However, the pure demand drove the creation of new technologies, not just to facilitate traditional banking services, but also to create new ones. Better domestically made mobile phones, new data centers dug into hills in Guizhou, a zillion websites in support of modern Chinese life styles—these all laid the foundation for a consumer-driven economy, a policy goal the party publicly supports as a replacement to investment-driven growth. Well, P2P, WMPs, *Yu'e-Bao*, the now enfeebled STAR market in Shanghai, and the universe of online services represent just that: the emergence of a world-class consumer-driven, technology-based economy supported by onshore capital.

In two short decades the very nature of China's economy had begun to change and had done so without the massive injections of capital enjoyed by the state sector. In 1997 the country was an afterthought; articles in influential journals asked whether China really mattered.[19] The country's accession to the WTO in 2001 made all the difference; foreign capital and management poured in, employment soared as Chinese built world-class supply chains as the party stepped back.[20] Chinese people for the first time had money as the middle class broadened to over 300 million across the country's eastern seaboard: the same size as the US population!

Now that the party has put itself directly back into the heart of much of this, will such innovation continue? As for the Chinese financial sector, the result is already clear: it is settling back into its old ways in the grasp of the party's thinking that control is equivalent to stability. This search for stability has strengthened Beijing's capacity to channel funds in directions it likes—uncompetitive SOEs, the military and police—but it has also reinforced the already strong trend toward localism and self-reliance. As the past decade has shown, and with the exception of the overbuilt bullet railway system, local power has meant new airports and train stations, but also 100-story buildings, amusement parks, ghost cities, and the creation of 64 million empty apartments.

There is a larger problem. As the population rapidly ages in the very near future, the 92 trillion *yuan* in savings they have squirreled away in banks and under mattresses will just as rapidly disappear as oldsters use it up to support their retirements. According to a draft OECD study,[21] people over the age of 65 will exceed 200 million in 2026, 300 million in 2038 and 330 million in 2050, of which 100 million will be age 80 or older. In 2050 these oldsters will represent 25 percent of the total population. By 2100, some analysts project that China's population will be equal to that in 1975, 940 million and some project even lower levels. The math is clear, unless fertility rates change or the returns on social security funds increase dramatically, household savings are in for a long decline. Are the assets of China's banks and the government itself sufficiently liquid to withstand a pay-down of this major funding source?

Notes

1. Only the Bank of China, the specialized foreign exchange bank, and the People's Construction Bank of China (now China Construction Bank), an arm of the MOF that channeled budgetary grants, existed during the prereform years.
2. See the voluminous 刘德福, 谢志强, 主编, 垂直领导体制下金融系统党委书记工作全书 (The complete volume on party secretary work in the banking system under a vertical leadership structure), (北京, 当代中国出版社, 1999).
3. All entities listed in Hong Kong had these revisions approved by annual meetings of shareholders so they are part of the public record.
4. "Jack Ma's Bund speech," https://interconnected.blog/jack-ma-bund-finance-summit-speech/.
5. GSIBs are banks whose health may have an impact on the global financial system. The Basel Committee's assessment methodology for GSIBs requires a sample of banks to report a set of indicators to national supervisory authorities. These indicators are then aggregated and used to calculate the scores of banks in the sample. Banks above a cutoff score are identified as GSIBs and are allocated to buckets that will be used to determine their higher capital adequacy

requirement. For more, see Bank for International Settlements, https://www.bis.org/bcbs/gsib/.

6. Christine Wong, "The Fiscal Stimulus Programme and Public Governance Issues in China," *OECD Journal on Budgeting*, 11, no. 3 (2011), http://dx.doi.org/10.1787/budget-11-5kg3nhljqrjl; also see Chong En-bai et al., "The Long Shadow of Fiscal Expansion," Working Paper 22801, National Bureau of Economic Research, http://www.nber.org/papers/w22801.

7. National Audit Office, 2011年第35 号:全国地方政府性债券审计结果 (2011, no. 35; results of the national audit of local government debt), http:www.audit.gov.cn/n1992150/n1992500/2752208.html.

8. National Audit Office, 2013年4公号: 36 地方政府本级政府性债券审计结果 (2013 24th public document: 2013 24th public document: results of the audit of the provincial level debt of 36 governments), http:/www.audit.gov.cn/n5/n25/c63632/content.html.

9. 关于加强地方政府性债务管理的意见 (2014) 国法43号 (Opinion on strengthening the management of local government debt (2014) Guofa No. 43).

10. Longmei Zhang et al., "China's High Savings: Drivers, Prospects and Policies," *IMF Working Paper*, WP/18/277, December 2018.

11. Based on Holz (2001), pp. 353–354; *China Statistical Yearbook*, author's calculations. The *China Statistical Yearbook*, which provided wage data, no longer carries post-2018 private sector wages.

12. For data leading to this conclusion see Carl E. Walter, "Was Deng Xiaoping Right? An Overview of China's Equity Markets," *Journal of Applied Corporate Finance* 26, no. 3 (Summer 2014): pp. 7–10.

13. Longmei Zhang et al., "China's High Savings," p. 6.

14. Assuming that the loan-to-deposit ratio overall was 60 percent.

15. Qing He and Xiaoyang Li, "The Failure of Chinese Peer-to-Peer Lending Platforms: Finance and Politics," *Journal of Corporate Finance* 66 (February 2021).

16. Weidong Chen and Xiaohui Yuan, "Financial Inclusion in China: An Overview," *Frontiers of Business Research in China*, no. 4 (2021), https://doi.org/10.1186/s11782-021-00098-6.

17. The comparison would be appraised value of state assets per share to offered market price per share. If the market is valuing bank shares below the asset per share ratio, then the bank cannot get approval to sell new shares. Of course the asset appraisal industry in China is wholly corrupt. For a thorough discussion see Ling Huawei and Yu Ning, "Manipulation of Asset Appraisals," *Caijing*, June 5, 2002.

18. Subordinated, hybrid, and Tier 2 are all debt securities that are designed to be close to equity. That is, in the case of bankruptcy or illiquidity, investors in such securities would receive payments only after depositors and other creditors have been paid out. In this way, they are like equity. "Perpetuals" are just that, debt securities that have no maturity but pay a steady stream of interest payments to investors. As such they are considered equity, not debt.

19. Gerald Segal, "Does China Matter?," *Foreign Affairs,* September–October 1999.

20. The bureaucracy stepping back from dealings based on patronage to allow a greater role for the rule of law and markets may be a key to China's brief periods of modernization; see David Faure, *China and Capitalism: A History of Business Enterprise in Modern China* (Hong Kong: Hong Kong University Press, 2006), pp. 93 ff.

21. Organisation for Economic Co-operation and Development, "The Silver and White Economy: The Chinese Demographic Challenge," Chapter 6 in a forthcoming report titled, "Fostering Resilient Economies: Demographic Transition in Local Labor Markets," https://www.oecd.org/employment/leed/OECD-China-report-Final.pdf.

Chapter 4

Trees Can Grow
to Heaven!

Discussions (on rectifying WMPs) went back and forth between
regulators . . . "It was like walking on eggs."

—*Regulatory official, 2017*[1]

The truth about making banks look good by using "bad banks"
is that the bad banks are usually very bad. In the case of China's
four national asset management companies (AMCs) the fact
that the largest of them burst like a balloon with an estimated US$300
billion in bad assets is a reflection on the banks, not just the balloon's
corrupt management. How could state banks grow at double-digit
rates over a decade when the size of China's economy in 2008 was 30
percent of that of the United States? There just couldn't have been that
much to lend to and, over time, where the money did go to was increasingly redundant, the principal example here being the real estate

sector and the bullet train network. The banks lent to them because they provided scale opportunities to lend, and lending, said the party, equals economic growth. High-speed lending, however, creates bad loans, and the AMCs alone were simply not sufficient to absorb the volume banks wanted to send their way. There had to be other channels, and with the help of regulators and support of the party over time there were.

Regulators had little choice but to find ways to protect the major state banks since they are the critical financial foundation of the party's ability to govern by patronage. And as results have shown, their efforts appear to have succeeded. China's banks, the largest in the world by assets, continue to meet and even exceed domestic and international regulatory requirements, even Basel's. The techniques banks use to achieve this are not new, just new to the Chinese market. They have been developed domestically over the last decade as more and more financial engineering has been required to prevent the reality of their asset quality from bursting out. After all, the listing rules of the Hong Kong Stock Exchange still require disclosure under certain conditions, even if those conditions are increasingly narrow. Even less acceptable, the National People's Congress will require answers to any major recapitalizations. The defaults of minor fringe banks and finally that of China Huarong, however, suggest that the system is close to reaching a level of problem asset saturation. It seems that bad assets once removed from bank balance sheets just don't go away. They are simply pushed around between different holding boxes without ever being fully resolved. To throw light on possible saturation, this chapter identifies and seeks to quantify the techniques and volume of bad assets that have been stripped from bank balance sheets.

Evolution of Chinese Balance Sheet Management Techniques

The road to financial wizardry in China took a decade to develop and then reached a dead end. Historically state bank operations after restructuring remained straightforward; their ability to operate as real commercial entities was then in the early stages. The policy makers sought to create the conditions to encourage financial creativity and in 2006 issued "Guidelines on financial innovation by commercial banks."[2] At the same time, regulators were in the early stages of approving a number of products, some of which were detailed in Chapter 2. The "new" products regulators initially approved included asset-backed securities (ABS) and the now famous wealth management products (WMPs). The timing was bad; the impact of the first stimulus tsunami in 2008 caught regulators as flat-footed as the bankers and in the next years compelled far more financial innovation Chinese-style.

The enthusiasm of local governments for stimulus money should have been expected since China's leaders largely have backgrounds running provinces. Local government applications for Beijing's approval of new infrastructure projects numbered in the thousands and overwhelmed the central bureaucracy. There was no time for the National Development and Reform Commission (NDRC, the old State Planning Commission with a new name) to select wisely. In the rush to implement the 2008 stimulus, there could be no well-chosen projects, the high-speed rail being perhaps an exception.

China's leaders should have well understood that the economic driver, indeed the very model they would now rely on, was state investment intermediated by and decided upon by local governments. Putting aside the internet giants and the property developers, in the private sector there were and are no large-scale truly private companies, only myriad small- and medium-sized enterprises that form parts of the global supply chain. The system over time simply does not encourage entrepreneurs to grow large private companies; *large* means political risk as the current rolling takeover by the party shows.

For its part, the central bank has steadfastly promoted financial liberalization aimed at creating costs for using capital as the best way to constrain bank lending and improve enterprise management. Even after 2012 and the onset of the China Dream, the PBOC persisted in lobbying for a policy package that would internationalize China's financial markets. These policies, in fact, were meant to have been the follow-on to bank commercialization and included liberalization of the capital account, interest rates, and the currency itself. Instead of restructuring internal bank operations, the PBOC sought to change their operating environment. Previous efforts in 2010 to internationalize

China's currency as a reserve currency had proved a diplomatic and political coup for Zhou Xiaochuan, then the head of the central bank. Unfortunately, a loosening of the capital account from 2014–2017 as part of this package removed nearly a trillion US dollars from the country's foreign reserves. This ensured that this "reform" would not happen again.

But PBOC's partial liberalization of interest rates for both loans and deposits had a major impact domestically by reducing bank interest margins as the cost of deposits rose while interest on loans remained under tight political control. This of course created pressure inside banks for higher yielding assets. At the same time, the unforeseen combination of cell phones, the Internet, and on-line shopping gave rise, almost overnight, to China's booming, and lightly regulated, fintech industry. This, in turn, was used by the major banks to win support for expanded use of WMPs, arguing that these products enhanced their competitiveness in attracting and retaining deposits.

In short, the years following the outbreak of the crisis saw the valuation genie come alive in new products and combine with the outpouring of credit to create a world of so-called "shadow banking" products. The regulatory efforts to manage the problem had contrary effects and, in any event, ran up against the party's pressure for higher growth. Continual stimulus may have ensured that China was the first to recover economic growth after the crisis, but the stimulus did not ease off. And in China, as the saying goes, once the window is open, everyone rushes in for a piece of the action before it slams shut again.

China's financial engineering was approved tentatively and then developed rapidly. As Table 4.1 illustrates, many products and specialist entities became active as pressure built on bank balance sheets in the years following 2008. Until 2021 the party still believed it could manage this jerrybuilt structure of products supporting the status quo; such was stability after all. The deleveraging effort of 2016–2019 appeared to slow things down, but Covid-19 has saved the day as loose credit resumed. There is always a reason for loose credit. The sections that follow track each product's use starting with an introductory summary of their total impact.

Table 4.1 Evolution of asset management techniques for banks.

Non-performing asset management channels	On/Off bank balance sheet	NPL or other asset	Date established/ approved	Date first active/used
State AMCs	Off	NPL	1999	1999
Huida AMC and other structured entities	Off	NPL	2005	2005
Trust plans	Off	All	1980	2007
Wealth management products	Off	All	2005	2007
Asset exchanges and online auctions	Off	NPL	1996	2013
Asset-backed securities	Off	All	2005	2014
Local AMCs	Off	NPL	2014	2014
Debt for equity swaps	On	NPL	2017	2017

Outcomes in Financial Engineering Chinese-Style

To the extent possible, Table 4.2 summarizes the quantitative information developed in the various sections that follow. The products in this table were created to enable banks to remove problem assets from their balance sheets. In combination with other measures described in Chapter 5, banks have been able to present sound performance metrics to domestic and international regulators as well as investors. Where no data can be found, the product is not included in the table but is still described in a section later in the chapter. This suggests that the figures in the table represent an underestimate. State agencies or official industry associations provide the bulk of the data, but this does not mean it is accurate, only illustrative. For example, in 2016 the total of the various risk assets spun off (and possibly disposed of, 处置)reached a peak of just above 36 percent of total risk-weighted assets. This is a huge number, but it is comparable to the 35 percent figure noted by a vice-premier of finance in 2001 just prior to the state bank restructuring effort. The amount of WMPs outstanding at the various year-ends stands out, its contribution by far the largest of any product that can be quantified. This makes sense, because individual investors enthusiastically welcome

Table 4.2 Summary of estimated spun-off banking assets, 2010–2019.

Note	RMB bn	2010	2011	2012	2013	2014	2015	2016	2017	2018	2019
1	Sales to state AMCs at full face value	NA	NA	265	524	862	975	1,559	1,555	744	562
2	Trust Cos. cooperation with banks	1,661	0	359	155	911	971	686	1,417	0	1,529
3	Wealth management products outstanding at year end	2,950	4,500	7,950	10,240	15,020	23,500	29,050	29,540	22,040	23,400
4	Asset-backed securities	NA	NA	NA	NA	269	530	576	872	1,480	1,975
5	Asset exchanges and online auctions	NA	NA	NA	NA	NA	NA	NA	NA	142	110
6	Implemented debt for equity swaps	NA	NA	NA	NA	NA	NA	NA	230	458	1,400
7	NPL write-offs and	NA	NA	NA	NA	101	237	433	430	730	1,055
8	Estimated spun-out assets	4,611	4,500	8,574	10,919	17,163	26,214	32,304	34,044	25,594	30,031
8	Total on-balance-sheet risk-weighted assets	35,537	43,142	50,660	69,658	76,391	88,471	101,326	112,525	122,396	136,920
9	Average bank assets = (Prior year + Current year)/2	88,525	104,974	123,737	143,081	162,339	199,229	229,255	223,136	240,376	288,071
	Estimated spun-out assets/prior-year risk assets	10.3%	12.7%	19.9%	21.6%	24.6%	34.3%	36.5%	33.6%	22.7%	24.5%
	Estimated spun-out assets/avg. banking assets	5.2%	4.3%	6.9%	7.6%	10.6%	13.2%	14.1%	15.3%	10.6%	10.4%

NOTE: (1) State AMCs from Cinda/Huarong annual reports, author's calculations; (2) China Trust Association; (3) Wind, China Asset Management Report; (4) China Banking Wealth Management Market Report; 2007–2013, 2007–2013 IMF No. 14/35, 2014; (5) Petersen Institute and MacroPolo; (6) Reuters, January 13, 2020; (7) CBIRC, 2018, 2019 are all banks' prior years; only listed banks 2013–2017; PBOC; (8) CBIRC; (9) CBIRC.
SOURCE: Author's calculations and as noted.

92

opportunities to earn a better return on their savings. It is also the case that bank balance sheets are far larger by a multiple than they were in 1997. But despite all that, these WMP figures are likely to be low since banks typically will plan to have the bulk of them mature before year-end audit dates so that deposit figures will be as high as possible.

Whatever the incompleteness or accuracy of the data, the overall trend and scale feel correct: as risk assets ballooned and continue to balloon, banks made strenuous efforts to rid themselves of both good and bad assets. Even so, risk-weighted assets[3] increased nearly *300 times from 2010 to 2019,* and this is an official CBIRC number; has anyone thought about this?! The various ways of dumping assets have, with the support of the various regulators and, it must be said, accountants, enabled banks to meet regulatory requirements and to even produce eye-popping ratios in line with the guidelines of international regulators. Nevertheless, state bank balance sheets stick out like sore thumbs, as was seen in Chapter 3, and call out for far deeper probing than they have received.

Channels to Support State Bank Performance Metrics

State Asset Management Companies

The four (now five or maybe even more[4]) state AMCs were the crucial part of bank restructurings during the reform era and were meant to be dissolved after a 10-year period, which would have meant 2008. The assumption was that, over that time, the old bad assets would all have been managed away, and that any new bad loans could be worked out or charged off by the banks themselves. This plan was always highly disingenuous; was the party really going to dissolve entities with tens of thousands of staff? Zhou Xiaochuan, then chairman of China Construction Bank, had used the creation of Cinda AMC as a way to eliminate over 20,000 positions in the bank, and the other banks had followed the example. But in 2008, as in any other year, outright termination of workers was untenable given large-scale unemployment in Beijing. Demonstrations by laid-off bank workers can still be seen around the banks' head offices at year-ends. So winding up the employment of perhaps 80,000 people mainly in the capital city was never going to happen.

As 2008 approached, the outbreak of the global financial crisis and stimulus provided the opportunity for the four AMCs to lobby for full universal banking licenses, and in 2010 they succeeded, being approved as China's first financial conglomerates.[5] This approval opened the way for the state banks themselves to seek other financial licenses including asset management, life insurance, indeed everything except for underwriting securities and brokerage. Each already had a trust subsidiary from the early 1980s. Financial licenses proliferated during these years at all levels of the economy.

The bankruptcy of Lehman Brothers was the salvation of the AMCs and their staff, but AMCs, like the banks, became huge capital drains. No problem; three years later in December 2013 Cinda successfully launched Hong Kong's largest IPO of that year. The AMC took in US$2.5 billion supported by 10 major foreign fund managers tagging along as "cornerstone" investors and holding 44 percent of the offering. Two years later, Huarong also listed, raising US$2.3 billion, but only with the massive support of China Reinsurance Group taking 55 percent of the shares and a second domestic group of "cornerstone" investors another 15 percent. Even so, the MOF continued to hold 61 percent of Huarong's expanded equity. Not very successful, but still ranking in a lot of new capital as well as demonstrating why Beijing retains the stock exchanges. The weak showing of Huarong guaranteed that deals from China Orient and Great Wall IPOs were unlikely to see the light of day. The Cinda and Huarong IPOs were financial failures for investors; Figure 4.1 shows the price performance of the two companies from year-end 2013. AMCs were likely never again to raise "public" capital, but perhaps profit from shares was not what the keystone investors, foreign or domestic, had in mind anyway.

The listings in Hong Kong and continuous professional auditing of two of the four state AMCs makes it possible to estimate how China's banks have disposed of a portion of their bad loans. Figure 4.2 shows the full book value and related losses to banks of loan packages that banks sold. The calculations are based on the audited statements of Cinda and Huarong and assume that Great Wall and China Orient acquired the same amounts. It is also assumed that the acquisition price paid by each AMC is based on banks selling batch loans at an average 40 percent of carrying value. This is a generous assumption, but it means that banks

Figure 4.1 Cinda and Huarong AMC share performance.
SOURCE: Wind Information, based on HKEx data.

wrote off 60 percent of the loan value; it could be more.[6] Banks also "work out" problem loans themselves, but the process is time consuming; easier to let the "professionals" do it. In their peak years of bad loan acquisition, the four AMCs were buying up US$200 billion annually, but the impact on bank balance sheets was still not enough, as Table 4.2 shows.

Book value assets sold and net losses are then divided by average total loans to illustrate the scale of the disposals. The figure shows that AMC acquisitions peaked in 2016 at the start of the deleveraging campaign. At this point, loans disposed to AMCs represented about 2 percent of average loans. This figure, had it remained on bank balance sheets, would have doubled the banking system's NPL ratio, reducing profit and so negatively impacting capital.

But if AMCs acquire bad assets from banks, the key question that will shed light on the entire business is *how do they finance such purchases*? Table 4.3 shows an estimate of the funding the four AMCs accessed to operate their bad loan business. This funding for the four AMCs grew

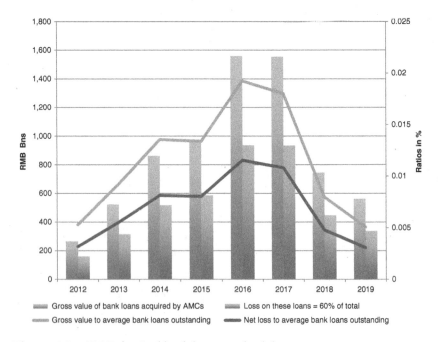

Figure 4.2   AMC acquired bank loans, net bank losses.
NOTE: Assumes average price to AMCs = 40 percent of bank loan book value.
SOURCE: Cinda, Huarong and CBIRC annual reports; author's calculation.

from an estimated 1.3 trillion *yuan* to almost 5 trillion *yuan* in five years, or about four times. Of course this growth in AMC balance sheets reflected the equally large growth of bank balance sheets and, inevitably, bad loans. Loans came largely from the banks themselves from US$200 billion in 2014 up to nearly US$800 billion in 2019. Then from 2016 "Due to customers" became a major source of funding. Who were these customers? They can also only be banks; it appears that the AMCs were giving banks IOUs in return for the "purchase" of their bad assets. In reality, this means that banks had offloaded bad assets and taken the high risk of AMC IOUs in return; nothing was accomplished except in an accounting sense.

As for the AMCs, it is apparent that they lacked the actual funding to operate. So it is not surprising that Huarong defaulted due to illiquidity and was then shown to be bankrupt. But its bankruptcy is not the end of the story: Who will bear the losses involved with its huge pile of bad assets? China Citic, which took over the hulk, is not going to lose

Table 4.3 Estimated funding sources of state asset management companies.

RMB Bns	2009	2010	2011	2012	2013	2014	2015	2016	2017	2018	2019
Cinda Asset Management											
PBOC loans	23.4	16.5	11.3	7.1	4.9	1.0	1.0	1.0	1.0	1.0	1.0
Bank loans	21.5	19.9	25.2	76.1	173.8	263.5	317.0	450.5	580.4	570.8	536.6
Bonds	0	0	1.0	12.5	13.3	43.7	111.8	152.5	206.5	283.1	304.9
Due to customers	0	0	0	0	0	0	0	204.6	226.2	254.0	275.2
Huarong Asset Management											
PBOC loans	NA	NA	NA	4.0	5.2	8.0	0	2.0	4.6	2.4	3.6
Bank loans	NA	NA	NA	97.7	87.9	171.9	295.0	511.3	773.1	760.9	761.5
Bonds	NA	NA	NA	3.5	17.9	48.0	143.1	243.1	332.0	353.3	367.3
Due to customers	NA	NA	NA	70.0	87.9	117.2	139.9	172.4	202.3	209.1	226.8
Total	44.9	36.4	37.5	270.9	390.9	653.3	1,007.8	1,737.4	2,326.1	2,434.6	2,476.9
Great Wall, Orient Asset Management	44.9	36.4	37.5	270.9	390.9	653.3	1,007.8	1,737.4	2,326.1	2,434.6	2,476.9
Total All AMCs	89.8	72.8	75.0	541.8	781.8	1,306.6	2,015.6	3,474.8	4,652.2	4,869.2	4,953.8

SOURCES: Cinda and Huarong audited financial statements; author's calculations.

money; losses will have to go back to those providing the funding: banks, bond holders and the so-called "customers" who, on taking AMC IOUs, exposed themselves to AMC risk. Where did these funding estimates come from? The *audited* numbers from Cinda and Huarong are estimated to be equal to what Great Wall and Orient borrowed.

The inability of a bank to make another loan must have led to Huarong's default in 2021. The Ministry of Finance majority owns and supposedly controlled Huarong. Why didn't the MOF see to it that this problem was solved before it became public? Although it may seem otherwise, in China there is a process and very detailed budgetary rules bind the MOF. It can't simply lend money it hasn't been approved to have (at least in such a public situation) and it will certainly not ask the National People's Congress for permission. Nor can it order banks, which are outside of the MOF system, to make a loan. Besides, there was a scapegoat at hand in Chairman Lai.

Acquiring bank assets is not the whole story; the AMCs were also used to mop up failed enterprises, keeping the licenses, staff, and other assets needed to operate, of course. The existence of these wholly uncompetitive zombie entities was the basis the AMCs used to lobby for financial conglomerate licenses. Armed with the approval to continue to operate, the AMCs set up as universal banks. This was, in fact, quite easy since the zombies included bankrupt securities, trust, insurance, and other nonbank entities. These failed companies had all been transferred to the AMCs, but failing to restructure and sell them, the AMCs now set them up as subsidiaries and over the next years used them to park their own bad assets. The effort to become super-banks inevitably failed and the zombie companies stagnated because they had always been noncompetitive and the AMCs were not equipped to change that.

The collapsing share prices of Cinda and Huarong suggest that the AMCs either paid too much or failed to recover the acquired assets profitably. It seems the latter may have been the case. The AMC business model is straightforward: buy low and recover value high. The bad loans an AMC might acquire from a bank include rights to collateral and owning the entire 100 percent face value of the loan even though it has been sold to it at a discount, say 60 percent. AMC staff will then negotiate with borrowers with the aim of recovering a value greater than the purchase price. Borrowers are incented to deal, since they can settle debt at a cost significantly less than full value.[7] Of course, banks also can do this work, but they prefer not to, perhaps because recoveries of collateral can mean using force.

On to the scapegoat: in 2017 the head of Huarong AMC, Mr. Lai Xiaomin, known inside the company as the "God of Wealth," was put under investigation and removed from his position on charges of corruption. He had reportedly taken 1.8 billion *yuan* in bribes. Lai had been chairman of Huarong from its IPO in 2012 until his removal in mid-2017—a period of five years. It was more than money; it was said he was charged with the "three 100s:" 100 suites, 100 related persons, and 100 mistresses.

His apartment was found stuffed with 200 million *yuan* in cash and his mother-in-law's bank account also bulged with money, yet he claimed he never spent a penny. Prior to his appointment to Huarong, Lai had been a regulator at the PBOC and CBRC; he was small and unprepossessing, yet he managed such a lifestyle! He was sentenced to death and executed in January 2021, or so the newspapers reported. Shortly thereafter on April 2, 2021, the trading of Huarong's shares was suspended due to a failure to file audited 2020 financial statements. The interim president stated that auditors needed more time to review certain transactions.[8]

The only facts in this story may be Mr. Lai's execution and the halt in Huarong's share trading, and Lai's execution itself is not confirmed. The financial performance of the two listed AMCs since their IPOs has been nothing short of incredible: Huarong's total assets grew at a compound rate of 43 percent per year, while Cinda lagged behind at 37 percent. Huge amounts of capital were raised in the markets and from banks. Their organizations extended beyond China's borders to Hong Kong, New York and billion-dollar amusement islands in South Korea. Figure 4.3 is an abbreviated Huarong organizational chart deploying 12 principal subsidiaries, 31 domestic branches, and 21 "group entities," and no doubt hundreds more. It included such things as hotels in New York and that US$3.4 billion investment through British Virgin Island holding companies in a gambling island in South Korea.[9] The number of unconsolidated entities is unknown. There is no doubt that the Huarong head office had no visibility into the operating balance sheets of its subsidiaries. The possibilities for stashing away countless problem assets are huge with a bank and two subsidiary asset management companies, but in the end limited by how much Huarong itself could borrow.

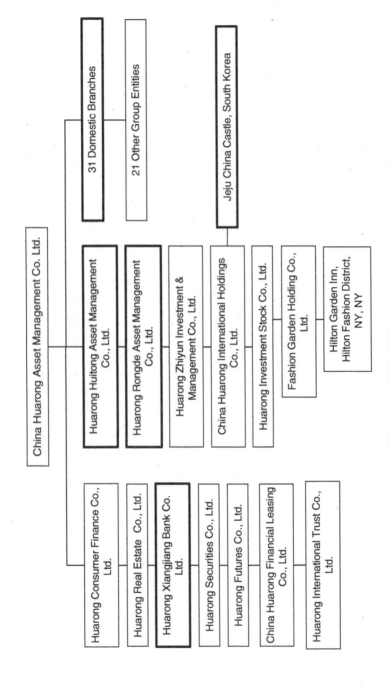

Figure 4.3 Organization structure of Huarong AMC, 2017.
SOURCE: Huarong AMC financial reports.

The figure shows the organization structure of China Huarong Asset Management Co. Ltd., with the following entities:

- 31 Domestic Branches
- 21 Other Group Entities
- Huarong Huitong Asset Management Co., Ltd.
- Huarong Rongde Asset Management Co., Ltd.
- Huarong Zhiyun Investment & Management Co., Ltd.
- China Huarong International Holdings Co., Ltd.
  - Jeju China Castle, South Korea
- Huarong Investment Stock Co., Ltd.
- Fashion Garden Holding Co., Ltd.
  - Hilton Garden Inn, Hilton Fashion District, NY, NY
- Huarong Consumer Finance Co., Ltd.
- Huarong Real Estate Co., Ltd.
- Huarong Xiangjiang Bank Co., Ltd.
- Huarong Securities Co., Ltd.
- Huarong Futures Co., Ltd.
- China Huarong Financial Leasing Co., Ltd.
- Huarong International Trust Co., Ltd.

What does Mr. Lai's story really tell? It tells the story of a man caught up in circumstances and, under no supervision from his presumed owner, the Ministry of Finance, losing control of himself. Over the years leading up to the start of the deleveraging campaign in late 2016, the AMCs were sold increasing amounts of non-performing banking and other assets. Their balance sheets were at the mercy of not just government demands, but also the demands of banks and other institutions. Lai could not ignore these demands. The pile of cash in Lai's apartment and elsewhere shows his weakness and the poverty of his life. The poor performance of both listed companies' shares is an indication of failed management. Huarong was just another balloon in a financial system packed with failed assets and beset by feckless management and regulators. Of course, it must be swept away under the carpet; it is, after all, a sovereign entity. Reports confirm that China Citic Group is the lucky receiver that is planning to provide new capital, take over its operations, spin off assets, and recover losses.[10] These assets, however, are worth very little.

Of course Citic itself had little choice since it was the only other central government financial entity besides China Investment Corporation/Huijin, but the latter was able to refuse. So why would Citic Group accept the cleanup job? It wants something back. Citic Group belongs to the State Council, which should make it sovereign. In 1995, however, Beijing removed the State Seal from its logo, thereby demoting it to semisovereign. Taking on the Huarong problem from the MOF may in the end restore Citic's position in the hierarchy. As for Cinda, perhaps it has been better managed, as has been its reputation. Its financial condition as well as that of the other two unlisted AMCs no doubt will require shoring up quietly, which will add to the state's overall debt load.

Why look at the Huarong case in such detail? China Evergrande generated far more attention, but Huarong is a key piece of the central government, of the system itself. Its default and failure tells far more about how the party manages capital than Evergrande, which, after all, is a private business. And the picture Huarong presents of the party's management is not pretty.

Trust Companies and Trust Plans

From the 1980s and the start of reform when there were over 750, trust companies have always meant trouble for regulators in China. In the late 1990s, their numbers were drastically reduced after the collapse of Guangdong International Trust and Investment Company in 1998. By the time of the financial crisis, a decade later, only 68 were left, mostly owned by provincial governments, a couple of cities, SOEs, and a few banks including all state banks. It is no wonder that these entities are difficult to oversee. The flexibility of their business licenses allows for securitization of virtually any type of asset. Consequently trust companies are clear targets for banks looking to offload loans or enterprises looking to fund projects.

Trust transactions known as single-fund (单一) trusts were designed for this. Mostly banks and trust companies create trusts based on bank loans, bonds, or virtually any asset that throws off cash. Once the trust is set up, the assets are placed into it as collateral, and the bank or enterprise creating the trust receives the funds paid for the trust plan by investors. Thus, in one quick transaction, banks found an efficient way to manage their balance sheets, and enterprises or local governments found a way to finance their projects, particularly real estate. Investors are largely high-net-worth individuals and banks themselves. Trust plans make up 17 percent of nonstandard assets in the WMP pool.

The trouble with trusts, like everything financial in China, lies in the valuation of the assets entrusted or the projects that trust funds finance; from the outside both are entirely opaque. Regulators intervened in late 2011 and again in early 2013 to issue guidelines that limited the use of single-fund trusts, the most popular form of trust plan. The new rules reduced these plans from over 70 percent of total trust assets to less than 40 percent (see Figure 4.4). In terms of absolute values, however, it wasn't until after 2016 and the start of the deleveraging effort that single trusts were really put under pressure. Table 4.2 includes only single trusts done with banks.

There is another aspect to trust companies. For banks that own a trust subsidiary, the creation of trust investments creates structured entities that are unconsolidated on the bank's balance sheet. These exist still associated even if loosely to the bank because regulations require the originating trust company to retain 10 percent of any trust plan it creates; so small an interest should indicate the trust company has no control

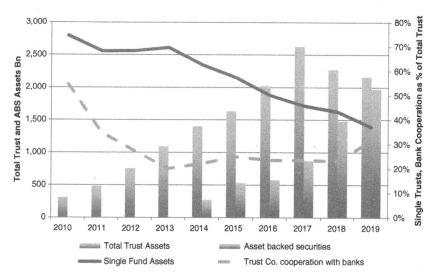

Figure 4.4   Trends in trust and ABS assets, 2010–2019.
SOURCE: China Trust Association and *China Bond*.

over the trust plan. Over time, however, this can create a huge amount of off-balance-sheet assets for which the parent bank may still end up being responsible in the event of a plan default.

Asset-Backed Securities

Similar to trust products, asset-backed securities (ABS) give banks a way to manage their balance sheets by offloading assets. Industry pressure to approve asset-backed securities began in the late 1990s. Regulators, however, proved reluctant to deal with this product even before the financial crisis in 2008; trust plans were hard enough! The first two experiments with ABS-like products were approved in 2005, but given the complex regulatory scrutiny that typifies China, these led to very little issuance until 2013. At that point the need for liquidity and the large bank books of consumer-related loans (cars, homes, credit cards) created pressure for change. There emerged two different product paths for ABS, one supported by PBOC/CBRC and the other by the securities regulator, the China Securities Regulatory Commission (CSRC). The CSRC applications were not subject to the regulator's typical prolonged scrutiny; instead, new ABS issues had only to be registered.

In contrast, the PBOC/CBRC path required a special-purpose vehicle and review. It was not surprising, then, that most issuers chose the CSRC channel. It is hard to understand how CSRC-registered ABS represent securities wholly separate from the issuer.

In any event, this led to an explosion of issuance that by 2019 had reached nearly US$2 trillion, making China's market for asset-backs the second largest in the world and nearly equal to single-unit trusts (see Figure 4.4). As single-unit trusts came under regulator pressure and their use began to fall in 2017, ABS issuance began to pick up. In contrast to trusts, the ABS product is typically backed by car loans, mortgages, and credit cards, and their prospectuses arc available on the China Bond website. They are also used to dispose of bad assets, with these accounting for perhaps 10–15 percent of total issuance. Single-unit trust assets, in contrast, are nontransparent and typically end up in WMP asset pools.

Huida Asset Management Company and Structured Entities

In August 2005 the PBOC created a structure that has successfully flown beneath the radar all these years. Nonetheless, it has been widely copied by banks and AMCs. Named Huida AMC, this entity was designed to take "problems left over from history" off the central bank's balance sheet.[11] Huida (汇达) was described as the original fifth AMC, and its operations have understandably remained mysterious.[12] Created and staffed by the PBOC's Financial Stability Bureau, Huida was the twin to Huijin, the entity holding state interests in the big state banks and other parts of the financial sector. Unlike Huijin's investments in good banks, Huida was designed to manage bad assets, removing them from PBOC's balance sheet. Consequently, Huida had to be capitalized by a third-party investor to avoid issues of consolidation. Due to its close connection with PBOC, Cinda AMC was the logical choice, but the capital and subsequent financing came from PBOC (see Figure 4.5). Note that the funds put in by PBOC were used to buy assets from PBOC; Huida held the assets, but PBOC got its money back. Although it is majority owned, Huida cannot be found anywhere in Cinda's thick audited financial statements, although as an ostensibly wholly owned subsidiary its balance sheet should be fully consolidated into Cinda's statements.

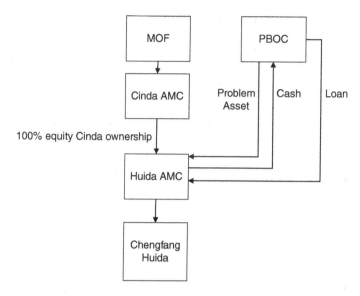

Figure 4.5 Transfer of PBOC problem assets to Huida AMC.

This suggests it is not audited; it is entirely a shell company stuffed with bad assets and no capital.

What type of assets would Huida hold? Its original business license specified real estate loans in Hainan and Guangzhou and portfolios assumed as part of the Guangdong International Trust and Investment and Guangdong Enterprise bankruptcies. This structure made sense; PBOC simply passed these problem assets over to an entity theoretically specializing in dealing with them. Huida then went silent for 15 years before it suddenly emerged under a new name, Chengfang Huida (成方汇达), a subsidiary of Huida also controlled by the central bank.[13] The central bank used the new Huida entity to acquire a controlling interest in a failed city commercial bank, the Bank of Jinzhou. There was also news that Huida would acquire 100 billion *yuan* in assets from Huarong and that the delay in this transaction was what prevented Huarong from filing its annual statement.[14] This suggests that the PBOC is using Central Huijin as the shareholder of "good" banks, while Huida holds assets as well as equity of bad banks.

The Huida structure itself, however, is the point of this bit of history. The absorption capacity of the four state AMCs is obviously limited by the amount of funding they can access from the banks and PBOC. The overall

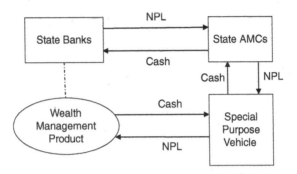

Figure 4.6   The bank use of SPVs as a channel to sell NPLs as WMPs.

volume of non-performing assets, however, is most certainly not decreasing and still needs workable paths off bank balance sheets. With the cognizance of the bank regulator, banks began to set up special-purpose vehicles (SPVs) similar to Huida together with the major AMCs (see Figure 4.6).

The transactions involved are straightforward. Banks sold NPLs to the asset management companies that, in turn, sold it to the special purpose vehicle. The SPV, in turn, completed the transaction by selling the NPLs on to a WMP asset pool controlled by the bank. The result is that these assets simply disappeared not only from bank balance sheets, but also from the AMC balance sheets and even from the SPV balance sheets becoming part of the so-called investment portfolio of unknowing retail investors. A glance at Table 4.5 showing the makeup of non-standard assets provides an idea of the sorts of things involved and their volume. In theory, regulators have now stopped this type of arrangement.

Wealth Management Products

Trust products and ABS securities alone could not manage the volume of bad assets large banks were creating. Banks needed a more efficient way to manage their balance sheets and they found it in the so-called wealth management products (WMP). WMPs at the start in 2007, however, were based on the idea that the product would allow banks to manage their asset scale at the margin. So little thought was given to this measure that, until five years later, there were no reliable figures about the size of assets involved other than what was recorded by the Wind platform. There was no central depository and there appeared to be little regulatory oversight. If you can't measure it, how can you regulate it? By 2012, however, the "tree" had grown too large to ignore. Demand by retail investors for products with better yields than bank deposits plus pressure from the new fintech companies discussed previously drove WMP scale larger and larger. Of course, China's financially repressed masses would pile into WMPs; they had little place else to go with their money. This was especially the case because they believed that Beijing would never allow retail investors to lose money. This firm belief in moral hazard paid off again!

Table 4.4 shows just how fast this product grew. From about five trillion *yuan* (US$850 billion) in 2010, in 2017, their peak year, net issuance of WMPs reached 73 trillion *yuan* (US$13 trillion).* The figures are enormous and in their biggest years represented around half of average total bank deposits. The sheer scale of WMPs together with trust plans generated concerns about the rise of "shadow banking" in 2010. Shadow banking can be defined as a system of credit disintermediation outside of the regular banking system.[15] In China wealth management products became the major part of this activity. They also demonstrate that the funding source for the bulk of shadow banking products is the banking system itself. In China, what else can it be since the major banks control the largest chunk of retail and corporate deposits? Consequently as attacks on shadow banking grew, an effort arose to demonstrate that WMPs played a positive role contributing directly and indirectly to what in China is called "the real economy (实体经济)."

Table 4.5 is designed by the semi-official *China Wealth Management* team to show that WMP assets contribute directly to the real economy. This data is provided only for the years shown when the topic was still hot among Chinese regulators. Each year, the contribution averaged two-thirds of the proceeds of all new WMP issuance or around five trillion *yuan* (US$900 billion). It is obvious that in the first two years the report could not avoid stating that proceeds were directed to investments in capital markets, foreign exchange, or other financial products (most likely equity of some sort). These financial "services" accounted for 25

---

*Issuance is presented as an accumulating figure in Chinese reports. Depending on the year, WMP investments matured on average anywhere from three months to 12 months and more. The issuance figures are adjusted based on the average maturity and the assumed turnover. For example, if the average maturity is six months, the official issuance is divided in half, as this is the actual amount of money invested in the product at the given time; until 2017 and the effort to rectify the product they are assumed to roll over. In Table 4.2, data for month-end outstandings are used.

Table 4.4 Trends in WMP issuance, investors, and asset composition, 2010–2020.

RMB bn	2010	2011	2012	2013	2014	2015	2016	2017	2018	2019	2020
Net wealth management products issued	4,917	8,700	8,833	17,620	45,788	66,116	69,755	72,912	59,840	55,800	78,498
Average retail and corporate bank deposits	58,276	78,004	84,400	96,595	112,216	127,685	145,892	140,927	162,213	187,825	205,844
WMP issued/average bank deposits	8.4%	11.2%	10.5%	18.2%	40.8%	51.8%	47.8%	51.7%	36.9%	29.7%	38.1%
Average maturity in months	6 mos.	7 mos.	4 mos.	3 mos.	3 mos.	9 mos.	9 mos	141 days	161 days	186 days	228 days
Total number of WMP issuing banks	170	NA	NA	427	525	426	526	591	439	377	331
Investor composition %											
Retail	NA	NA	NA	50.9%	59.6%	58.6%	46.3%	63.6%	78.5%	NA	99.7%
Institutional	NA	NA	NA	38.8%	29.6%	26.5%	25.9%	28.4%	16.8%	NA	3.5%
Private banks	NA	NA	NA	5.0%	7.6%	5.5%	7.2%	0.0%	0.0%	NA	0.0%
Banks' asset pool composition	NA	NA	NA	2.5%	3.3%	9.5%	20.6%	8.0%	4.7%	NA	0.0%
Asset pool composition %											
Bonds	NA	NA	NA	38.6%	43.8%	51.0%	43.8%	42.2%	53.4%	59.7%	64.3%
Nonstandard assets	NA	NA	NA	27.5%	20.9%	15.7%	17.5%	16.2%	17.2%	15.6%	10.9%
Equity products	NA	NA	NA	6.1%	6.2%	7.8%	7.3%	9.5%	9.9%	7.6%	4.8%
Interbank and repo products	NA	NA	NA					9.9%	6.6%	6.6%	6.6%
Deposits	NA	NA	NA	25.6%	26.6%	22.4%	16.6%	13.9%	5.8%	6.5%	9.1%
Funds	NA	NA	NA		1.3%	1.8%		2.1%	3.4%	2.0%	2.8%
Derivatives	NA	NA	NA	1.1%	0.5%		13.1%				

SOURCE: *China Wealth Management Report*; PBOC; CBIRC; author's calculations.

Table 4.5 Use of WMP proceeds to invest in "real economy."

%	2012	2013	2014	2015
Construction	6.0%	6.2%	21.1%	12.8%
Infrastructure	9.5%	7.8%	7.7%	12.3%
Real estate	5.9%	5.0%	3.6%	9.7%
Roads and transport	6.4%	5.5%	9.1%	6.0%
Power and heat	8.5%	7.3%	13.2%	5.7%
Coal	5.4%	5.6%	9.3%	4.8%
Agriculture	NA	2.2%	10.2%	4.6%
Housing	NA	NA	NA	2.6%
Wholesale	2.9%	2.6%	2.9%	1.9%
Ferrous metal refining	1.8%	1.8%	4.3%	1.8%
Chemicals	NA	NA	2.8%	1.7%
Retail	NA	NA	2.2%	1.6%
Oil and gas	NA	NA	1.4%	1.6%
Railways	4.2%	3.3%	3.9%	1.6%
Water transport	NA	NA	2.1%	–
Other transport	NA	NA	1.9%	–
Business services	6.4%	8.5%	–	–
Capital markets	3.6%	3.1%	–	–
Foreign exchange	6.6%	7.1%	–	–
Other finance	17.7%	14.8%	–	–
Other	14.9%	19.3%	–	–

SOURCE: *China Wealth Management Report*, various.

percent of the total funds made available—such frankness could not have scored points with the regulators! Consequently, for the two later years, such activity disappeared from the presentation replaced by construction, infrastructure, and real estate, all of which accounted for over one-third of such "real economy" investments. Chapter 5 demonstrates how local governments directed these funds. Viewing the composition of the WMP asset pools, it is difficult to see how the Chinese analysts uncovered the ultimate users of WMP proceeds; no one can tell where the proceeds of a bond issue are used, for example, since money is fungible.

There is information on just what are non-standard assets, defined as those that cannot be traded on the interbank market. Table 4.6 provides a breakdown for the years 2015 and 2016, the only years data are available. There are 10 categories of assets plus "other," of which the largest in 2016 were participations, "other," and trust loans. Participations represent

Table 4.6   Composition of nonstandard assets.

As a percent of year-end values	2014	2015	2016	2017	2018
Nonstandard assets/funds invested in WMP %	20.9%	15.7%	17.5%	16.2%	17.2%
Value nonstandard assets 100 mm	28,150	32,971	37,201	50,808	47,914
Broken down into:	NA	–	–	NA	NA
participations	–	35%	29%	–	–
trust loans	–	18%	17%	–	–
exchange entrusted	–	16%	9%	–	–
entrusted	–	11%	8%	–	–
repurchase equity investment	–	6%	6%	–	–
exchange of credit assets	–	3%	0%	–	–
receivables	–	2%	1%	–	–
notes	–	1%	1%	–	–
private placements	–	0%	0%	–	–
Letters of credit	–	0%	0%	–	–
Other nonstandard assets	–	8%	26%	–	–

SOURCE: *China Wealth Management Report*, various.

part of a loan for which the risk is shared among banks. The "entrusted" category represents assets created on behalf of a third party; the third party supposedly takes all risk. It is hard to imagine just what sort of equity investment would be repoed but they are not on the interbank market! This is likely a transaction in which a borrowing party presents the lending party with equity as part of an overall fund with the understanding that it will want it back at the fund's maturity. If the list looks like everything but the kitchen sink, it is. As of 2018, the book value, assuming banks kept accurate track of off-balance-sheet asset pools, approached US$1 trillion. Data on the maturity of such products is unavailable, but their value is knowable: very little. More on this topic in Chapter 5.

As mentioned, investors in WMPs are mostly individuals, who doubtless did not care what assets they "owned" since they believed that the WMPs, whether guaranteed or not, were implicitly backed by Beijing. Retail made up for half of all numbers, and institutions (单位) accounted for 20–30 percent until the new regulations forced the market to become entirely retail in 2020. Figure 4.7 shows the category of banks issuing WMPs. The state banks and shareholding banks are, unsurprisingly, the principal issuers with city commercial banks growing

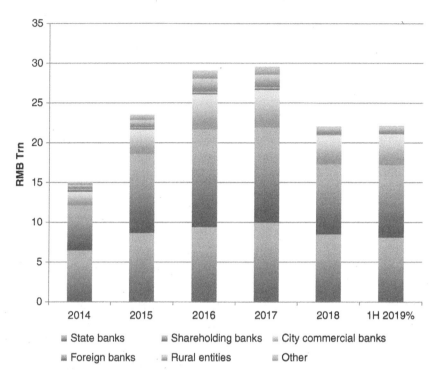

Figure 4.7   Bank issuers of WMP and size of investments.
SOURCE: *China Wealth Management Report*, various.

quickly. The shareholding banks are best understood as quasi-investment banks. With only a small branch network, meaning low levels of deposits, these banks create product invested in by other institutions either for their own books or through the interbank market. What is surprising is the size of rural commercial banks and cooperatives participation: farmers buying into the China Dream!

The number of banks involved is also telling. In 2010, a mere 170 banks arranged WMPs; by 2018 the number had more than tripled to 591. Since there aren't that many banking institutions in all of China, what does this number represent? It means that bank branches were the principal market players. Presumably the head office organizations placed a policy template on their activity, but it is questionable whether major bank branches and sub-branches adhered to this in practice, given local political pressure. As for the small banks, it is very likely to be a free-for-all and for the same reasons. In short, the WMP market must have been chaotic up until the 2017 effort to rein it in, and banks were made to report their balances to the regulators. But then again, it was the banks reporting, not third parties.

Local government pressures drove the eager participation in this market by the city and rural commercial banks. On the one hand, they faced their local government owners or sponsors who needed financial support, but with little to no deposit base funding such projects had always been difficult if not impossible. Wealth management products enabled them to match local government projects paying relatively high interest rates with yield-hungry retail depositors with money in other banks. Figure 3.6, discussed previously, illustrates just how successful these small local banks were in attracting deposits away from the state banks.

There is a significant difference in type of WMP product offered between the state and shareholding banks versus the city commercial banks. The city banks typically offered investors a product made up of a single asset—perhaps a utility or an airport project. The state banks, on the other hand, offloaded all sorts of assets from their own balance sheets creating multi-layered products. The fun had to come to an end and in late 2017, a draft of new regulations for WMPs was circulated for industry comment[16] and laid out significant changes to the market[17] as is discussed in the next chapter. With the financial limitations of the major AMCs likely after Huarong and these new rules, it is difficult to see how banks would have efficient ways to shape their balance sheets.

Asset Exchanges and Online Auctions

At the same time that the first five local AMCs were approved, the Zhejiang Provincial High Court approached Alibaba, which is based in that province, to ask if Alibaba's Internet superstore would host judicial auctions of bad loans as well as their collateral. At the time, such auctions were held in physical asset exchanges that are located all over the country, with the Tianjin and Shandong exchanges being the more active. Alibaba agreed, and so in 2015 Taobao, China's Amazon, began to auction problem assets on line.

Statistics for the activity at these various exchanges and platforms are not collected, so it is difficult to determine the scale of their contribution. Dinny MacMahon and his team, however, meticulously put together data by hand for the last quarter of 2017.[18] At that time the 20 exchanges and platforms that they monitored recorded the sale of 126 billion *renminbi* (about US$2 billion) of bad loans, which was 7 percent of total official bank NPLs. The asset sources for the physical asset exchanges were the smaller banks; for example, Industrial Bank accounted for 55 percent in value. On Taobao, 81 percent of loan value came from AMCs; among these Cinda AMC accounted for 55 percent, and Great Wall AMC 14 percent. These statistics provide only a small glimpse of this activity. Another research institute monitored 40 local AMCs during 2018 and arrived at 142 billion *yuan* in bad loan sales; of these about 40 percent were acquired by the state AMCs.[19] So these exchanges and TaoBao seem to play significant roles at the margin in passing along non-performing assets, but the numbers and trend line are unknown.

Local Asset Management Companies

Burgeoning problem loans at the local levels compelled Beijing to approve local asset management companies in 2014.[20] As with local bonds, in the beginning the window was opened just a crack and only five provincial applications met the regulatory guidelines. The pressure was such, however, that another 53(!) or so were approved in the next four years. Provincial and local governments were required to put up a designated amount of capital and maintain capital ratios. This was hardly a problem, since without (and sometimes even with) professional audits anything is financially possible. It was thought that such entities, being a part of local governments, would be able to operate more effectively than the big national AMCs and so manage down the level of bad loans.[21] This was the party believing its own dream.

These entities were limited in capital and expertise, could not access the interbank markets and could only operate within their own provinces.[22] Moreover, although Beijing approved the licenses, it left their supervision to local regulatory offices. In other words, these entities are unregulated. Gradually the barriers were removed so that private capital and national companies edged in. Although there are many types of operation, in general, these AMCs act as warehouses for local bank NPLs. Similar to the Huida arrangement, an AMC borrows from a bank, acquires the same bank's problem assets, and holds them while the bank reworks the terms of the asset and then sells it on as a WMP. Although this was banned by Beijing in 2016, the arrangements continued for some time. In the same year the regulator opened the door to sales to third parties outside the province, including asset exchanges and electronic auction houses such as TaoBao.

In sum, because this band of operators' activities are local and unregulated, the scale of their contribution to bad loan "disposals" is unclear. This is why analysts, for example, Standard & Poor's, estimate that there may be as much as 30–40 trillion *yuan* (US$4.5–6 trillion) in hidden local debt.[23] It could be a lot more. No one knows and in Beijing no one really wants to know; it is the provincial governor's baby.

Debt-to-Equity Swaps

From 2017, China's major banks were allowed to establish subsidiaries, asset investment companies (AIC) specializing in acquiring debt and restructuring it into equity and then selling the result into various investment channels.[24] In practice, this work is very similar to the efforts in the 1990s to assemble profitable companies out of the shambles of state enterprises that could sell shares publicly. As the entire 1990s experiment showed, however, this kind of restructuring is extremely difficult. It requires discovering a profitable or at least sustainable operation within the operations of a larger state enterprise that was designed to act as a part of a state structure that no longer exists. In the old state, SOEs could operate without concern for profit, but with concern for maintaining employment. In a restructuring a workable collection of businesses and assets must be assembled and then fenced off from the things that will not be included, and that includes people. How, then, can these people, both workers and retirees, be supported?[25] In the 1990s this could be done due to the full support of national policy. In the new century, conditions are different.

If the social hurdle can be overcome and a workable business found, the problem becomes one of valuation: What is the conversion factor of an enterprise's debt into equity? Put another way, what is the value of the debt and what is the value of the new equity? It is difficult to use international techniques in such cases, either because the enterprise has no active market for its debt or because the subject enterprise has never been transformed into a company limited by shares; that is, it literally has no shares to value. To attribute value to hypothetical shares, the company must first be profitable. Even so, international methods are being used, but it will all come down to a difficult negotiation with enterprise management.

If a sustaining enterprise can be designed, there is the problem of arranging funding for any exchange or acquisition of debt for shares. Regulations require that these AICs acquire non-performing assets from enterprises with no relationship to their banking parent and self-fund through bond sales, interbank borrowing, and their own capital. They are, in short, to operate at arm's distance from their own bank. This is not a problem, since the state bank AICs can be mutually supportive as is the typical case; anyway, they are, after all, virtually the same bank.

To date the AICs have experienced difficulties gaining scale. Consequently, the regulators in 2020 allowed them to sell "investment plans" using the debt-to-equity transactions as the underlying assets. These plans are nothing but wealth management products using a fancy name with far riskier assets and with no standardized data available. Because of the difficulty involved in valuation and restructuring, the debt-to-equity effort must remain a marginal tool although its contribution in 2019 suggests that it is gaining some traction.

Implications

The list of financial tools reviewed earlier shows how quickly China's financial practices began to converge with many aspects of the Anglo-American model. Barely a decade after their restructuring and listing, China's banking system was actively developing products similar to those of the US experience in the runup to 2009. The circumstances, however, were very different. In the United States, the pressure of too much money led to a desire for higher yields in an environment of sustained low interest rates, unsophisticated ratings agencies, weak regulators, and political enthusiasm for cheap housing; the market drove events. In China, Beijing reacted to the crisis in the United States and globally by urging banks to lend in order to support the economy. This was initially successful as China was the first major country to resume growth. But the demand pull of local governments for capital quickly led to continued, if slower, lending and severe pressures on balance sheets. This in turn led to the creation of a range of shadow banking products and the institutions supporting them. The party may have laughed at the near meltdown of the Western financial system in 2008, but it had little choice but to follow in its footsteps, either that or delisting the banks.

The array of these products suggests that the underlying problem assets were not being actively managed. As banks grew ever larger, the volume of bad assets inevitably increased. It may simply have been the case that there was simply too much stuff out there to manage, as the China Huarong case suggests. So it seems that the state at all levels followed in Beijing's footsteps and invented new products with longer maturities and new boxes to store them in. Problem assets were simply shifted around inside the economy, working their way out from the major state banks to lesser local institutions out in the provinces. In the process, everyone involved in this game kept their heads down and moved on; after all, no one seemed to be keeping count except perhaps the banks. Has any major institution involved in this shell game ever actually taken a loss? Even Huarong had been profitable until the end despite holding US$320 billion in bad assets that apparently just sat there. And did Huarong's auditor only just find these things? All these spun-off assets must be seen as the cost of maintaining a banking system that from the outside appears like any other. But it is not. Chapter 7 pursues this matter in more depth.

Beijing has shown that it will throw away the things it no longer wants, for example, Didi Chuxing, Ant Financial, HNA, Anbang, Evergrande, P2P, and the entire teaching and entertainment sector, but there will be a cost to the economy that the party alone cannot replace. Now, banks, even the central bank, are facing the political challenge of the Central Disciplinary Commission for the error of lending to private companies that the party believes are injurious to China: political errors! Well, banks in the manner of market-based economies are no longer needed when the party calls all the shots. They simply become entities filled with accountants keeping track of the party's decisions, but not too closely. And, as the next chapter shows, accounting principles, even international ones, are flexible and are made to suit many situations. Zhu Rongji may have wanted his National Champions to dominate the *Fortune* Global 500; this new gang of one does not seem to care.

Notes

1. Wu Hongyuran, Han Yi, and Han Wei, "In Depth: Financial Regulators Seek to Tame China's $15 Trillion Wild West," *Caixin*, https://www.caixinglobal. com/2017-11-27/financial-regulators-seek-to-tame-chinas-15-trillion-wild-west-101268691.html.

2. CBRC, "Guidelines for Financial Innovation of Commercial Banks," December 6, 2006, https://www.cbirc.gov.cn/en/view/pages/ItemDetail. html?docId=406&itemId=981.

3. Given asset classes are assigned different risk weights by accounting principles, thus a loan is assigned 100 percent, bonds only 20 percent.

4. "China Approves Fifth National Asset Management Company," *China Banking News*, December 18, 2020, https://www.chinabankingnews.com/2020/12/18/ china-approves-fifth-nationwide-asset-management-company/.

5. Carl Walter and Fraser Howie, *Red Capitalism*, 2nd ed. (Singapore: John Wiley & Sons, 2010), pp. 82 ff.

6. In these loan sales to AMCs, the AMC buys a loan at a discounted amount from the bank. The AMC also receives the rights to the full loan value. Thus, the AMC believes it can recover over what it paid by negotiating with the creditor, who still owes the full 100 percent, or selling off loan collateral, or both.

7. For a colorful description of one foreigner's experience collecting loans to the business see Karen Richardson, "In China Foreign Firms Chip Away at Mountain of Bad, Overdue Debt," *Wall Street Journal*, January 13, 2004, https:// www.wsj.com/articles/SB107393717164647800.

8. John Cheng, "China Huarong Delays 2020 Results Past April Deadline," *Bloomberg*, April 25, 2012, https://www.bloomberg.com/news/articles/2021-04-25/china-huarong-delays-release-of-2020-results-past-april-deadline.

9. Yue Yue, "In Depth: Huarong's $3.4 Billion Debacle on a South Korean Tourist Trap," *Caixin*, September 8, 2021, https://www.caixinlobal.com/2021-09-08/ in-depth-huarongs-34-billion-debacle-on-a-south-korean-tourist-trap-101770726.html.

10. *Bloomberg News*, "Huarong Said to Plan Assets Sales, Avoid Debt Restructuring," April 8, 2021.

11. Yu Ning, "Huida Takes the Stage," *Caijing*, July 25, 2005, p. 65.

12. Huida in late 2019 had a website with not much on it, but it was there. In late 2021 it is no longer available for "security reasons."

13. Wu Hongyuran and Timmy Shen, "PBOC to Become Bank of Jinzhou Biggest Shareholder in Latest Bailout," *Caijing*, March 12, 2020; *Wall Street Journal*, April 6, 2020.

14. Reuters, "Bond Investors on Edge as China Grapples with Huarong Restructuring," April 22, 2021, https://www.reuters.com/article/idUSL8 N2MF2GH?edition-redirect=ca. The article even notes that Huida is under Cinda but managed by PBOC.

15. See Country Analyst Unit, "Shadow Banking in China: Expanding Scale, Evolving Structure," *Asia Focus*, Federal Reserve Bank of San Francisco, April 2013.

16. 人民银行, 银监会, "关于规范金融机构资产管理业务的指导意见 (征求意见稿) (Leading opinion on regularizing the asset management business of financial institutions—Draft for comment), November 17, 2017, http://www.pbc.gov.cn/rmyh/105208/3420439/index.html; 银保会, 商业 银行理财业务监督管理办法 (Method on supervising and managing commercial bank WMP business), No. 6, September 29, 2018, https://www.waizi. org.cn/doc/41534.html.

17. See Carl Walter, "Convergence and Reversion: China's Banking System at 70," *Journal of Applied Corporate Finance* 32, no. 4 (2020): 8 ff.

18. Dinny MacMahon, "Collateral Returning to Its Roots: The Role of Taobao Auctions in Resolving Delinquent Loans," *MacroPolo*, July 25, 2018, https:// macropolo.org/cleanup_analysis/returning-to-its-roots/.

19. ShoreVest, *China Debt Dynamics* 3, no. 5 (October 16, 2019).

20. Dinny MacMahon, "The Clean Up: China's Local AMCs Making a Mark," *MacroPolo*, March 12, 2018.

21. For a good, if dated, overview, see Zuhe Rong and Shiyi Zhou, "Local Asset Management Companies in China: The New Frontier to Tackle China's Local Debt Problem," Orient Capital Research, June 14, 2014, http://www.orient-capitalresearch.com/wp-content/uploads/2014/07/Chinas-Local-AMCs-Tackling-Local-Debt.pdf.

22. Wu Xiaomeng and Han Wei, "Beijing Sets Up Second 'Bad Bank' in Partnership With JD.com," *Caixin*, November 14, 2019, https://www.caixinlobal.com/ 2019-11-14/beijing-sets-up-second-bad-bank-in-partnership-with-jdcom-101483441.html.

23. Zia Khan, "S&P: Chinese Local Governments' Hidden Debt Could Be as High as US$6 Trillion," S&P Global, October 16, 2018.

24. Peng Qinqing and Han Wei, "China Expands Funding Sources for Debt-to-Equity Swaps," *Caixin*, May 7, 20220, https://www.caixinlobal.com/2020-05-07/china-expands-funding-sources-for-debt-to-equity-swaps-101550801.html.

25. See Carl Walter and Fraser Howie, *Privatizing China: Inside China's Stock Markets* (Singapore: John Wiley & Sons, 2005), Chapter 5 for a full discussion of SOE restructuring.

Chapter 5

Beautifying Bank Balance Sheets

> In our opinion the consolidated statements of XX Bank and its subsidiaries . . . give a true and fair view of the financial position of the bank . . .
>
> —*Bank audit opinion, 2018*

All publicly listed companies provide audited financial statements to their investors. In China, these statements may be the most important contribution of the entire experiment with shares and stock markets. Before public listings of state enterprises, the government had no idea where its investment capital had gone or how it was being used. Now there is a clearer but still partial picture. But all publicly listed companies try to put their best foot forward. Enron in 2000 is a perfect example of how management can manipulate accounting principles to produce better financial performance. Banks are no different, especially because management's judgment is such a huge part of setting asset valuations. Not only are assets hard to value, banks have many ways of transforming bad assets into good assets; the global financial crisis if nothing else demonstrated that accounting standards, auditors, regulators, and ratings agencies can fail to keep up with financial innovation. Why should it be any different in China? It is not. This chapter examines a number of examples of financial flexibility on the asset and contingent liability sides of the Chinese bank balance sheet.

Parking Assets—the Interbank Market and "Repos"

In China the interbank market is a way to park unwanted assets on someone else's balance sheet typically over a critical time period—for example the last day of the audit year. Internationally, however, the interbank market is a very matter-of-fact way for banks to balance that last bit of their balance sheet at the end of each business day by borrowing short-term funds from other banks. Banks with excess cash lend to other banks, and transactions are very short term. Interbank transactions are generally thought to be very risk free, since banks are, in theory at least, heavily regulated. Credit losses in the interbank market should not happen except if banks lend excessively and consistently to illiquid banks. In China this means that the head offices and provincial branches of the big state banks and the shareholding banks share the burden of oversight with the central regulators, while local offices of the bank regulator oversee the small city commercial banks. These local offices are susceptible to the influence of local governments. As a result, local bank balance sheets are questionable; even such short-term monies as obtained from the interbank market commonly are used in support of long-term non-performing assets.

"Repos" are a common product in all financial markets. A repo is the borrowing of money against the collateral of bonds, usually central government bonds. In this market, the motivations for participation are not simply to find liquidity for a bond portfolio. Transactions are also used to borrow money to buy more bonds, so repos can be used and are used internationally as a trading product to generate profit.[1] Trades are called "repo" transactions when Bank A "sells" a bond to Bank B, which "purchases" it. It is called a "repo (回购; for repossession)" because Bank A will, at the trade's maturity, repossess the bond, which has served as collateral, when it repays the "loan" to Bank B. If Bank A does not buy back the securities, Bank B can keep the bond, sell it, and presumably cover the loss of its loan to Bank A. There is also a trade called the "reverse" repo (逆回购). This is just the flipside of a repo trade from the point of view of Bank B. Here Bank B receives ("reverses in") a security or securities from Bank A as collateral for its "loan" and on repayment of the loan "reverses out" those securities to Bank A.

In the Chinese context, such transactions allow Bank A to remove bonds from its balance sheet for a time, say, over an accounting period.[2] In the parlance, this is called "parking." Thus, accountants may see only cash on the bank's balance sheet, not some questionable asset the value of which may be less than its book value. In other words, if you are Bank A and want to unload certain securities or even other products (trust plans and WMPs are allowed[3]), you simply "repo out" these things temporarily to another bank and take in a short-term "loan" that appears as cash on the asset side of your balance sheet and as part of a trading liability. The unwanted asset is subtracted from your security (or other investment) portfolio. *Poof*, it is gone; the overall balance sheet has not changed in value except that risk-weighted assets have decreased and been replaced by cash, which, of course, has no risk but, of course, your liabilities have increased.

From the name and the discussion it might be thought that this is a market for banks only. Nothing could be further from the case. In China the market includes all banks plus insurance companies, securities companies, funds, finance companies, trust companies, financial leasing companies and asset management companies (state and local).[4] In short, the entire Chinese financial system is in there, with special notice going to the state and local AMCs. In short, in China the interbank market is not what you might casually expect from its name.

Table 5.1 shows the average monthly outstanding value of reverse repo transactions at year-end from 2007 to 2016. The volume of reverse repos directly indicates the need of the "repo" bank to remove undesirable assets from its balance sheet or the need for liquidity. The average value of such trades was steady as a percent of total banking assets at around 5 percent until 2014 when demand for funding increased

Table 5.1 Average monthly reverse repo transactions: moving securities out.

100 mm	2007	2008	2009	2010	2011	2012	2013	2014	2015	2016
State banks	14,200	14,211	22,505	25,278	21,483	56,899	47,095	73,002	177,463	180,965
Other banks, including	16,220	19,379	23,798	23,940	31,430	42,475	59,411	79,769	145,297	222,198
CCBs	0	0	0	0	0	0	0	21,494	53,763	82,990
Other financial institutions	4,312	10,594	9,565	18,328	21,361	7,397	10,633	14,506	31,069	57,056
Insurance companies	904	964	95	1,407	2,147	2,794	3,162	2,602	1,211	10,446
Securities companies and funds	823	1,324	255	1,084	2,034	2,283	3,299	3,655	4,870	18,600
Foreigners	264	514	200	507	1,683	2,000	3,047	3,460	433	1,647
Total	**36,723**	**46,986**	**56,417**	**70,544**	**80,137**	**113,848**	**126,647**	**198,488**	**414,105**	**573,903**
Total bank assets	961,609	1,137,867	1,336,863	1,524,752	1,722,010	1,991,557	2,303,756	1,722,030	2,262,557	2,322,532
Reverse Repo as %	4%	4%	4%	5%	5%	6%	5%	12%	18%	25%

SOURCE: *China Banking Almanac.*

significantly. The value of average monthly transactions soared more than four times from 2013 to 2016, driven by total borrowing hitting 25 percent as measured against total bank assets.[5] Some of these trades ended up in bank WMP asset pools; in 2017 such interbank repo assets constituted 11 percent of total underlying WMP assets (see Tables 4.4 and 4.5).

The data in Table 5.1 includes "other financial institutions"—the National Social Security Fund (NSSF), mutual-type funds, urban and rural credit coops, finance companies, trust companies, financial leasing companies and AMCs. It is easy to narrow this group down to the actual players. Trust companies do not have large balance sheets; they exist to securitize assets and earn management fees, not hold assets. The finance and financial leasing companies are also tiny. As for the AMCs at fiscal year 2019, the two publicly listed companies together show only 32 billion *yuan* in reverse repo transactions, suggesting the four state AMCs would have around 64 billion yuan. This result is surprisingly small, but then again what acceptable, standard assets do they hold? The bulk of NSSF liabilities consist of reverse repo, but the amount is not large either, at FY2018 only 138 billion *yuan*. Adding all of these up totals just over 234 billion *yuan*.

This leaves the small cooperative banks. By 2016, the urban coops had nearly all been consolidated into city commercial banks. Rural coops, however, had just started the process of becoming rural commercial banks. Consequently, rural coops taken as a whole still had a sizable balance sheet on which there were 861 billion *yuan* of securities of the total sold as part of repo transactions, making them the largest component of the "other" category. These insignificant entities located out in China's puckabrush were being stuffed with securities of uncertain value that they financed with the money of peasant farmers.

What of the other 70 billion *yuan*? Only mutual funds, WMPs, and trust plans are left. These three products share a similar structure: there is a fund manager. Mutual funds all have fund managers setting an investment strategy. Bank-appointed staff manage the off-balance-sheet WMPs and their need for liquidity from time to time is obvious: they borrow funds from the market against their provision of standard assets. Trust plans are similar: a trust company appoints a manager to handle the trust funds of two or more investors. Again, one can understand the need for liquidity in such operations in which the fund manager would borrow funds from the market against standard securities. It is reasonable to assume that these product managers might borrow the remaining 70 billion in the "other" category. Next to the "other" category comes "other banks" of which city commercial banks constitute 96 percent, borrowing via reverse repo some 53 trillion (about US$9 trillion) over the course of 2016 or $740 billion a month.

To sum up, this little observed but very common transaction had, as of fiscal year 2016, the last time data was made available, removed 1.6 trillion *renminbi* (US$230 billion) of assets from the balance sheets of Chinese financial entities in China. These assets included central and local government bonds, but also WMPs and trust plans, both of which have highly questionable value. Of these, over half were being held by individual rural credit coops.

In addition to these coops, others must also be lending the money in these transactions. Table 5.2 shows the position of each bank category after netting out borrowing from lending—banks do both all the time. Negative numbers mean the bank on a net basis lent money; positive numbers mean the bank borrowed on a net basis. Given their lock on deposits, the biggest lenders had to be the state banks and the biggest borrowers city banks and "other" institutions. As shown, the lending and, consequently, the *monthly* borrowing amounts shot up in 2015 and 2016 with state banks providing around 16 trillion yuan (US2.4 trillion) in net financing. In comparison, the *daily net repos* in the US market in 2020 were US$700 billion of which US$2.6 trillion were reverse (lending) repos. As in the US market, Chinese transactions have maturities largely of one day, although the latter market does extend to a year.

Flexible Loan Agreements

The analysis has not finished with bonds yet; when loans were handed out in 2009 and 2010, the urgency was such that banks took little care about the details; time was of the essence. Projects were approved by Beijing in bundles.[6] As a result, nearly half the loans extended were short term, that is, a year or less. From a borrower and a lender viewpoint

Table 5.2 Average monthly net bank repo lending and borrowing, 2007–2016

100 mm	2007	2008	2009	2010	2011	2012	2013	2014	2015	2016
State banks	−11,071	−10,764	−19,924	−18,970	−15,341	−45,084	−35,754	−66,561	−154,323	−160,942
Other banks, including city banks	987	1,306	−405	7,599	4,847	22,341	14,819	31,267	62,522	46,000
	0	0	0	0	0	0	0	15,940	48,772	44,183
Other financial institutions	3,511	2,255	8,150	2,413	3,157	8,406	5,481	6,856	63,980	94,288
Insurance Cos.	2,607	2,220	3,363	1,820	2,076	1,939	4,629	7,464	10,245	−2,620
Securities Cos. and Funds	1,134	2,391	6,027	4,498	4,858	8,653	9,883	17,039	8,846	0
Foreigners	2,833	2,591	2,456	2,641	820	1,661	942	3,944	8,731	5,919

NOTE: A negative figure means lending, positive means borrowing. *Source: China Banking Almanac.*

short-term loans were unworkable in the long run; once things settled
down, both would be scrambling with the repayment of "old" loans, the
extension of new loans, and all the administrative work that went with it.
Moreover, these short-term loans were meant to support longer-term
projects—highways, water works, airports, and, especially, bullet trains.
So the loans should match the maturity of the project creating the cash
flow to pay it back.

In 2012, the bank regulator sent out work teams to help provincial
bank branches restructure existing local loans. The consequence was a
rollover of all bank debt as shown in Figure 5.1 and the extension of loan
maturities. As of fiscal year 2010, outstanding local debt according to the
National Audit Office (NAO) was just over 90 billion *yuan* at the end of
the first stimulus package and the same amount as at year-end 2012.[7]
The middle columns show the original net loans outstanding as *if principal had in fact been repaid as scheduled*. Instead, loans had been restructured
to suit the character of investment projects.

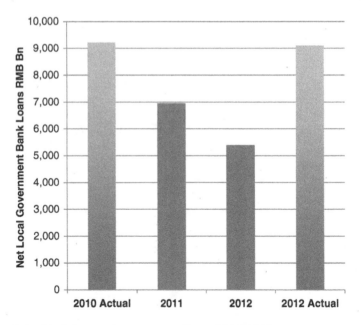

Figure 5.1   Bank loan and guarantee rollover, 2010–2012.
SOURCE: National Audit Bureau, 2011 and 2013.

This is a particular example of a common Chinese practice of revising loan terms not just to adjust errors, but also to avoid a borrower's default and the necessity to increase non-performing assets. In this case, the extension of loan maturities turned out to be just the first step in transforming the original loans into bonds with much, much longer terms and so more manageable for everyone involved—banks, local governments, regulators, auditors and, of course, the party.

Local Government Bonds

Chapter 2 explored the relationship between local governments and banks and demonstrated the historical dependency of local budgets on bank and enterprise loans. In 2010, the PBOC dispatched study groups to the United States to explore the US municipal bond market. The central bank's interest seemed obvious, first to promote the further development of the nascent domestic bond market, one of its major policy goals. The more important objective, however, was to lay the groundwork for creating a Chinese version of "munies," the securities issued by municipal government entities in the United States. The creation of such a market in China would require an amendment to the 1994 Budget Law, eliminating the clause that forbade local governments from borrowing. A municipal bond market, therefore, would be *de facto* recognition that the Budget Law compromise had failed. On the other hand, the PBOC argued that munies offered a way to make already-existing local debt transparent and local government borrowing controllable by Beijing, a step toward hard budgets. They also offered a way to extend once again maturities for all those long-dated infrastructure projects.

The explorations by the PBOC team in the United States also had the support of the MOF. Adding to this came pressure from local governments; the lobbying came together in the MOF's tentative steps to allow "muni" issuance. In 2009 the MOF initiated a pilot project in which the ministry issued bonds in the name of a handful of the strongest provincial governments, for example, Shandong and Shanghai. But as Beijing continued to use bank loans to drive economic growth, pressure grew to throw open the bond door to every sort of local issuer. This became the so-called "Close the back door while opening the front door" policy. All told, local government debt grew rapidly from 2010, reaching some RMB14.7 trillion (US$2.3 trillion) by 2015, nearly 19 percent of GDP.[8] The front door was wide open (but so was the back door).

What is meant by "local government bonds"? The usage in the China Central Depository and Clearing Co. includes only provincial-level governments, certain cities like Beijing and Shanghai that have provincial status, and a small number of wealthy second-tier cities such as Suzhou, Shenzhen, Qingdao, and Ningbo. Local government bonds do not include bonds issued by local government financing platforms (LGFP) of which there is a vast and probably unknowable amount. Therefore, in speaking about local government bonds, the reality is that the numbers, without doubt, underestimate local debt.

From the very start, it was obvious that everyone in Beijing, not to mention the party leadership, was fully aware of the precarious fiscal situation of most local governments. They could hardly have failed to know since most senior government officials' career includes a stint at the provincial level. This explains the tentative approach by the MOF. At the same time, the big state banks were facing a huge challenge in their burgeoning loan portfolios: too much local debt with too little quality and not enough capital to support it all. Consequently, they also eagerly supported local bond issuance and proposed using them to refinance the existing local debt already on their balance sheets. In 2011, munies were a concept whose time had come in China.

Based on international accounting principles this product seemed a no brainer. Loans attract 100 percent risk weightings; the calculation of risk-weighted assets is used in calculating a bank's capital adequacy.[9] Bonds are different and, according to international accounting standards, bonds attract only a 20 percent risk weighting. In the China financial wonderland, bonds of all provincial issuers are rated investment grade[10] by official "third-party" credit agencies and all call only for 20 percent weightings and minimal provisions against interest rate movements.[11] From the design of the Chinese state, this makes sense, but everyone in the financial sector knows that not all provinces are created equal. And the maturities of local bonds were long. As of fiscal year 2019, less than 5 percent had maturities of less than three years, while 10 percent were 30-year bonds, 29 percent were 10-year, and 17 percent were seven-year.[12] Provincial credit risk plus long-term market risk suggest that loss provisions should be far higher than audited statements provide, since, in the absence of a liquid trading market, the bonds are more akin to loans than securities.

In any event, this accounting approach enabled Chinese banks to manipulate their balance sheets, aided and abetted by their auditors and regulators. As for ethics, from the party's viewpoint, this was never involved. The approach reduced financial risk, at least from an accounting angle, and so should be fully supported. The logic always was "I am the majority shareholder of these banks and this approach improves my financial position." The question is never, what is best for minority shareholders or is this going to be a problem later on. "Later on" can take care of itself. So the alliance of local governments and banks plus the central bank and the party organization accelerated the volume of local borrowing in the guise of bonds in the name of risk reduction and transparency. All told, local government debt grew from RMB11 trillion in 2010 to RMB22.8 trillion (nearly US$4 trillion) by 2019, 23 percent of GDP and around 17 percent of total risk-weighted banking assets.[13]

Only in 2016 did a concerted effort begin to control leverage throughout the system. At this point, 60 percent of local debt had been transformed into bonds and all of it held by banks (see Table 5.3). The new deleveraging policy led to an explosion of issuance, but only within limits now imposed by Beijing.[14] By FY2019, the year the bond for debt program was to end, nearly 90 percent of local debt had been transformed into bonds. With maturities of up to 30 years, the investor market for local debt also expanded a bit to include funds and insurance companies. Even so, there is no doubt that the Big 5 state banks held most of these issues. Of course, banks can select which local bonds to carry, but in the end somebody has to pony up for the weakest issuers either directly or through the repo market.

As mentioned, swapping loans for bonds relieved significant pressure on bank capital adequacy calculations. As Table 5.3 shows, in 2018 local debt totaled around 16.6 trillion *yuan* (US$2.5 trillion). The loans for bond swaps released over 12 trillion *yuan* (US$2 trillion, Column F) in capital—only around 4.3 trillion *yuan* (US$700 billion, Column G) was used in calculating capital adequacy. Had the swaps not happened, the banks would have had to treat 15.3 trillion *yuan* (US$2.5 trillion,

Table 5.3 · More local government bonds less risk weight.

100 mms	Local Gov't Bonds Held by All Entities	Local Gov't Bonds Held by Banks/ Total Local Debt	Total Local Debt	Net Local Debt Risk Weight 100%	Bank Held Bonds Risk Weighting 20%	Total Risk Weight Removed	Net Risk Weighted Local Debt
	A	B	C	D C – A	E A × .20	F A – E	G C – F
2013	8,498	6.3%	135,515	127,017	1,700	6,798	128,717
2014	11,472	7.4%	154,074	142,602	2,294	9,178	144,896
2015	44,557	30.2%	147,568	103,011	8,911	35,646	111,922
2016	93,631	61.0%	153,558	59,927	18,726	74,905	78,653
2017	127,556	77.3%	165,100	37,544	25,511	102,045	63,055
2018	153,272	92.3%	166,100	12,828	30,654	122,618	43,482
2019	211,183	86.3%	228,219	17,036	42,237	168,946	59,273

SOURCE: *China Bond*, PBOC; nonfinancial loans include corporate and retail; author's calculations.

Column A) as loans attracting 100 percent risk weighting; the pressure to raise new capital would have been huge. Swapping into bonds meant that the banks could lend *five times* more than if these local credits had remained loans.

This was a very big deal for capital-strapped state banks, and it was also a huge thing for a government seeking to deleverage the economy: in the flash of an accounting policy, bank-wide leverage had been reduced! And nobody paid any attention even among the foreigners!

Bank Bond Portfolios

In 2019, portfolios of commercial bank bonds accounted for 14 percent of total banking assets and one-third of total bank loans. Figure 5.2 shows all financial entities holding fixed-income securities in 2109. The figure shows that China's commercial banks hold the bulk of the

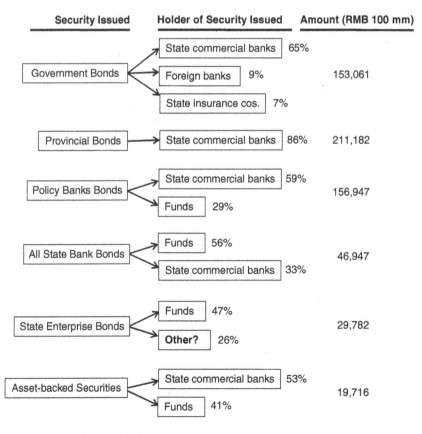

Figure 5.2 Principal holders of issued securities, 2019.
Source: China Bond.

country's debt securities: 65 percent of central government bonds, 92 percent of provincial government bonds, 59 percent of policy bank bonds, 33 percent of commercial bank bonds, and 53 percent of asset-backed securities. In short, China's commercial banks finance the bonds of the Chinese government with the exception of corporate debt. Any thought that China's banks do not finance the national budget is blinded by detail.

Figure 5.3 shows bank bond portfolios growing rapidly after the financial crisis. The figure separately includes bonds of the China Development Bank (CDB), which has been a principal lender to local governments since its establishment in 1993.[15] China Development Bank funds itself primarily by these bonds and by borrowing from the central bank. Its bonds plus provincial government bonds in 2019 equaled nearly two-thirds of bank bond portfolios. Central government debt itself is half of provincial debt; the remaining enterprise (or corporate) bonds total less than 10 percent of provincial debt. Enterprise bonds have been crowded out of bank portfolios and into mutual funds.

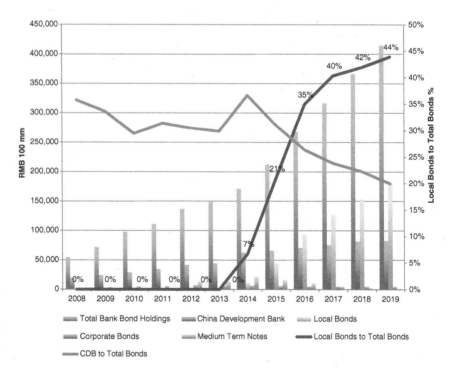

Figure 5.3   Local bonds in bank bond portfolios, 2013–2019.
SOURCE: China Bond.

From a risk viewpoint, bond portfolio exposure to CDB is a semi-sovereign risk. Its then powerful head, Chen Yuan, had sought to turn CDB into a financial conglomerate with the ultimate goal of listing as an investment banking group.[16] In 2008 he succeeded in turning it into a company limited by shares, the move just prior to listing. This threw the market for the bank's bonds into a tizzy: the bank was no longer a strict semi-sovereign, but what was it? Even in the China bond market, participants are aware of risk. The global crisis put *paid* to Chen's listing ideas and in 2013 he was made chairman of the symbolic Chinese People's Consultative Congress and CDB reverted to a clear semi-sovereign in 2017 and the market settled down.

Risk and Bank Provincial Bond Holdings

As for provincial government bonds, China's "unitary" administrative system suggests that all provinces plus the central government are equal parts of a single entity. This is the reason Chinese credit-rating agencies rate all provincial debt triple A. No one in the market is fooled. Figure 5.4 illustrates the inequality among provincial economies, showing provincial bonds plus local government financial platform placements to provincial GDP. LGFP placements (but not their entire debt, which would include bank loans) are now a matter of record and can be found in the Wind database. As of fiscal year 2019, such placements total a mere (as compared to local bonds) 6 trillion *yuan* (US$900 billion), but this number is surely an underestimate.

With the exception of Tianjin, the provinces with outstanding debt of 40 percent or more of GDP are not surprising; they are border provinces mostly in the far west. As for Tianjin, the "Manhattan City" project is the best illustration for why the city's debt is so high. This project involves the creation of an entire new city on the Bohai Bay coast modeled after Manhattan with the same street and place names, even a Central Park. There is an electrified model that takes up the floor of a large building. Tianjin's new port is another example: the cranes designed to lift containers off huge ships are as shiny-new as Christmas toys. If they build it, they will come. Tianjin is a financial disaster waiting to happen.

A second group of provinces enjoy debt of nearly 30 percent of GDP. It is not surprising that the strongest provinces (excepting Tibet,

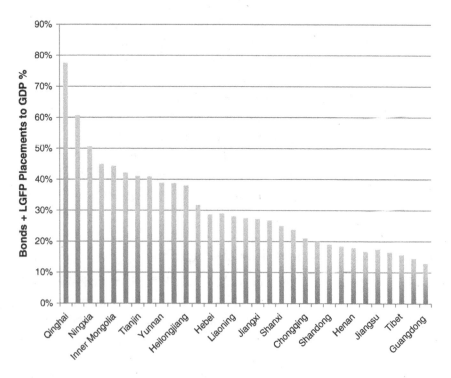

Figure 5.4   Provincial bonds and LGFP placements to provincial GDP, 2019.
SOURCE: Wind and *China Statistical Yearbook*; author's calculations.

which has no economy and also little debt) show the lowest levels of debt. On the other hand, these same provinces led by Jiangsu and Zhejiang had the highest numbers of LGFPs and related LGFP placements. Even the lowest layers of local government know how to borrow in Jiangsu.

From a geographic viewpoint, all the strongest provinces are on the coast of East China from Shandong in the north to Guangdong in the south. These seven provinces and two provincial-level cities account for 57 percent of total outstanding bonds. This means that the remaining bonds, accounting for 43 percent of the total and 22 issuing provinces, are poor credits, certainly not triple A. From this financial viewpoint China's geography has remained largely unchanged from time immemorial notwithstanding the billions of dollars of foreign and domestic investment over the past 30 years. Anyone traveling outside the East Coast can soon come to the same conclusion.

Estimating the interest expense on local debt and comparing it to total budgetary revenues shows even more clearly where the risk lies. As shown in Table 5.4 those provinces with high debt levels are the same as those with low budgetary revenues. There are nine provinces with interest expense ratios of 20 percent or more of official budgeted

Table 5.4   Provincial budgetary revenues vs. debt expenses 2019.

100 mm	2019 Budgeted Revenues	Bonds + Placements 6/2020	Coupon at 5%	Coupon/ Budget %
Qinghai	273	2,300	115	42%
Guizhou	1,727	10,175	509	29%
Shaanxi	2,243	11,495	575	26%
Yunnan	1,994	9,035	452	23%
Gansu	871	3,682	184	21%
Inner Mongolia	1,858	7,641	382	21%
Heilongjiang	1,283	5,166	258	20%
Guangxi	1,681	6,725	336	20%
Ningxia	437	1,746	87	20%
Jilin	1,241	4,807	240	19%
Shanxi	2,293	8,826	441	19%
Xinjiang	1,531	5,273	264	17%
Sichuan	3,911	12,476	624	16%
Hainan	753	2,388	119	16%
Hebei	3,514	10,053	503	14%
Jiangxi	2,373	6,750	338	14%
Tianjin	2,106	5,802	290	14%
Liaoning	2,616	7,107	355	14%
Fujian	3,007	7,783	389	13%
Henan	3,766	9,697	485	13%
Hunan	2,861	6,998	350	12%
Chongqing	2,266	4,962	248	11%
Zhejiang	6,598	13,784	689	10%
Jiangsu	8,630	17,404	870	10%
Hubei	3,307	6,633	332	10%
Shandong	6,485	12,186	609	9%
Anhui	3,049	4,244	212	7%
Tibet	230	264	13	6%
Guangdong	12,105	13,872	694	6%
Beijing	5,786	5,900	295	5%
Shanghai	7,108	6,278	314	4%

SOURCE: Wind and *China Statistical Yearbook*, author's calculations.

revenues. Excepting Tianjin, these are also the provinces with some of the weakest economies and, therefore, lowest actual budgetary revenues in the country. Bond coupons depend on maturities and creditworthiness, so the 5 percent figure used in the table should be seen as an estimate only; actual market rates would be much higher if there were a market.

Trading and Valuation of Provincial Bonds

The discussion of provincial bonds to this point relates only to valuations of creditworthiness. The data has shown that administratively equal provinces in fact have significantly different credit characteristics. These differences should be brought out in the values the bond market assigns to each security.[17] China's bond market, however, is dysfunctional: there is very little trading among the 800,000(!)-plus participants. The participant number is so high because each branch of every market member belongs to the interbank market; there are no effective central treasuries as there are for international banks. In fact, over the past decade, as provincial debt boomed, whatever trading there was became concentrated in central government debt, including that of China Development Bank. But even in those bonds trading has come nearly to a standstill (see Figure 5.5). A decade earlier in 2010 government bonds had turned over one time a year and CDB bonds 4 times,[18] whereas in 2020 the relative turnover numbers were approximately one-tenth of the 2010 totals.

The huge increase in securities outstanding and the mispricing of all bonds account for the nonexistent trading activity. For example, say Party A wants to sell to Party B a bond that he underwrote when the bond was issued. Party B is likely to ask for a price much cheaper than the price set by regulators when A underwrote the issue. If he sold the bond, Party A would take a loss, while Party B would gain a bond with a price closer to what the market might demand. Actual trading would become active if the bond prices were close to what market participants, and not regulators, demand.

Put another way, there are few buyers for Chinese securities at their current price levels. For the foreign institutions now buying central government bonds, they do so since the coupon is greater than what is now available internationally, and they expect the currency to increase in value, but they could be wrong. Of course, bonds of Chinese entities issued out of Hong Kong into international markets, for example, those of Huarong and Evergrande, all were priced at the market and trade at the market.

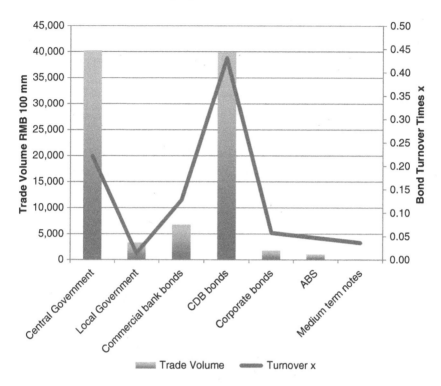

Figure 5.5   Interbank market bond trading volume and turnover, 2020.
SOURCE: *China Bond*, author's calculations; for comparison with 2010, this same chart can be found in Carl Walter and Fraser Howie, *Red Capitalism*, 2nd ed., Figure 4.8, p. 111.

For Chinese banks, however, the absence of a market means that their bond portfolios,[19] and especially their provincial bond portfolios, are materially overvalued. In the event active trading were to begin, if, for example, a provincial bond were priced at a true market clearing level, these portfolios would have to be revalued by bank auditors and significant losses would result. Or, looked at another way, all these bonds are little more than disguised loans and should be treated by accountants as such.[20]

Government "Guidance" Funds

In 1998 the district government in the university section of Beijing, Zhongguancun, established the Beijing Zhongguancun Venture Capital Development Fund to help finance the new technology zone it had just established. The Fund became a forerunner of over a thousand funds set up by the central and local governments all over China. Some, like the National Integrated Circuits Fund and the Silk Road Fund, are well known; others, such as the Jilin Government Industry Investment Guidance Fund, not so much. The funds were set up as limited partnerships with investors holding equity portions. The fund periods were generally meant to be a decade.[21] They mark a return to state-planned investing but without any state plan.

State banks and the larger shareholding banks became investors in the funds organized by agencies of the central government; the banks were compelled to support the latter's policy efforts. These funds were just another way to increase extra-budgetary financing. Nor did these funds provide rich returns; whereas a venture capital fund in the United States would expect a return of many times, these China funds paid out below 10 percent. They were more similar to a loan than to equity.

In fact, these equity investments are hidden inside the loan category on bank balance sheets. Investment agreements describe the transaction as some sort of convertible loan instrument. On investing, the equity assumes a loan-like character even though it is equity in the partnership itself. At maturity, sometime in the distant future, the equity investment becomes a loan and is paid off. This arrangement exists to avoid banks having to make a capital provision of 400 percent, if the transaction had been approved by the State Council, and 1250 percent if not. For this reason, a significant amount of such funds were placed in WMP asset pools, well away from bank balance sheets (such assets constituted 6 percent of WMP non-standard assets; see Table 4.6).

While guidance funds are not a large category on bank balance sheets, the fact that the government knowingly twists regulations to turn equity into debt provides insight into the quality of bank assets overall. From the start of the deleveraging campaign, regulators required banks to employ loan-type risk weights to these funds.

Off-Balance-Sheet Items

Entrusted Loans

An entrusted loan is a very simple transaction involving an enterprise making a loan through the agency of a bank. To do this the enterprise provides the funds to a bank, which then transfers them to the target enterprise.

It does this because, in China, enterprises, whether state-owned or private, are not allowed to operate a true central treasury function. For that matter, Chinese banks also do not have such a function. A central treasury finances the overall operations of an enterprise and its group-deploying capital in the most efficient way possible and is the face of the enterprise to its banks. Some large state enterprises and auto sales companies do have finance companies, but their function is more to provide consumer finance (autos) or to act as a financial consultant and arranger on a project basis working with individual members of an enterprise group and financial institutions, for example, China Power Finance.

The ban on central treasury functions is based on how state enterprises have been traditionally organized. Prior to making use of stock markets to raise funds, state enterprises were overseen or "owned" by local governments. During the 1990s many of the larger ones were transferred to central government oversight, yet, at the same time, local governments could not be ignored since the enterprise staff and workers were a local responsibility.

Large enterprises may operate subsidiaries in many provinces and these historically have had their own local financial arrangements. A central treasury function would weaken local authority and even remove the local operation's finances from the influence, if not control, of the local government. On the other hand, it is common to have one larger enterprise in a group with the ability to borrow large sums from state banks. Often the head of central enterprise groups is minister-level, whereas the heads of state banks are only vice-ministers; this gave the enterprise head significant leverage. These larger group enterprises commonly over-borrow and then arrange with a bank to make an "entrusted loan" to fund another subsidiary part of its operations. To a certain extent it acts as the group's central treasurer.

From the agent bank's viewpoint, an entrusted loan is not a loan since nothing appears on its balance sheet; the money merely passed through its hands for a small fee. It had merely been "entrusted" by the large enterprise to pass funds on as instructed. From a risk perspective, there are a couple of problems with such transactions. First, what if the subsidiary borrower fails to repay the loan: the bank, even though it has acted only as an agent, received the money and the central enterprise will expect the funds back. The big problem is that such funds often ended up in financial rather than operational transactions.

As Chapter 2 suggested, local governments often pressure state enterprises to make funds available; sending an entrusted loan down to a local subsidiary is a way to achieve this. The subsidiary takes the underlying paperwork related to the investment and, working with a trust company (which the enterprise group or the local government or both may have an interest in), sells it as part of a trust plan to third-party investors of a second bank. Part of the proceeds from this sale may eventually be used by the subsidiary to repay the entrusted loan. The eventual repayment of the original transaction restores the liquidity of the entrusting state enterprise (See Figure 5.6).

Remember that the large enterprise over-borrowed in the first place and so increased its own debt-to-equity ratio, or leverage. So in late 2009 it was entirely natural for banks, faced with the political command to provide huge amounts of funds to stimulate the economy, sent large

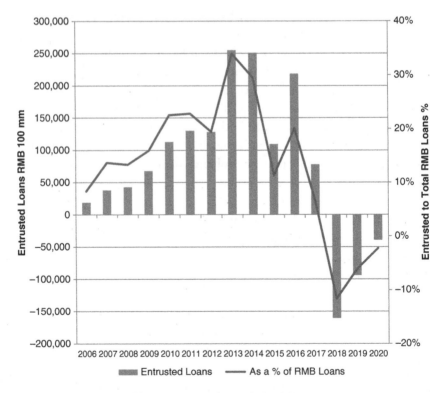

Figure 5.6   Entrusted loans to RMB loans, 2006–2020.
SOURCE: *China Banking Almanac*; figures show new financing; negative figures represent repayment.

chunks of money to state enterprises, including China Railways. These enterprises naturally used entrusted loans to channel money to subsidiaries around the country. In the years after 2009, entrusted loans grew rapidly, equaling around 35 percent of total RMB loans in 2013 and 2014. Come 2016 and the deleveraging campaign, the story changed and entrusted loans became an easy target for regulators aiming for quick results. Figure 5.7 shows this story clearly. The 2016 deleveraging effort included new rules drawing specific limits around the product issued by the bank regulator in 2018. With enterprises paying down their loans, the politicians could claim victory, but perhaps not for long.

Debt-to-Equity Swaps

As part of the same 2016 deleveraging effort SASAC, the nominal overseer of central state enterprise groups, required its enterprises to reduce their leverage by 2 percent by the end of 2020. Paying down entrusted loans was one method. There were other ways as well, including debt-to-equity swaps. It should be noted that there was never a mention, just as there has never been any mention, of real privatization. Enticing private capital into a group company as a minority stakeholder was, however, allowed since, by introducing third-party capital, it would reduce the burden on the state. Real privatization, meaning the sale of a controlling stake to a non-state investor, is never a solution in China . . . yet.

It is a good question how leverage in the state enterprise groups is measured, since most, if not all of them are not listed anywhere as consolidated entities. As a result, the campaign's focus was probably on outstanding debt of the largest group enterprise. To kick off the debt-swap program, five state banks applied for and, in 2017, were quickly approved to set up subsidiaries to handle these swaps. These subsidiaries generally had a billion *yuan* as seed capital; thereafter, they had to rely on the market for financing, not being allowed to borrow from their parents. Well, it was all the same: Sub A of Major Bank 1 issued debt bought by Major Bank 2 and vice versa for Sub B of Bank 2. Some of this debt ended up in the WMP asset pools. According to the bank regulator, by the end of 2017 the five subs had raised 2.5 trillion yuan in funding and signed 1.6 trillion in deals, enough to get started!

These subsidiaries generally worked with their bank's own borrowers raising financing from the market to acquire the loans from their parent. This would not reduce the parent bank's total assets since the 100 percent owned subsidiary would be consolidated in its financial statements. If a transaction were successful, however, it would reduce total loans. How? The answer is complicated but once swapped for equity, the bankers would seek to sell the equity to third parties, maybe even listing the enterprise on the Shanghai exchange. If this process were completed, then the parent bank would have reduced its book of problem loans. By 2020, when this program was meant to have ended, some five trillion *yuan* worth of these transactions were to have been signed of which three trillion completed. By mid-year 2020, however, only 910 billion *yuan* had been finished.[22]

This approach to deleveraging state enterprises and reducing bank problem assets was never going to have a material impact. The valuation process for the equity and the ensuing haggling with the troubled state enterprise would be incredibly time consuming. How can the value of an equity stake in an unincorporated, unlisted (and bankrupt) enterprise be calculated? To start with the problem enterprise may not yet have been restructured as a company limited by shares. If it has not, then it is impossible to carry out any kind of legitimate swap.

Versions of international valuation techniques are being used in these transactions, but they do not work in China. First, there is no yield curve; as a result, cash flows (if there are any) cannot be discounted to arrive at a price per share. For the same reason, the use of comparable listed companies in the same industry as the target enterprise is inappropriate as well; listed Chinese state enterprises in Hong Kong have been thoroughly restructured whereas the target enterprise is likely to be an unrestructured, pure state enterprise.

For these reasons many of the original transactions included a repo clause; if bankers found the subsidiaries to be worthless, they could exercise the repo to get their investment back, but this obviously wouldn't help the leverage problem. As a result, some recent transactions have done equity swaps with a listed parent of the troubled enterprise. While this may have provided assurance that the bank might receive shares of value, it does not solve the problem of valuation of the subsidiary.[23]

Other Contingent Liabilities

There are many unconsolidated transactions that represent contingent liabilities. *Contingent* means that a possibility exists that someday they may cause trouble. Wealth management products are a prime example, except the product was always considered a final sale to the investor and so had never carried in bank financial statements as a contingent risk. Other types of banking transactions that create contingent liabilities include foreign exchange trades, guarantees, letters of credit, interest rate swaps. These are all valued at regulatory-set risk weights. "Unconsolidated structured entities" are another type of financial transaction that, from an accounting viewpoint, are not considered even contingent liabilities.

1. Wealth Management Products In Chapter 4, WMPs were discussed as *a flow*, the value of assets transferred into the wealth management asset pool. The point of revisiting WMPs here is to give an idea of what the outstanding size of off-balance-sheet asset pools might be. Presumably these assets were transitioned from the balance sheet to the asset pool to an invested product at the same time. Over time, the value of total invested products changed. If investment in WMPs continued to increase as it did until 2016, then the invested asset pool equaled the total value of the asset pool as shown in Figure 5.7. So long as investor demand grew, this situation was fine. If, however, the value of invested assets shrank, the pool

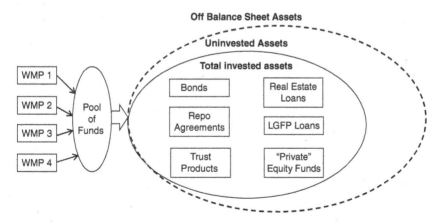

Figure 5.7   Schematic of wealth management product asset pools.

of assets would continue to exist and remain off balance sheet *but with no funding!* This was not so good: Who now owned these assets? A discussion began within the industry on this topic.[24]

This led in early 2017 to the regulators circulating a document seeking industry opinion, usually done before a significant change is introduced.[25] After what must have been heated discussions, the final document sponsored by five heavyweight ministries, including the central bank and the banking, securities, foreign exchange, and insurance regulators, was put forth in 2018 (this took place before the merger of the banking and insurance regulators).

There were five crucial points that, if followed by the banks, would have a major impact on their balance sheets (author's italics):

1. Existing WMP asset pools must be eliminated by the end of 2020. The assets can mature or be sold or *be brought back on bank balance sheets.*
2. The asset management business going forward can only be done in a single-purpose subsidiary that banks (or other institutions) may apply for. Such subsidiaries must start out with clean balance sheets—that is, *old assets cannot be stuffed into new boxes* unless the assets comply with the new regulation.
3. WMPs may *no longer be designed with maturity mismatches,* that is, the maturity on the WMP itself must equal that of the underlying asset.
4. *Layering of assets* to create a WMP is forbidden.

The regulations would make it very difficult for banks to arrange a product with a yield over straight debt: no maturity mismatch and no layering. Bringing securities back on balance sheets also posed massive administrative, accounting, and regulatory problems, not to mention possible losses. It meant that by the end of 2020 all existing asset pools totaling at least 8.51 trillion *yuan* (US$1.3 trillion) and at most 30 trillion yuan (not quite US$5 trillion) would be completely cleaned up. This huge range is due to how the official numbers lowball the problem.[26] In any event, the complexity of the cleanup ensured that 2020 would not be the terminal date. Events may have given the banks extra time: Covid-19 broke out, spread rapidly internationally, effectively reducing global trade and led, once again, to a command injection of liquidity into the financial system.

Table 5.5   Outstanding wealth management products and their composition.

100 mm RMB	2013	2014	2015	2016	2017	2018
Amount of funds raised	70,480	150,200	158,410	270,100	173,590	98,450
Amount of nonstandard assets	19,375	39,893	24,918	47,240	28,156	16,963
Asset composition %						
Debt	38.6%	43.8%	51.0%	43.8%	42.2%	53.4%
Nonstandard debt assets	27.5%	26.6%	15.7%	17.5%	16.2%	17.2%
Cash and bank deposits	25.6%	20.9%	22.4%	16.6%	13.9%	5.8%
Interbank repoed assets	NA	NA	NA	NA	0.11	6.6%
Currencies	NA	NA	7.8%	13.1%	NA	NA
Rights assets	6.1%	6.2%	NA	7.0%	9.5%	9.9%
Public funds	NA	NA	NA	NA	NA	NA
Derivatives	1.1%	1.3%	NA	NA	NA	NA
QDII assets	0.4%	0.5%	NA	NA	NA	NA
Other	0.4%	0.3%	NA	NA	NA	NA
WMP financing tools	0.2%	0.3%	NA	NA	NA	NA
Credit assets	2.0%	0.2%	NA	NA	NA	NA
Other investment assets	1.0%	0.2%	NA	NA	NA	NA

SOURCE: *China Wealth Management Report*, various.

Table 5.5 shows outstandings and the makeup of the non-standard products included in WMP asset pools. Data is not available for all products in all years, but what there is gives an idea of the huge variety of things banks transferred into the asset pool.

Unconsolidated Structured Entities

Unconsolidated structured entities—this is a concept that just screams out for transparency. Like WMPs, these entities represent pools of assets located off balance sheet. How do they exist? All large state banks have trust company subsidiaries that take bank assets, wrap them up in a trust plan and sell to third parties, just like WMPs only with largely institutional investors. Regulations require that arrangers retain a 10 percent portion of such trust plans. Otherwise, based on close auditing, the trust company is no longer supposed to be involved in any way with the management of the plan that has been sold. Since it does not manage or control the trust plan in any way it can be unconsolidated. The likelihood of this arrangement begs belief.

How much of these entities are out there? Since they are unconsolidated, there is no need to disclose data about them in bank financial statements. However, auditors are required by Hong Kong listing rules to make note in their audit letter of four "Key Audit Matters." These form a part of the audit letter attached to the financial statements. In its audit letter for Bank of China's 2018 statements, Ernst & Young include structured entities as a key matter noting,

> Due to the significance of the unconsolidated structured entitles and the complexity of judgment exercised by management, consolidation or non-consolidation of structured entities is considered a key audit matter.[27]

The auditors accepted management's signed statement that everything was as it should be—namely, unconsolidated. The fact that auditors mention this as a "key issue" and not only for this one bank is the point. It strongly suggests that there are large whales lurking out there in the financial sea for which banks may ultimately be liable, as the analysis of WMPs demonstrates.

Comments

Banks everywhere are extremely complex entities that are poorly understood by those outside the industry and even by most of the people working inside them. From 2009 the party put huge pressure on China's newly recapitalized banks to stimulate the economy, when this fiscal role better belonged to the central bank. As will be discussed in Chapter 7, in China banks executed what is known in the United States as a program of "quantitative easing" by buying up loans. Bank management, of course, had no choice.

At the same time, the major state banks are public entities and so need to provide semi-annual public financial statements that audited with "clean" opinions. These were then examined globally by myriad investor analysts and international regulators. In the words of pre-reform China, banks needed to be both "red and expert (又红又专)" during times when the "expert" part of the equation was rapidly weakening. Now, in the early years of the 2020s, the party seems increasingly bent on reversing the order that Deng Xiaoping had worked so long to put in place. It would not be surprising if this continues that the state banks would be, one after the other, delisted. They could still be audited, but the reports would be solely for the use of their sole owners, the party. Or abbreviated statements with no footnotes could be published, as is the case now with China Development Bank. After all, it might be argued, China has plenty of capital; it doesn't need foreign capital in its critical institutions anymore. It could happen.

Notes

1. For a full explanation of the US repo market, the largest in the world, see the classic by Marcia Stigum, *The Money Market* (New York: Dow Jones-Irwin, 1983), Chapter 2.
2. In China transactions can extend as far as 6 months, whereas internationally such trades are usually quite short, typically overnight. The accounting transactions are clear on every bank balance sheet. On the asset side for repo transactions, Bank A increases cash (the securities are "sold"), decreases its securities portfolio, and a liability called "financial liabilities sold under repurchase" is created.
3. Products that can be traded in the interbank market are called standard products and those that are not allowed are non-standard. Not all trust plans or WMPs can be used to borrow money in the repo market.
4. For definition see footnotes in 人民银行 (PBOC), 中国金融年鉴 2014 (China Banking Almanac 2014), p. 404.
5. The percentage for banks alone would have been somewhat lower given the participation of non-bank financial entities.
6. Christine Wong, "The Fiscal Stimulus Program and Public Governance Issues in China," *OECD Journal on Budgeting* 11, no. 3 (2011), http://dx.doi .org/10.1787/budget-11-5kg3nhljqrjl.
7. . National Audit Bureau, 全国地方性债务审计结果公告2011年(2011 Report 鸥鸟National Local Debt Audit results); 35号(总第04号); and 36个地方政府 本级政府性债务审计结果 2013年 (2013 Audit Results of 36 Local Government Level Local Debt), 第4号(总第166号).
8. Raphael Lam and Jingsen Wang, "China's Local Government Bond Market," *International Monetary Fund Working Paper,* WP/18/219, p. 4 ff.
9. The capital adequacy ratio of a bank equals total regulatory capital divided by risk-weighted assets.
10. Gabriel Wildau, "Half of China's Provinces Deserve Junk Ratings, S&P Warns," *Financial Times,* November 20, 2014. S&P was allowed to begin domestic ratings work officially in 2019.

11. The minimal loss provisions relate to interest rate market risk and assume that there is a liquid bond market, that is, there is somebody else out there to buy the bond. This assumption that in China there actually is a secondary market for these bonds is false. See Walter and Howie, *Red Capitalism*, pp. 105–112.

12. *China Finance Almanac* 2019, p. 545.

13. Raphael Lam and Jingsen Wang, "China's Local Government Bond Market," pp. 4 ff.

14. Actually a total annual limit to local government borrowing was imposed as of 2010 as part of the formal budgetary process and approved by the National People's Congress. Not that this in any way limited local borrowing. See 中国财政发展报告2010 (上海, 上海财政经济出版社, 2010), pp. 381 ff.

15. See Henry Sanderson and Michael Forsythe, *China's Superbank* (Singapore: John Wiley & Sons, 2013), pp. 29 ff. This book makes a good stab at showing the symbiotic relationship between China Development Bank and local governments.

16. For the story, see Carl Walter and Fraser Howie, *Red Capitalism*, 2nd ed., pp. 126 ff.

17. The character of the bond market is fully brought out in Walter and Howie, *Red Capitalism*, 2nd ed., Chapter 4.

18. See Walter and Howie, *Red Capitalism*, 2nd ed., Figure 4.8, p. 111.

19. Bank balance sheets carry bonds based on intention. They are either recorded as investments or as trading securities. In either case, they are improperly valued, since their carrying value does not reflect a market value. In this sense they are just loans, but in China a secondary market for loans doesn't exist.

20. Bonds and loans internationally are very different. Bonds issue a prospectus to all potential buyers that lays out all the transaction details. Loan information is proprietary to the bank, so it is difficult for potential buyers to properly value the loan. Bonds, on the other hand, are transparent commodities so that a market can build up around them. Because there is an active market, it is simple to value the bond on a bank balance sheet. Of course markets change and the bank may lose money, so there are provisions for this. In China, there is no trading because there is no market. How can these "bonds" be accounted for as bonds internationally?

21. Shuli Ren, "China's $856 Billion Startup Juggernaut Is Getting Stuck," *Bloomberg*, https://www.bloombergquint.com/view/china-s-856-billion-startup-juggernaut-is-getting-stuck; Emily Feng, "China's State-Owned Venture Capital Funds Battle to Make an Impact," *Financial Times*, https://www.ft.com/content/4fa2caaa-f9f0-11e8-af46-2022a0b02a6c.

22. State Council, 银保监会规范保险资金投资债转股投资计划 (CBIRC standardizes insurance capital swapping into equity investment plans), September 10, 2020, http://www.gov.cn/xinwen/2020-09/10/content_5542303.htm.

23. See also Tianlei Huang, the Peterson Institute, "Tracking China's Debt-to-equity Program," June 2019, https://www.piie.com/blogs/china-economic-watch/tracking-chinas-debt-equity-swap-program-great-cry-and-little-wool; and Cindy H. Huang, "Is China's Great Debt-for-Equity Swap Working? A Reality Check at Year Three," Standard & Poor's, May 2019, https://www.spglobal.com/en/research-insights/articles/is-china-s-great-debt-for-equity-swap-working-a-reality-check-at-year-three.

24. Gabriel Wildau, "China Regulator Launches Fresh Shadow Banking Crackdown," *Financial Times*, July 29, 2020.

25. See "China Steps Up Management of Wealth Management Products," *Reuters*, July, 20, 2017.

26. In 2017, principal guaranteed WMPs were still sold and the 2017 outstanding figure includes them. The regulators terminated these products in 2018 leaving only nonguaranteed WMP products officially outstanding. But the asset pool for the guaranteed products continued to exist, hence the higher number of assets needing to be cleaned up one way or the other.

27. Ernst & Young, "Bank of China Audit Letter," Bank of China financial statement, December 31, 2018, p. 135.

Chapter 6

After 30 Years, Was Deng Xiaoping Right?

Are such things as stock markets good or not?

—*Deng Xiaoping, Shenzhen, January 22, 1992*[1]

In Shenzhen in late January 1992, Deng Xiaoping, China's last emperor, was fleeing the political disputes fracturing his party in Beijing. The left wing had identified the financial reforms of the 1980s as the main source of the social chaos at the decade's end. Deng had come to Shenzhen to see if its special economic zone, bustling with Hong Kong companies, might present a way forward for mainland China. The spot he was standing on is now a vacant lot with a huge billboard showing only his face in profile. Surrounded by the same white tiled buildings he had seen in 1992, his portrait is placed against a deep blue background; shouldn't it be red? This lot, in a not-so-modern part of town and despite the terrible events of June 4, remains a hallowed

piece of ground in a China where there are very few. It is the only me-
morial to Deng anywhere in the country save, perhaps, for his home-
town in Sichuan.

Standing there surrounded by reporters and his entourage, Deng was
asked about the social function and effects of stock markets. He famously
replied, "Are such things as stock markets good or not? Do these things
exist only in capitalist countries or can socialist ones use them too? It is
permitted to try them out . . . If they work out . . . then we will open
up . . . If they are mistakes, just correct them or close the markets."

These words provided political cover for the actions of a group centered
around Zhu Rongji, then vice-premier in charge of economics and finance,
to make use of China's recently opened, but moribund stock exchanges in
Shanghai and Shenzhen. Perhaps equally important, Zhu followed up on
a recent proposition by the Stock Exchange of Hong Kong to list several
state enterprises on the Stock Exchange of Hong Kong as an experiment.
Zhu agreed with the exchange's reasoning that overseas listings would subject state enterprises to additional regulatory and investor oversight, raise
capital outside of the awkward joint venture framework, and promote
greater efficiency.

This chapter assembles information from previous chapters to provide an overview of the major factors of the past 40 years that have led
to the state's excessive leverage today. This overview starts with the creation of a rough balance sheet for the state (party-owned) sector showing
assets and their sources of funding. Using this balance sheet, the chapter seeks to respond to the question posed by Deng Xiaoping: Was the
Anglo-Saxon system of capital markets, that is capitalism itself, good for
China or not? Has listing had a positive impact on how banks operate?
Did it improve corporate governance and economic efficiencies? What
role has China's debt capital market, the second largest in the world,
played in the rise of the world's second largest economy? Have Deng's
heirs managed these capitalist tools effectively? What have been the costs
associated with financial markets, and how should success be measured?

A Summary State Balance Sheet

The financial balance sheet in Table 6.1 shows the value of all assets,
financial and non-financial, that the state has invested in as well as all its

Table 6.1   Summary consolidated balance sheet of the Chinese state sector.

RMB 100 mm	1978	1990	2000	2008	2010	2018
Financial assets	4,729	28,930	175,095	485,414	831,799	1,930,225
Non-financial assets	4,794	18,738	100,639	740,938	774,595	2,024,629
including:						
Fixed assets adjusted for market	3,364	12,917	74,664	272,253	468,397	828,054
Inventory	1,430	5,821	22,275	57,788	106,325	415,854
Non-productive assets	0	0	3,700	410,897	199,873	780,721
Total Assets	**9,523**	**47,793**	**275,734**	**1,226,352**	**1,606,394**	**3,954,854**
Financial liabilities	5,731	37,932	215,499	1,047,728	1,263,414	3,501,780
Total Liabilities	**5,731**	**37,932**	**215,499**	**1,047,728**	**1,263,414**	**3,501,780**
Net Worth	**3,792**	**9,861**	**60,234**	**178,624**	**342,979**	**453,074**
of which:						
Minority interest	0	0	28,231	99,715	209,322	256,967
State net worth	3,792	9,861	32,003	78,909	133,657	196,107
Note:						
Net Financial Assets (Liabilities)	−1,002	−9,002	−40,404	−562,314	−431,615	−1,571,555

SOURCES: See Appendix 2.

sources of financing on a consolidated basis. This balance sheet is modeled after the formats used by the IMF in its "Government Finances" database.[2] It summarizes all financial assets, which include cash and the debt owed by third parties, and all financial liabilities; these are the money it has borrowed. Non-financial assets include all the capital goods owned by state enterprises, their inventory, and a category called non-productive assets.[3] The value of assets and liabilities plus net worth should be equal.

The 40 years shown in the balance sheet documents China's extraordinary rise from nothing to the second largest economy in the world. It also clearly illustrates that this rise has taken place largely since the year 2000. Just prior to its accession to the WTO in 2001, China's GDP was US$1.2 trillion, its foreign reserves around US$150 billion, and the state's balance sheet, including all SOEs, state banks, and government assets, about US$3.4 trillion.

The question this chapter asks is, how did China go from nowhere in 1978 to an economy with a GDP of US$5.6 trillion in 20 years? The balance sheet seems to provide a simple answer, the state borrowed! By 2018, the volume of obligations as compared to the state's net worth was a whopping 21 times. Even worse, its financial net worth, financial assets less financial liabilities, was negative 157 trillion *yuan* (about US$24 trillion) as against the state's net worth of 20 trillion *yuan* (US$3 trillion). But borrowing is not the whole story, so the sections that follow show the key factors that provide a more nuanced answer to the question.

Inefficient Investment Equals Extrabudgetary Funding

At the start of economic reforms in 1978, the party saw its biggest challenge as reforming poorly performing state-owned enterprises. SOEs dominated the economy and their planned "surpluses" were the primary source of budgetary revenue. The first reform efforts, with some justification, were efforts to make their investments more accountable for capital costs, and so lead to more efficient production. In 1985, profits funded 80 percent of total investment, but then the state began to charge interest on what had always been budgetary grants; these latter at once became called loans. This reduced SOE capital and cash accounts that had been used to invest in fixed assets. Over the next decade, the profit to capital investment ratio shrank rapidly; by 1997 less than 9 percent of SOE profits went for investment purposes.

As shown in Table 6.2, in 1985 profit constituted 81 percent of capital investment, but as the new capital charges cut into profits, "internal" financing was replaced by other sources. The idea after Deng's 1992 "Southern Tour" became more explicitly to induce state enterprises to become independent commercial entities and, if possible, to raise capital on public markets. Budgetary funds that had earlier financed investment were directed elsewhere.

As a result, the sources of investment funds had to change since overall investment was growing at a vigorous and steady 15 percent rate during the 1978–1997 period. By this point in time, SOE profits and state budgetary grants contributed less than 10 percent to SOE investment.

Table 6.2   Investment financing sources and efficiency, 1978–1997.

%	1978	1980	1985	1990	1995	1997
Industrial SOEs						
Profit/total investment	–	–	80.80	22.21	14.71	8.63

	1980/ 1978	1985/ 1980	1990/ 1985	1995/ 1990	1997/ 1995	1997/ 1978
Investment rate of increase %	1.01%	1.62%	2.13%	3.40%	1.27%	15.08%

Investment financing sources %	1978	1980	1985	1990	1995	1997
All state agencies						
State budget	62.16	44.66	23.98	13.20	5.00	4.68
Domestic loans	1.69	11.67	23.04	23.60	23.66	22.98
Foreign funds	4.21	7.19	5.27	9.10	7.89	5.07
Self-collected funds	31.94	36.48	47.71	43.18	48.70	52.73
Other	0.00	0.00	0.00	10.91	15.89	14.25
Investment efficiency * %						
All state agencies	–	–	69.3	80.65	67.81	79.6
Industrial capital construction	–	–	69.3	77.41	61.22	75.13
Industrial technological updating	–	65.58	64.35	86.68	76.89	81.89

* Efficiency = Completed investment/investment expenditures.
Source: Holz (2001), pp. 361–362; see also the discussion around Table 2.2.

The rest, as seen in Chapter 2 and also shown in the table, was funded by bank loans. And the impact on SOE and bank balance sheets was obvious: in support of investment they became increasingly burdened with debt. This was especially so since capital investment loans had long maturities. For banks this meant that such loans sat on their balance sheets for a while, limiting funding for other projects.

How much invested capital was actually getting into the economy and being used to increase productivity, as opposed to being siphoned off by various kinds of middlemen, including local governments? In the 1985 to 1990 period, the data for all investment by industrial enterprises suggests that only two thirds of capital expenditures actually went to financing capital investment, and 30 percent went elsewhere.[4] The trend in the ratios for all state agencies shows that, in general, investment efficiency was around 80 percent by 1997.

Where did the other 20 percent go? It could be that there was a large volume of unfinished investment on SOE balance sheets or perhaps these were loans that would eventually go bad. A more likely explanation, as made in Chapter 2, was that local governments derived a part of their "extrabudgetary" revenues from skimming off a portion of investment capital. The reverse side of this local government activity is unfinished or inefficient investment. The consequence over time of such capital "leakage" has been lower capital investment and diminished assets reported on the state balance sheet and increased financial liabilities.

The Promise of the Stock Markets

Deng's 1992 support of stock markets and the quick follow-up by his team of reformers raised expectations for further, and this time more decisive, changes for SOEs. On the heels of Deng's trip south, China's first corporate law was enacted and a specialized securities market regulator was established in October 1992. At the same time, the government announced a list of nine large state enterprises as candidates for listing on the Hong Kong Stock Exchange. This decision, which was taken by Zhu Rongji in the spring of 1992, had the effect of internationalizing China's experiment with shares and placed the development of the two mainland exchanges in subordinate positions, where they remain today. The status of the Shanghai market would have been raised immeasurably had Ant Financial completed its dual Shanghai–Hong Kong listing in 2021.

These actions and a host of supporting legislation led to the incorporation of SOEs as companies limited by shares with the aim of recapitalizing them with "other peoples' money." This was openly conceded in a book published in 1999 to celebrate the 50th anniversary of the People's Republic. The author, a vice-governor of the central bank, noted, "Looking at the current situation in our country, no matter whether the regulators, government departments, or the listed companies, all treat public offerings and listing of shares as a cheap source of funding."[5] The plan worked—but very little, including the state's view of the claims and rights of outside investors, has changed since then as recent events demonstrate.

The impact of this incorporation process on the face of Chinese economy, however, has been further reaching than the more than $1 trillion in capital raised. China's corporatization process combined China's best state companies with the best capitalist expertise on Wall Street. Working together, Chinese authorities, Wall Street bankers, accountants, and lawyers transformed unprofitable and uncompetitive SOEs into listable companies and, almost at once, these companies became *Fortune Global 500* behemoths the Chinese deemed as "National Champions." (The bigger the deal the more the fees.) The October 1997 listing of China Telecom was the first significant transaction, raising $4 billion in its IPO and a massive $36 billion in a secondary offering in 1998. Beijing had never seen such money! Many state enterprises followed this model in the next few years.

As Chinese SOEs gained the attention of global investors, the process of tailoring China's domestic markets to suit local conditions became clearer. Table 6.3 and Figure 6.1 demonstrate that shares issued in Shanghai IPOs have been consistently and deliberately underpriced, which after persisting for so long can only be seen as a matter of

Table 6.3   A-share listing-day performance 1998–2010.

	Number of Listings	Average First-Day Jump %	Average First-Day Turnover %
2010	127	47	69
2009	99	74	79
2008	77	115	80
2007	126	193	65
2006	66	84	70
2005	14	48	58
2004	100	70	55
2003	67	72	52
2002	68	134	62
2001	77	138	64
2000	135	152	59
1999	93	113	60
1998	92	149	62

Note: Turnover = amount of shares sold as a percent of first day shares allowed to be sold; strategic investors shares may be "locked up" for a period.
Source: Wind, author's calculations.

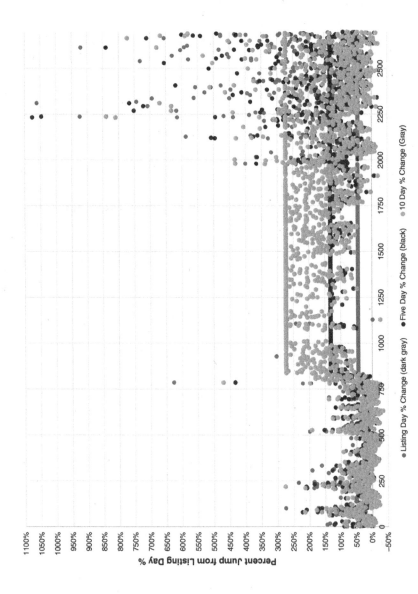

Figure 6.1 IPO price jumps 2010–May 2021.

NOTE: The three horizontal lines correspond to the related price-limit point, with the bottom line representing the listing price change, the middle line the fifth-day change, and the top line the change after the tenth-day change.

Source: Wind; author's calculations.

state policy. Shanghai is the market of choice for Chinese SOEs and regulators, not bankers or the market, set the formula by which shares are priced. Although the exact method has been tinkered with over the years, what might be characterized as a *shocking* degree of underpricing—orders of magnitude larger than what has been the case in the U.S.—has prevailed throughout the entire 1998–2021 period.

For example, in 1998 there were 92 IPOs of Chinese SOEs on the Shanghai Exchange that experienced an *average* first-day price jump of 149 percent, as compared to 281 IPOs in the United States that were underpriced by 21.9 percent.[6] In the Chinese IPOs, moreover, 62 percent of all so-called investors dumped their shares on the first day that such shares were deemed tradable. By 2010, the picture was similar, but with an average first day price jump of only 47 percent—the maximum allowed—and 69 percent selling their shares. In short, it's not hard to see why "investors" fought to get as many IPO shares as they could—typically using illegal bank loans—and then selling out immediately to repay those loans, thereby minimizing their economic risk. This is not investing; it is speculation encouraged by the state and coming at the expense of the state.

Things did not improve. Figure 6.1, which shows the price movements over the period 2010–2020 for all 2,700-plus Shanghai IPOs, also illustrates the futility of the efforts of Chinese regulators to limit such underpricing. As can be seen in the figure, there was a major cessation of IPO activity during the years 2010–2013 due to the global financial crisis. In fact, in 2013 there were no IPOs at all. In 2014, the market reopened, but with new listing rules limiting the first-day jump to *only* 44 percent; for each day thereafter, the usual 10 percent price limit remained in place. The result was predictable—*all* IPOs popped 44 percent on the first day, then spent each of the next 10 trading days going 10 percent limit up until they reached their "equilibrium" trading level. During the period through 2018, this level seems to have been a remarkably stable 250 percent of the listing price.

Then starting in mid-2019, such predictability vanished when listings on the new Shanghai STAR market for tech stocks were no longer limited to the first-day limit, and limits on daily price movements were doubled from 10 to 20 percent. In 2020, ChiNext, the market for small and medium-sized "private" companies, also adopted these rules, leaving only the Shanghai Exchange still subject to the 44 percent limit. In this fashion, rampant, unrestrained IPO underpricing became the rule once more.

In sum, during the nearly 25 years since the adoption of its Securities Law in 1997, the Chinese state, that is, party has as a matter of policy deliberately sold down its own investment in state enterprises too cheaply. The question is why? The party may have seen itself as protecting retail investors from the rapacity of underwriters, and protecting underwriters—all owned by the state of course—from losing money. And Beijing, it's true, has always sought, but largely failed, to control the level of the market index to prevent crashes and any associated social unrest. But all that considered, the state would appear to benefit *least* from the huge first-day price jumps coupled with heavy turnover thereafter. While the listing company succeeds in raising capital with the underpriced shares, some investors get to walk off with fortunes. There is no doubt but that the listing enterprise is the biggest loser in this arrangement—and, as the owner of such enterprises, so, of course, is the state. Though the loss on a single enterprise IPO may seem immaterial, over time and with thousands of IPOs, the loss of value to the state becomes enormous.

Such an IPO underpricing policy amounts to a huge transfer of real wealth from the accounts of ordinary Chinese citizens not just to a handful of lucky retail investors, but to a galaxy of "Friends of the Family" who might be related in some way to the state sector and, of course, the party. From a public finance perspective, the critical point is that the gains of these investors—which might include distant subsidiaries of state enterprises called "strategic investors" and obscure investment companies—are *not going to be invested back into the state.* Even worse, it is taking money from the bank accounts of the small players who lose in this zero-sum game. This *takes deposits directly away from banks* that would have been used to fund the state and its enterprises.

Even while recognizing this dissipation of SOE value through IPO pricing, the analysis here is premised on the assumption that the state's ownership position is maintained at roughly 60 percent of total domestic market capitalization.[7] Beijing has always, by policy and regulation, insisted on holding at least a majority (over 50 percent) stake in its enterprises. This 60 percent is, therefore, an assumption based on market data; it is likely to be overstated for a number of reasons.

Table 6.4 explains this by showing different categories of shareholders and shows just how complicated the ownership of the major assets of the state has become. For A shares alone, five major investor categories

Table 6.4 Categories and values of equity shares, 1995–2018.

RMB 100 mms	1995	1998	2000	2005	2008	2010	2015	2018	% A share market cap
Minority Shareholder Interest									
Domestic retail held A shares	577	4,052	11,744	7,662	26,397	70,244	99,471	85,204	26.3%
"Friends of the Family" held A shares	214	1,499	4,344	2,834	9,763	25,981	36,791	31,514	9.7%
Foreign held H and Red Chip shares	445	764	12,143	28,732	63,555	113,097	122,838	128,732	NA
Foreign held A shares	0	0	0	0	0	0	5,987	11,517	3.6%
Total Minority Interest	**1,236**	**6,314**	**28,231**	**39,227**	**99,715**	**209,322**	**265,087**	**256,967**	**39.5%**
State Net Worth									
Original domestic LP shares	0	0	0	0	6,381	78,730	173,860	150,537	46.4%
Shares held directly by state agencies	22,593	21,935	32,003	21,454	72,528	54,927	55,328	45,570	14.0%
Total State Net Worth	**22,593**	**21,935**	**32,003**	**21,454**	**78,909**	**133,657**	**229,188**	**196,107**	**60.5%**
State Net Worth + Minority Interest	**23,829**	**28,249**	**60,234**	**60,681**	**178,624**	**342,979**	**494,275**	**453,074**	**100.0%**

NOTE: The so-called B-shares, an early and abandoned foreign currency share, are not included due to immateriality.
SOURCE: *China Banking Almanac*, Hong Kong Stock Exchange; author's estimations for "Friends of the Family" and Domestic LP shares.

can be named, and it is impossible to know to what degree the hand of the state can be found in each. The offshore shares are even more opaque. The table suggests this by including Friends of the Family and domestic LP shares as discussed later.

It is extremely difficult to deal with the Hong Kong listed H shares, yet they must be included because Hong Kong has become the major international market for large state enterprises. Some Chinese companies are listed in Hong Kong, but not in Shanghai, and some are listed on both exchanges. With the "Through Train (通车)," moreover, mainland retail investors can buy Hong Kong shares as can retail Hong Kongers buy A shares. Moreover, offshore Chinese company subsidiaries, state agencies, and other investment vehicles can also buy these shares. As a result, estimating the value of the unlisted shares of these Chinese companies is extremely difficult. The Hong Kong exchange solves the problem of H and Red Chip market capitalization by valuing only what is listed in Hong Kong. It is not very satisfactory, but for purposes of this analysis Hong Kong shares are carried on the state balance sheet as Minority Shares and at market value as per the exchange.[8] The result, however, is that, on the state balance sheet, the value of the minority interest exceeds state net worth, but conceptually and in reality some mix of state entities still controls the majority of shares and share value.

As regards the Shanghai A shares, overall true retail investors are estimated to hold about 72 percent in 2018, while "Friends of the Family" hold 17 percent.[9] These numbers are likely to be reversed during an IPO since applications for shares must be backed by cash, and an investor is limited to one application per 10,000 shares held in his account. Those with access to the most cash and those who hold the most shares always succeed in being allocated large allotments of shares in the IPO. The value of such shares does not show up in the account data since the bulk are sold almost immediately.

The shares called "Original Domestic Legal Person (LP) shares" are a huge part of the state's own net worth. They are broken out and shown here even though after the 2005 share reforms, they no longer exist as an independent share class. But they are still there and are estimated here for reference. These shares come about when SOE groups hive off and list a portion of their operations; then, after listing, the group continues to hold the controlling shares on behalf of the state.[10] In the course of such IPOs, state agencies, the remnants of the old Soviet-style ministries, may also have provided investment funds in the new company, and so they also hold shares, what were called officially State Shares. Since it never actually invested in such entities, SASAC does not hold any domestic LP shares.

Also it is important to note that although the chairmen of SOE group companies are always senior party members and sometimes even ministers, it is not entirely accurate to say that the state controls all these shares; there may be entities in the background that cannot be seen. If it ever comes to a real privatization, the state itself could end up being a minority shareholder in many of its largest enterprises.

So that brings us back to the question at the start: Did the Deng-inspired experiment with incorporating and publicly listing state enterprises work from a macroeconomic view? The short answer is, probably not. Analysts have concluded that the state sector generates only 23–39 percent of China's GDP.[11] If the social stability sustained by full employment is the key, then it is important to recognize that employment in state entities represents only 16 percent of the total; the rest are in the non-state, private sector.

Does the state itself profit from the earnings of its enterprises? The answer again is no. Although roughly two out of three SOEs were profitable in 2018, the state budget receives less than 2 percent of its total fiscal revenues from enterprise profits; of course, it does receive taxes.[12] SOE profits stay with enterprise groups as a down payment on social stability.

So did China's real reformers make a wise decision in the early 1990s when they kicked off the shareholding experiment? After all, in 1978 the state held nearly 100 percent of the capital invested in its enterprises and financed the entire national budget with their surpluses. Putting aside the billions of US dollars raised in share offerings, the answer must still be yes; it would have been impossible for the outside world to have so thoroughly engaged with a China that, in the 1980s, had an amorphous economy papered over by Five Year Plans.[13] Incorporating and publicly listing Chinese enterprises has put China on the map internationally and enabled both the Chinese bureaucracy and international leaders to speak the common language of international capitalism, no matter how they understand it. Moreover, it has given China's leadership a powerful lobbying group in Washington—American investment banks and fund managers. In the end, whether the communist party persists or a new political group emerges, all now speak the language of capital. The only question is just a matter of how well they use the capital they succeed in attracting.

Massive Growth in Deposits

As shown in Chapter 3, Beijing could raise large amounts of capital in IPOs and on the domestic bond market during the decade after the Global Financial Crisis. With this capital in hand it could lend huge amounts of money and all because of the massive accumulation of household and corporate deposits in the years following China's entry into the WTO in 2001. Figure 6.2 shows deposit trends for the period 1995–2020 as well as changes in the critical loan-to-deposit ratio used by the PBOC to manage lending levels. The PBOC uses this ratio to limit bank use of deposits to finance loans with the aim of ensuring price stability and the liquidity of the financial system.

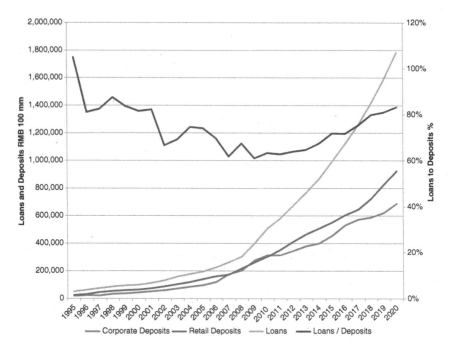

Figure 6.2   Deposits, loans, and loan-to-deposit ratio, 1995–2020.
SOURCE: *China Banking Almanac*; author's calculations.

This ratio in 1995 was 104 percent; in other words, banks were making more loans than they had deposits to support them; too much money was being created. Unsurprisingly, this was the same year China's national inflation rate reached around 25 percent. During the period 1997–2010, which saw the major restructuring and public listings of the largest state banks, the central bank mandated a much lower loan-to-deposit ratio of about 60 percent; that is, banks could then lend out only 60 percent of their total deposits, both corporate and household. But even at this extremely conservative level,[14] the absolute amount of loans outstanding began to grow steadily because of extraordinarily rapid deposit growth. When the outbreak of the financial crisis put an end to regulatory conservatism, the ratio climbed steadily, reaching over 80 percent in 2020. During this decade, loans outstanding rose by a factor of four. For this reason alone, it shouldn't be surprising that China's state banks place four out of five on the *Fortune* Global 500 in terms of total assets. There may be a deleveraging campaign starting in 2016, but it cannot be seen in these numbers.

And these numbers do not even include the deposit reserves accumulated by the central bank. Starting in 2004, the PBOC began to subtract deposits from the banking system to control lending and the money supply during the boom years following accession to the WTO. As can be seen in Figure 6.3, in 2008 when reserves reached a peak of 21.5 percent of deposits, they began to drop sharply as Beijing chased GDP growth during the crisis years. After a brief nod to deleveraging, loan growth accelerated after 2016 with the help of the injection of deposit reserves into bank balance sheets. So, as bank regulators allowed higher loan-to-deposit ratios, the central bank was releasing ever more deposit reserves, providing a double charge of lending firepower.

In sum, lending, corporate, and retail savings grew in direct response to the huge social changes created by Beijing's policy shift in the late 1990s from a planned economy to a more market-driven one.[15] Traditional Soviet-style industrial ministries were closed as the focus of development turned to state enterprise profitability, a more supportive attitude prevailed toward private enterprise, and capital began to be raised through stock markets. The SOEs themselves were restructured, leading to the loss of over 25 million jobs. In rural areas, the old barefoot doctor medical support service disappeared as the cooperative farming

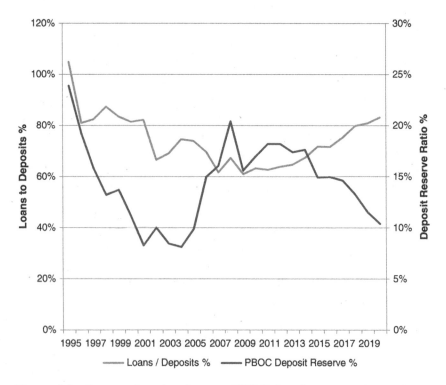

Figure 6.3   Loan-to-deposit ratio versus PBOC deposit reserve ratio, 1995–2020.
SOURCE: *China Banking Almanac*, Wind; author's calculations.

model was done away with. Finally, the one-child policy resulted in less consumption and more savings for two reasons: cheaper to raise one child than two; and parents could expect less support in old age. By the turn of the century, the old society and its social safety net had disappeared. In response to all this change and growing uncertainties about the future, people began to save and this saving went into loans to the party.

"Opening" the Door to Foreign Investment

China's accession to the WTO in 2001 added jet fuel to the government's policy of welcoming foreign investment. This encouraged widespread belief among foreign governments and companies that China was open for business, willing to abide by international rules and clearly set on the road to some sort of capitalist-style market economy. Perhaps a more important factor was the assumption of power in 2002 by men with little support across the bureaucracies and military. Their lack of support meant that the central government was weak vis-à-vis the provinces. In an effort to buy local support and also to address inequality, Beijing began to increase its budgetary transfers to the poorer provinces. While adding significantly to central government debt, such transfers did little to increase political clout. Over the decade that this group was in power, financial reform pushed forward on its own, and the economy simply boomed as the party and bureaucracy stepped back. China was blasting into the modern age because it was no longer being managed like a Soviet train station.[16] If China is a superpower today, it should give thanks to Hu Jintao, the party secretary, and Wen Jiabao, the premier.

With WTO and a weak central government, hundreds of billions of direct investment dollars poured into local economies and government coffers. Local governments needed the jobs coming from such investment and, with passive Beijing bureaucracies, proceeded to cut Western companies terrific deals in terms of taxes and land costs, even building factories to measure.

Along with jobs, foreign direct investment and an export-heavy current account created domestic liquidity from corporate savings. In the country's closed capital account, banks must sell to the central bank every US dollar brought in, with the given enterprise receiving RMB in return. The central-bank balance sheet shows the resulting dollar as reserves on the asset side and local currency as a liability. The net exports associated with and stemming from foreign direct investments (FDIs) have been *the* chief drivers of liquidity in the Chinese economy as well as a prime, if indirect, driver of the growth of corporate and household deposits.

In 2004, China began running a current account surplus—exports less imports—with the world that is commonly understood to have led to its huge foreign exchange reserves. The less recognized consequence of this FDI and export growth has been the huge amount of RMB released into the system. This new money went first into corporate deposits, whether those held by a foreign-invested enterprise or a Chinese SOE or private company. And part of this money was paid out in salaries to China's workers.

Excessive Reliance on Debt

At this point, little more needs be said about the debt that China's state sector has piled up; it is simply the converse of China's huge deposit buildup. Figure 6.4 shows the various components of state obligations. Household obligations including deposits, currency held, savings bonds and A shares are a basic part of the state's overall debt. Also included is an estimation of non-performing assets from a consolidated state viewpoint (see Appendix 1 for details). These are state obligations because they continue to be funded by third parties, depositors, and shareholders.

Figures of China's massive *local* debt are only estimates of indebtedness provided by local governments and not verified by any third party, which the MOF states outright in very small print deep in its *China*

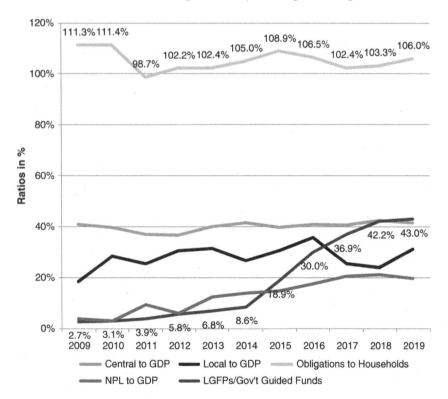

Figure 6.4   Central and local government non-current obligations to GDP.

SOURCE: OECD, *China Bond, China Finance Almanac, China Banking Almanac,* annual reports of China Huarong and China Cinda, *China Banking Wealth Management Report;* author's calculations. See Appendix 1.

Finance Almanac.[17] There can be little doubt the numbers should be materially higher. Taken altogether, total state obligations reaches around 198 percent of GDP, exceeding the levels attained by the EU countries and the United States (137 percent) and closing in on Japan's level (234 percent).[18]

One conclusion from this is that much of the state's borrowing must have gone to places that did not add to state assets, mainly consumption items in local budgets or simply to financial assets. To the extent these are loans, this means they are not going to be paid back. The few efforts that have been advanced to increase the capacity of the fiscal system by creating new taxes have largely wilted in the face of political indecision[19]— worry over whether such taxes would be acceptable to the people or would have a negative impact on economic growth, which has been the continuing fate with gasoline and now the effort to exact real estate taxes.

The official deficit reported to the NPC hovers around 3 percent, but if the borrowings of local governments plus funds raised by the so-called government guidance funds are included as *fiscal spending* and not commercial borrowing, then the deficit swells to multiples of the official number. The figures shown in Figure 6.5 are estimates made by the IMF staff in the annual IMF Country Article IV Consultation Reports, which also provide projections five years out.[20] The figure shows that actual "augmented deficits"[21] in recent years have come in far worse than their earlier estimates. For example, the 2016 estimate showed a 10.7 percent deficit, while the 2022 report showed 2016 as actually recording a deficit of 15.9 percent. The same report estimated the 2021 deficit at 16.5 percent, as compared to Beijing's official deficit of 3 percent. The system is running out of money.

Deterioration of State Finances

What has been the cumulative impact of these factors on the government's finances? An official answer is lacking, since China does not publish a government balance sheet. Figure 6.6 extends the summary of the balance sheet summarized in Table 6.1 to include the entire 1978–2018 period. It compares the value of the capital (SNW, or state net worth), the party's investment of its own funds (and not including Minority

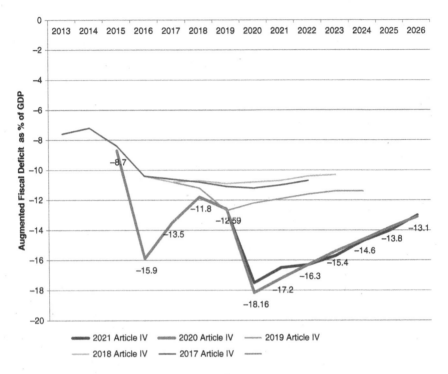

Figure 6.5   China augmented fiscal deficit to GDP.
SOURCE: IMF annual China Article IV Consultation Staff Reports.

Interest) in the state sector, from 1978–2018 to total liabilities. The figure shows the value of SNW in two ways: based on a *full* balance sheet (SNW/Total Assets); and based on a *net* balance sheet created by subtracting current liabilities from current assets, then adding the remainder to long-term assets, and from the resulting number subtracting long-term liabilities.

Netting out current items reduces overall assets and liabilities, but state net worth resulting from this calculation is based on accounting book values, whereas, in the full balance sheet, net worth data reflect *market capitalization*. Despite their huge differences, both calculations show the same trend, a sustained decline in net asset value. Although the state's *absolute* net worth in either case has increased somewhat, the weight of the debt it has taken on has more than offset it. By 2018, Chinese state liabilities in both calculations were roughly 20 times net worth; in other words, there were $20 of claims against the state for

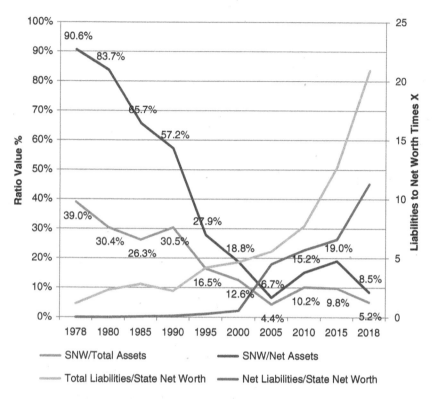

Figure 6.6   State net worth to assets, liabilities to state net worth.
NOTE: State Net Worth post-1995 does not include minority interests.
SOURCE: 1978–1997, Holz (2001); 1998–2018, author's calculations.

every $1 of state equity. In this sense, the state and the Chinese economy since 2018 should be facing financial difficulties. There are ways around this problem in the short run. The central bank has created money by releasing deposit reserves over the past few years. And China continues to enjoy a positive current account that also generates new liquidity in the system. But to the extent this money is directed overwhelmingly into the state sector itself, the end result will inevitably simply add to the state's overall leverage.[22]

What about the state's obligations to Chinese households that have financed a major portion of the state's investments? One of the most striking changes over the 40-year period has been the tremendous growth of household wealth. China's citizens have truly prospered since

2001, and household claims on the state, including deposits, currency held, and investments in state companies accounted for 22 percent of total state assets in 2018. The reform of real estate regulations beginning in 1997 opened up an entirely new investment category for the populace. The net value of their homes adds to household wealth, but because it is part of household balance sheets, it does not affect that of the state except by way of mortgages. A household balance sheet that in the 1980s and 1990s had little on it today would include, along with a house, mortgages, credit cards, share investments, and deposits.

These assets are the basis of China's large and growing middle class and the small and medium private enterprises that drive the economy and provide the party's political support. But private household wealth is not just the source of the party's political support; it has literally been absorbed into the party's own treasury, becoming a fundamental pillar of the state sector's financial system.

So the question that must be asked is this: Are there today sufficient state assets to meet household obligations that represent calls on those assets? Or to ask the same question another way: Has the party invested this money wisely?

As detailed in Table 6.5, the estimated accounting value of the best of China's state assets at the end of 2018, including the value of SOE fixed assets, investments, and loans that added up equal roughly a quarter of all state assets, appear to cover household claims against the state by a factor of 1.3 times. But if accounting principles are set aside for market values, we have to ask: Who would the loans be sold to—asset management companies?

If we generously assume that SOE loans are actually worth a discounted 60 percent of their book value and set the value of SOE investments at 50 percent (which is too high), can household claims still be met? The answer is no. Fairly recent Chinese financial history provides a suggestive demonstration of this. In 1997 the use of similar assumptions and numbers for the SOEs were the catalyst for the huge bank restructurings when written-off problem assets came close to 40 percent of the total.

But are such discounts large enough to reflect the actual loss of value? It would seem so; if we include net state current accounts—that is, current assets less current liabilities—we should have more than

Table 6.5 Household claims versus state assets, 2018.

100 mm	2018	Discounted Values	Discount Rate	Plus Net Current Assets
Household deposits	724,439			
Estimated currency held	57,102			
Savings bonds	7,218			
A share investments	85,204			
Total household claims	**873,963**	**873,963**		**873,963**
Foreign exchange reserves	212,557	212,557		212,557
SOE fixed assets	393,808	393,808		393,808
SOE investments	106,685	53,343	50%	53,343
Bank loans to SOEs	427,150	256,290	60%	256,290
Net current assets	0	0		764,128
Selected State Assets	**1,140,200**	**915,998**		**1,680,126**

enough to fund the deficit in longer-term asset values. In reality, if it came to netting current liabilities against assets, the best and most liquid current assets would probably have been used first to retire current debt obligations to the state itself. The remaining receivables and inventory may therefore not have full book value. Reviewing the rest of the balance sheet, there are no other assets with intrinsic value available to offset household obligations.

In sum, it appears that the value of state sector assets in 2018 may have been just enough to satisfy Chinese household obligations.

Summing Up

During the early years of the reform period, capital investments were gradually moved from the realm of budgetary grants to the banks, and they were classified as loans. The aim was to create a more market-driven environment to promote efficient SOE operations. Budgetary expenditures

therefore became largely consumption-oriented and so ceased contributing to increases in the values of state assets. Similarly, following the 1994
Budget Law, local government budgetary revenues were deliberately ren-
dered insufficient as compared to expanded budgetary responsibilities, also
largely consumption based. With the promised central transfers insufficient, local governments ended up borrowing from banks directly or indirectly even before 2009 to fill budgetary gaps and to fund capital investment.
Since much of this borrowing will have gone to consumption items, it did
not add directly to the state's net worth.

China Evergrande and Local Budgets

The slow-motion bankruptcy of China Evergrande Group, at one time
the most valuable real estate developer in the world, highlights the fiscal
difficulties of local governments and the failure of the national fiscal
system. What local governments have is the authority to use land; the sale
of land use rights to developers since 1997 quickly became a major generator of economic growth and local jobs. Evergrande was, without a
doubt, warmly welcomed and embraced by local party officialdom in
most places in China. But real estate development was not by itself a sure
revenue generator; as shown in Chapter 2 the local government had to
provide the infrastructure-related investment for projects. On top of that,
they had to pay relocation money to whomever had been living on the
land. So Evergrande was intimately involved in a process involving
developers, banks, trust companies, construction companies, and utilities,
each of which wanted to keep the process rolling so they could get paid.
Over time, real estate development became a Ponzi scheme in the sense
that revenue from the sale of one patch of land was typically used to
cover the expenses of the last development. This process helps explain
why in 2017 the China Household Survey found that 64 million, or
over 20 percent, of the country's apartments were empty.[23]

   Now if local governments are asked to step in to complete projects
that Evergrande cannot, where are they getting the money? At the behest
of the party, banks and enterprises will step up and help; all such "help"
will add to the state's leverage. Regardless of whether Beijing knew this
overbuilding was happening for the past eight years, and it most certainly
must have, it is responsible. Analysts have estimated that real estate

development as an industry contributed close to 30 percent of China's GDP.[24] There is no doubt that Beijing looked the other way until the problem became too large to ignore, after all, "homes are for living"! And little has been said about how the developers financed themselves; banks must be on the hook for huge amounts of loans. This has all proved to be an expensive way to provide social stability. Though it added to GDP growth, it contributed little or nothing to the state itself except stability. Once the land use fee has been paid, local governments receive little else; there is no real estate tax in China, not now, and unlikely for a long time.

This is part of the reason that during the period 1999–2018 the state's fixed assets plus current assets (which include inventories and receivables) increased at a compound nominal rate of only 13 percent *per annum*, while its long-term debt increased twice as fast at 26 percent. By 2018, total state liabilities reached about 90 percent of total assets. And just as it was in 1997, the state in 2018 had become overleveraged. China's entry to WTO in 2001 stimulated the rapid growth of foreign investment, related supply chains, and an export sector that benefited both companies and employees. Corporate deposits increased, as did household deposits. During these years, the wealth built up by China's growing middle class financed this massive party-led social security program in the second decade of the century.

But as Table 6.5 suggests, state assets may no longer be adequate to cover the claims of this middle class. Put simply, what one analyst found to be true in 1998[25] continues to be true 20 years later: the excessive borrowing by the state has left Chinese households (and a handful of foreigners) as the *de facto* majority owners of state sector assets. And this is not just rhetoric; the Chinese people today really *are* the effective owners of China's socialist state!

China Huarong: The Crack in the Foundation?

The recent China Huarong case throws even more light than Evergrande on the Chinese state's underlying illiquidity. In April 2021 China Huarong, one of the four original "bad banks" created in the restructuring of the four state banks, was unable to provide its audited annual financial statements as required by the Hong Kong Listing rules. When Huarong was created in 1999, the MOF had a 100 percent holding.

Even after its listing in October 2015, the ministry's share was still 61 percent after shares were sold to a number of state and foreign "strategic" investors (including Goldman Sachs) and to public investors. In April 2021 the market watched aghast when it was unable to submit its financials to the exchange because of an inability to secure a loan to fill a hole in its balance sheet. Such an excuse.

The China press's accounts of the government's actions placed all responsibility for Huarong's financial difficulties on its Chairman and CEO, Lai Xiaomin. Lai was placed under investigation in 2018, removed from the party the same year, accused of lurid dealings, convicted, and executed. Some 200 million *yuan* in cash was found in his apartment and this isn't easy since the largest bill in China is 100 *yuan*! (This is a man who placed first in the tough college entrance exam and was a senior official in the central bank before being sent by the party's Organization Department to Huarong.)

The problem with the story is that the Ministry of Finance had a controlling ownership interest in and thus oversight responsibility for Huarong. Keep in mind that this is also true for China Development Bank. Moreover, as a listed company, it boasted a Board of Directors including independent directors; this alone speaks volumes about the value of the shareholding experiment. Its semi-sovereign status was the reason it could borrow US$20 billion in Hong Kong, half of which it used to invest in a South Korean pleasure island. That's oversight.

From April to August 2021, it was entirely unclear what the Ministry would do. The drawn-out volleyball game between government departments on who would handle the default is a clear indication of the state's technical illiquidity. This difficulty should not have arisen as all of Huarong's debts are direct, central government obligations. The problem, however, is the process: the MOF, even if it had the capital in hand, was effectively prohibited from helping. Any large contributions of state funds to Huarong by the MOF would have required the approval of the National People's Congress (NPC) as part of the national budget. This would have proved embarrassing politically, and it explains why the Ministry sought to bury these obligations in Huijin or other state entities, until finally finding the China Citic Group, the last remaining centrally owned financial entity. Citic can easily borrow money (from other banks) and has access to the interbank markets without approaching the NPC! But Citic cannot be a long-term solution; it too will be forced by the low quality of Huarong's "assets" to borrow even more to support what the media say is "equity." Huarong is a clear and obvious example of the debt shell game in China and raises the question of what state entity has the capacity to take on the next major failure.

All this raises many more questions than may be addressed here. If the state makes investments in enterprises only to provide employment and social security, then Zhu Rongji has already demonstrated that this is a fallacy by closing down or selling state enterprises in the late 1990s. That decision left 25 million looking for jobs, but their children found better ones in a burgeoning private sector. The small SOEs that Zhu turned over to the workers have become the export dynamos that continue to flourish on the east coast of China. Though few are publicly listed, taken together they likely account for over half of GDP, while agriculture provides another 10 percent. This private sector has long since proven it can both employ and pay more, while making a profit as well.

Why, then, does the party cling to its SOEs? Is it a matter of power? Or history—since Lenin and Stalin did it, so should we? If it is simply power, then control of the military and police provide plenty of coercion when and as needed. On the other hand, a stronger economy is likely to provide the most reliable long-term basis for political support.

As for Lenin, does he matter? Beijing needs to do more than start a deleveraging campaign; it needs to decide to restructure its financial system as was done in 1997. The decades-long Chinese experiment to render state assets, banks, and enterprises more profitable has clearly failed. Perhaps the Japanese experience, discussed in Chapter 8, may suggest a way forward for China, but one that is likely to be quite difficult.

If nothing else, the examination of the main factors that have shaped China's state balance sheet suggests just how much the state itself—not to mention the Chinese and global economy—is exposed to financial risk by virtue of its owning and financing of assets that are, in reality, liabilities. Since it cannot inflate these problems away, one solution would be to privatize as much as possible to China's own private investors, who certainly have the money. As the man said, "Trees cannot grow to heaven." In China's state sector they already have. This suggestion is explored further in Chapter 8.

So Was Deng Right, Can Capital Markets Be Used in a Socialist Economy?

These comments, however, are those of an outsider. If Deng Xiaoping were around today and able to look back at the 30 years or so of China's experience with capitalist markets, he would almost certainly conclude that the effort had been worth it. Just compare China today (excluding the Covid-19 experience) with its situation in 1992! For the first time, China has a first-rate infrastructure supporting a national market for capital—and it has succeeded in using its control over the Hong Kong market to promote greater economic (and political) integration with the mainland. This effort has created national corporations that compare favorably in terms of scale and market capitalization with the world's largest multinationals. China's National Team would seem to be poised to leverage the country's huge foreign reserves to participate actively in the world's economy. Moreover, the operations and performance of these giants are more transparent than ever before—and to everyone—thanks to the legal and accounting standards they must maintain. Not to be forgotten, the sale of minority stakes in these companies has raised as much as $1 trillion. So what's not to like?

Starting with the state-owned companies, the domestic and overseas listing experience has helped improve corporate governance and management standards in exceptional cases only. For the most part, China's National Champions remain domestic, state-controlled enterprises and act like them. Institutions that are part of the state control the Shanghai market, which runs the main board containing China's biggest companies. The IPO lottery process limits the participation of retail investors in favor of these big institutions and their friends. The valuation of new shares takes place in a process that is closely supervised by the securities regulator and seems unable to prevent those first-day trading "pops" that enrich state institutions and the politically connected. Similar comments, absent the egregious "pops," could be made about the Hong Kong exchange.

It would seem little wonder, then, that the market seems to have flat-lined after the huge policy play on RMB appreciation in 2007 and 2008 and the fiasco with margin trading in 2015. But this is the way the party likes it. From 2012, the new government, bent on eliminating corruption, seems unable to figure out exactly what it wants to do with this piece of China's reform effort. When Zhu Rongji supported the listing effort back in the early 1990s, the hope was that the markets would create state enterprises able to compete internationally, while at the same time raising capital and all *without* requiring privatization. Judging the 30-year experiment on this basis suggests that China's adaptation of capitalist markets to its own circumstances has yet to yield the results its early promoters had hoped for, but in the end it may facilitate the necessary true privatization.

But 30 years is a short time in the country's efforts to modernize. It may be too early, perhaps, to suggest that Deng was wrong. What can be said is that the capital the Chinese state has raised whether from the markets or by co-opting corporate and household deposits has been directed to the state sector almost entirely; only 10 percent of the state's total assets are made up of loans for mortgages, credit cards, or to small enterprises. As Figure 6.5 suggests, the state's investments in its enterprises have failed to generate new capital to drive the economy forward. This has been the job of the non-state, private sector.

Had Beijing's intent in the 1990s been to gradually privatize—that is, sell majority stakes in its enterprises—then one might imagine that the TSMCs (Taiwan Semi-conductor Manufacturing Company) and Foxcomms, created in a single small province, might populate the Hong Kong and Shanghai exchanges in the place of the also-rans that do now.

China's government values control and stability over efficiency, and has paid dearly for it. But at some point, efficiency in the use of capital will have its say. Capital, after all, is a limited commodity even in China. As others have recently argued,[26] China's party stands with the support of Heaven's Mandate, an old saw that all Chinese firmly believe. One thing clearly has changed in the past 30 years: any loss of confidence in the party's management of China's limited capital resources would certainly have serious consequences not just for China but also for the world.

Notes

1. The date, the place, the time of day and who Deng was addressing are recorded in Li Zhangzhe, 终于成功:中国股市发展报告 (Success at last: report on the development of China's stock markets) (北京:世界知识出版社, 2001), p. 522. Li is the official historian of China's stock market experiment.
2. These statistics are founded on the methodologies laid out in the IMF's *Government Financial Statistics Manual 2014*, https://data.imf.org/api/document/download?key=60941310.
3. These non-productive assets appear to be a remainder of subtracting total assets of state enterprises from total liabilities plus equity in data provided by the MOF. Such a writeup in value of capital assets occurred in the original IPOs of the SOEs consolidated in the MOF data. There would be a writeup of value because Chinese regulations forbade the sale of shares at less than book value. The required surplus is added to capital and to assets.
4. An investment efficiency ratio is calculated from the data by dividing completed investment by total investment expenditures. Though figures may not be well comparable since expenditures may represent capital for a number of projects not yet completed, the large differences in the figures are suggestive.
5. Shang Ming, Editor, 新中国金融50年 (50 years of New China's banking), (北京, 中国财政经济出版社, 1999), p. 307.
6. See "Table 1: Mean First-day Returns and Money Left on the Table" in *Initial Public Offerings: Updated Statistics*; Jay R. Ritter, Warrington College of Business, University of Florida. October 1, 2021. https://site.warrington.ufl.edu/ritter/files/IPO-Statistics.pdf.
7. Until 2015 the breakdown of share types and, therefore, the owners of the shares was explicit. After the so-called "G-share" reforms of 2015, however, all shares were merged into a single category, just A shares. This made identifying the underlying owners difficult. For details see Carl E. Walter and Fraser J.T. Howie, *Privatizing China*, 2nd ed., Chapter 10.
8. Where listed company shares have been listed not only in Shanghai but also Hong Kong and New York it is a matter of judgment how to calculate the company's market capitalization. Table 6.3 uses Shanghai values for shares listed there and Hong Kong values for shares listed there. The important point, however, is that the state controls the absolute majority in terms of the number of voting shares. See Carl E. Walter and Fraser J. T. Howie, *Privatizing China*, 2nd ed., p. 182.
9. Based on data from the Shanghai Exchange's depository, we have shown in a number of places that the tradable segment of the A share market is about 17 percent held either by extremely wealthy individuals or by other types of investors, while the "moms and pops" of legend hold around 72 percent. For our most recent estimate, see Carl E. Walter, "Was Deng Xiaping Right? An Overview of China's Equity Markets," in *Journal of Applied Corporate Finance* 26, no. 3 (Summer 2014), p. 16.

10. See Walter and Howie, *Privatizing China*, pp. 186 ff.

11. For 23–28 percent of 2018 GDP see Chunlin Zhang, "How Much Do State-Owned Enterprises Contribute to China's GDP and Employment?," World Bank, 2019. © World Bank. https://openknowledge.worldbank.org/handle/10986/32306 License: CC BY 3.0 IGO; for 39 percent of 2015 GDP, see Carston A. Holz, "The Unfinished Business of State-owned Enterprise Reform in the People's Republic of China," *Journal of Economic Literature*, December 2, 1018, https://carstenholz.people.ust.hk/CarstenHolz-PRC-SOEreforms-2Dec2018.pdf.

12. Author's calculation based on MOF's "National State Capital Management Budget Final Accounts." A deep look at this shows the intense political infighting between national SOEs and the central government.

13. One need only review the difficult 1985 experience of Beijing Jeep, the first Sino-Foreign Joint Venture, to understand this point. See Jim Mann, *Beijing Jeep: The Short, Unhappy Romance of American Business in China* (New York: Simon & Schuster, 1989).

14. There are different loan-to-deposit ratios for different bank categories as well as different banks. This is a blended ratio calculated by total system loans and total bank deposits at PBOC.

15. Longmei Zhang et al., "China's High Savings: Drivers, Prospects and Policies," IMF Working Paper, WP/18/277, December 2018.

16. "We cannot manage the airport the same way as the railway station and we cannot manage the future with the ways of yesterday." This was the key remark in Jack Ma's comments in his final public speech at the Shanghai Bund Summit, October 24, 2020. Versions and commentary crowd Google and his speech can be seen on YouTube.

17. The footnote reads, "由于政府债券形式债务举借主体分布在融资平台公司等企事业单位，债务资金的举借和使用未经总预算会计核算，在完成地方政府债务置换前本表中地方政府债务余额数为地方统计数." (Because government debt types are held by local financing platforms and such enterprises, the debt and its use have yet to pass through overall budgetary accounts to be verified; until the completion of the loan to debt swap [ed: program] the local debt outstanding statistics in this table are local statistics). *China Finance Almanac* 2020, p. 357.

18. OECD, Data, "General Government Debt," 2018, https://data.oecd.org/gga/general-government-debt.htm.

19. Christine Wong, "Plus ça Change: Three Decades of Fiscal Policy and Central Local Relations," Working Paper WP22CW1, June 2021, East Asia Institute, National University of Singapore.

20. For example, see p. 53 of IMF, People's Republic of China: 2019 Article IV Consultation-Press Release; Staff Report, country report No. 19/266, August 8, 2019, https://www.imf.org/en/Publications/CR/Issues/2019/08/08/Peoples-Republic-of-China-2019-Article-IV-Consultation-Press-Release-Staff-Report-Staff-48576.

21. For a definition of augmented deficits see Yuanyan Sophia Zhang and Steven Barnett, "Fiscal Vulnerabilities and Risks from Local Government Finance in China," IMF Working Paper, WP14/4, January 2014, pp. 17 ff.

22. This is not to ignore the extremely negative net worth enjoyed by the United States as shown in IMF Government Finance data. The difference lies in the US dollar reserve currency the world still accepts as opposed to China's closed system.

23. Yoko Kubota and Liyan Qi, "Empty Buildings in China's Provincial Cities Testify to Evergrande Debacle," *Wall Street Journal*, October 4, 2021, https://www.wsj.com/articles/evergrande-china-real-estate-debt-debacle-empty-buildings-cities-beijing-11633374710.

24. Kenneth S. Rogoff and Yuanchen Yang, "Has China's Housing Production Peaked?," *China and the World Economy* 21, no. 1 (2021), p. 3. https://scholar.harvard.edu/rogoff/publications/peak-china-housing.

25. Carston A. Holz (2001), p. 363.

26. Logan Wright and Daniel Rosen, "Credit and Credibility: Risks to China's Economic Resilience," Rhodium Group, October 2018, https://rhg.com/research/credit-and-credibility-risks-to-chinas-economic-resilience/.

Chapter 7

China versus the United States: Comparing the Costs of Financial Crises

> . . . high leverage leads to high risk and . . . can cause the outbreak of a systemic financial crisis . . . and even result in "tossing the people's savings into the soup."
>
> —*Authoritative Person, Renmin ribao, September 9, 2016*

The previous chapters have taken a deep dive inside China's fiscal and financial systems and shown how the country's massive debt has come about. The several years since 2016 have seen some of China's leaders and regulators, if not its political leaders, engage in an attempt to bring their finances back under control. This effort has not been helped by the emergence of a "zero tolerance" policy aimed at Covid-19, nor have the bolts of lightning from Zhongnanhai, disabling the most vibrant parts of the private economy, helped. The Headquarters has truly been bombarding much of the country seemingly without any awareness of the need for constraint. But within the bowels of the state an effort to manage what could quickly become a real financial crisis is taking place.

After the past decade of financial stimulation, China's economy has grown to be the second largest in the world, roughly two-thirds the size of the economy of the United States. The country's technological achievements have surpassed anyone's expectations. "Wolf Warriors" from the Ministry of Foreign Relations demand that the world see that China is now Number 1, while also hoping to improve their own positions in the Chinese political sphere. Keeping in mind China's successes, it is important to consider the costs. In the calculations that come, costs are defined purely as financial costs; the political costs and costs to the populations involved are beyond the ability of this writer to calculate. The comparisons involve how the United States and China have addressed the challenges of financial crises and at what financial costs. Based on these, some conclusions are drawn about the nature of, at least, the Chinese system.

Summary Financial Crises, China and the United States

Over the past 40 years there are two fairly comparable examples when the United States and China faced major financial challenges. In the United States, the first was the savings and loan crisis of the 1980s, ending in 1994. This can be paired with China's reaction to the Asian Financial Crisis of 1997. The second set of crises stems from the global financial crisis itself. This book has shown how Beijing reacted to this crisis and has sought to quantify the measures taken by Beijing to protect its key state banks even while building up massive leverage within the system. In the United States the story was quite different, but proved to be no less expensive.

Table 7.1 provides a summary of cost outcomes for the four crises. The calculations are based on the following definitions.[1] First, crises

Table 7.1 Summary of crisis cost outcomes.

Note	Crisis	Record Year	Number of Entities	Average Total Assets US$ Bn	ex post Recap Cost US$ Bn	ex post Bad Debt Write-Off US$ Bn	Total ex post Cost US$ Bn	Fair Value Resolution Cost US$ Bn	Fair Value Net of Recoveries	Fair Value Cost to GDP %	Fair Value Resolution Cost/Total Assets %	Estimated Recovery %
1	US savings & loan/bank crisis	1980	747 S&Ls/1617 banks	$402/302	NA	NA	$160	$124	NA	4%	18%	82%
2	China bank recapitalization	1997	5 state banks	$1,560	$113	$443	$556	$422	$297	44%	27%	73%
3	US mortgage banking crisis	2008	Systemic	$1,532	NA	NA	NA	$498	NA	3%	33%	67%
4	China 2015–2019 deleveraging	2015	Systemic	$30,673	$576	$4,568	$5,144	$4,398	$3,630	42%	17%	–

NOTE: (1) FDIC; (2) Table 8.3; (3) Lucas (2019); (4) Tables 4.2 and 5.3 and *China Bond*.

become *bailouts* when a government subsidizes or implicitly guarantees financial institutions *undergoing financial distress* or when new legislation is passed that transfers value to institutions in distress. The start dates in the table refer to those years of record when a bailout is considered to have begun. The value, or financial support, provided by governments is then compared to the total assets of institutions *as of the bailout year* using the *present value* of all values transferred during the crisis. The objective is to compare *at the same value* all cash flows and subsidies associated with bailouts to the total asset values of failed institutions as of the year of their failure. In other words, the aim is to compare how much it cost to restore a broken institution or set of institutions to health.

Present value calculations require a discount rate. When market discount rates are not available or are unreliable, as is the case in China, a rate of 5 percent has been used to calculate what is called a *fair value* estimate. The fair value is the present value of all cash flows discounted back to the year the institution(s) failed and is meant to be a proxy for the market value of cash and subsidies provided.

It is true that China, as a matter of routine, guarantees and subsidizes its state banks. There can be no doubt, however, about the crisis Beijing faced in 1997 or the non-routine nature of its reactions to state bank weaknesses. Similarly, the rise of a complex shadow banking system following the initial financial stimulus of 2008 is also non-routine. The shadow banking system appears to have strengthened the major banks at first, but it did so at the cost of spreading financial risk throughout the entire system, and it has distorted the health of the state banks themselves.

There are other ways to calculate bailout costs; the table also shows the value of all cash flows between the Chinese government and the "resolved" entities to arrive at a simple cash figure, an *ex post* amount. The data for these figures are not easily arrived at in both US cases, and so not included. This approach ignores risk, as well as the time value of money, and is provided simply for reference. For the two US crises, the Congressional Office of the Budget (COB) has calculated their costs on a fair value basis; these are the official estimates provided to Congress. There have been no official Chinese crisis cost estimates made public for either case, and the present value results for China's responses approximate fair value. The *ex post* costs, however, can be estimated. Others may later arrive at more precise numbers for both Chinese crises.

Table 7.1 summarizes the four financial crises and compares fair value costs to respective GDPs as of the record year of the bailouts. All four cases involve clear bailout dates for the respective financial crisis. In the case of China's financial expansion since 2009, there is yet no clear-cut crisis, but a bailout date can be set at year-end 2015 prior to the announcement of the ongoing deleveraging campaign. This may not be entirely accurate, since Beijing began to put in place the shadow banking support system soon after the first stimulus package and also encouraged the accounting treatments described in Chapter 5. Nevertheless, the first attempt at managing the crisis began in 2016 with the "trees" article, and this date will be used to mark the beginning of the financial bailout in China. The end of this effort is considered to be 2019; after that year Beijing resumed its massive lending in order to offset the threat of Covid-19.

The first set of crises tells a story similar to the second set. In the United States, regulatory agencies resolved a huge number of failed thrifts and banks, recovering 82 percent of their total assets with estimated losses equaling four percent of GDP. The effort, however, was seen as a "debacle" by regulators and politicians alike. Had an earlier effort been more effective, the problems would have been resolved at a far lower cost and with far less political embarrassment. The failure to take decisive action early in a crisis is a common theme in these comparisons. In China, however, the cost of the bank restructurings reached over 40 percent of GDP and 27 percent of average 1997 banking assets. If recoveries on bad loans are estimated, then the costs to GDP would have been only 27 percent.

In sum, for the United States, even though the S&L crisis was the biggest financial challenge since the 1930s depression, its overall weight in the economy was quite small, but its political fallout was much larger. In China, the overall cost of the state bank bailout was huge and would most certainly have severely impacted the state's finances had there been a convertible currency and open capital account. These costs added up over the eight years it took to restructure and successfully recapitalize the banks. The process took too long.

The sheer scale of these Chinese costs makes the political resistance to the PBOC's restructuring plans far more understandable. China's politicians like those in the United States would only have understood the ongoing cash costs. In contrast to the PBOC, the Ministry of Finance's approach involved only IOUs and *no cash transfers* at all. This, no doubt, was seen as far more practical. Despite the disagreements, the numbers for China demonstrate the commitment of the party's controlling group of reformers to fundamentally altering the character and direction of Chinese development, if not its underlying ideologies. The irony is that their efforts enabled China to weather the global financial crisis with the world's best-capitalized banks in support of a traditional Soviet-style command economy lending operation. Moreover, the country's initial success in recovery undermined the political position of those who had worked so long to reform the economy. The tragedy for both China and the world is that the global financial crisis led to this reversion to old policies and political practices.

The second pair of crises was systemic in scale for both countries and related in that the one can be said to be the proximate cause of the other. The US mortgage crisis nearly tipped the Western financial system over. Its total cost ended up at 33 percent of all assets involved, but in comparison to the US GDP it again was quite small; the political and social costs domestically and internationally, however, were huge. In China, the party attempted to avoid its own crisis by engaging in a banking bailout *in advance* of any bailout. The costs to China through 2019 when calculated on a fair value basis, however, have been huge at 81 percent of 2015 GDP. Even if credit recoveries are considered, they would have little impact, given the size of WMP asset pools. The very scale of China's state banks, however, has also become huge, and fair value costs compared to total banking assets are again around 40 percent. And, of course, banks had to continuously raise new capital from each other, which on an *ex post* basis has amounted so far to about US$600 billion.

It is difficult to understand how the financial problems that have been created by the party's delay in taking real action can be resolved. It will take great political commitment and skill as was shown in 1997, but can this be found today? Chapter 8 reviews Japan's efforts to deleverage perhaps as a road map for China. One lesson from the United States and Japan is clear, however: the longer it takes to recognize a crisis and take substantive action, the higher the financial costs to the economy.

Comparisons of Crises

The US Savings and Loan (and Banking) Crisis, 1980–1994

The savings and loan (S&L) crisis in the United States is considered to be a debacle not because it threatened the US economy; it did not. In 1990, US GDP was almost US$6 trillion as compared to US$705 billion in failed thrift and bank assets, or 11.8 percent. But it was a debacle because it was the result of a years-long series of non-actions taken by regulators who, to some extent, had misunderstood the role of S&Ls and that financial change was coming.[2] Their actions, designed to help the industry, covered up its financial deterioration until increasing interest rates exposed its fundamental illiquidity. Consequently, the cleanup costs were far worse than should have been expected. The proximate cause of the crisis was continuous interest rate increases related to the raging inflation in the years after the 1974 oil crisis. These increases also had the same impact on hundreds of small-town banks across the country. As regulators worked through failed S&Ls, the Federal Deposit Insurance Corp. (FDIC) was doing the same with these small banks.

The trend in value by year of failed S&L and bank assets is shown in Figure 7.1. In 1980 there were almost 4,000 S&Ls with US$604 billion in total assets and tangible capital of US$32 billion (capital less intangible items). Over the next dozen or so years, 747 S&Ls were taken over to be "resolved" with total assets of US$402.1 billion. At the same time, 1,617 failed or failing banks were taken over by the FDIC involving US$302.6 billion in assets.

The original S&L regulator, the Federal Savings and Loan Insurance Corp. (FSLIC: Fizz-lick) had been established when the industry was seen as a kind of public utility for funding home mortgages. Its funding was limited by legislation, and staff were underpaid compared to other federal agencies. Moreover, its philosophy of regulation was rule-based and not based on principles of safety and soundness. Even worse, politicians in Congress stood on the side of S&Ls against intrusive regulatory investigation, believing that any losses incurred were "only on paper."

As interest rates increased, policy makers, lawmakers, and the legislature believed S&Ls should be granted regulatory forbearance until

THE RED DREAM

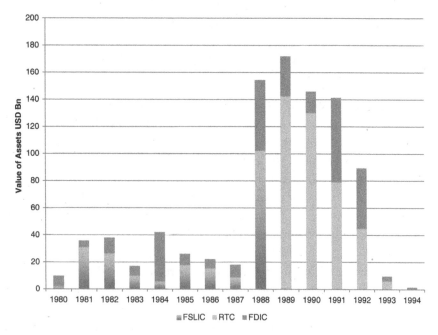

Figure 7.1 Value of failed S&L and bank assets, 1980–1994.
SOURCE: FDIC.

interest rates returned to "normal." In accordance, in the mid-1980s regulators *lowered* capital requirements significantly and S&Ls were allowed to issue "income capital certificates" to the regulator that were included in capital calculations. Even worse, they were allowed to amortize losses over a 10-year period with the net loss carried as an asset. Finally, regulators enacted the concept of "appraised equity capital," meaning S&Ls could count the increase in market value of their premises as capital. So it is certainly not the case that only regulators in China work aggressively in support of their supposed charges! But this is a case where the existing supervisory paradigm no longer suits a change in operating environment. As in Japan, so in the United States, and now perhaps in China—it takes time and major losses to demolish old thinking.

Table 7.2 shows the trend of S&L failures during FSLIC's existence, 1980–1989. Over these years, over 1,000 entities were closed. Then Reagan-era deregulation in the mid-1980s significantly eased entry into the industry. In 1984 and 1985 over 200 new entrants began to make use

Table 7.2 Savings and loan failures, 1980–1988.

US$ Bn	Number of S&Ls (Resolved, New)	Total Industry Assets $	Net Income $	Tangible Capital $	Capital/Total Assets %	Number of Insolvent S&Ls	Insolvent Assets $	Regulatory Reserves $
1980	3,993	604	0.8	32	5.3%	43	0.4	6.5
1981	3,751 (−242)	640	−4.6	25	4.0%	112	28.5	6.2
1982	3,287 (−464)	686	−4.1	4	0.5%	415	220	6.3
1983	3,146 (−141)	814	1.9	4	0.4%	515	284.6	6.4
1984	3,136 (+109)	976	1	3	0.3%	695	360.2	5.6
1985	3,246 (+100)	1,068	3.7	8	0.8%	705	358.3	4.6
1986	3,220 (−26)	1,162	0.1	14	1.2%	672	343.1	−6.3
1987	3,147 (−199)	1,249	−7.8	9	0.7%	672	353.8	−13.7
1988	2,949 (−11)	1,349	−13.4	22	1.6%	508	297.3	−75
1989	2,878	1,252	−17.6	10	0.8%	516	290.8	NA

SOURCE: FDIC.

of expanded S&L powers beyond originating simple mortgages. These "new" S&Ls became trading platforms aimed at arbitraging interest rates and soon ran into trouble of their own. By 1988 FSLIC's reserves were long gone and 516 S&Ls were still insolvent. The story was no better on the banking side.

The initial stage of the crisis ended in 1989 when the cost of events forced the new administration to pass the Financial Institution Reform, Recovery and Enforcement Act (FIRREA).[3] The Act terminated FSLIC and established the Resolution Trust Corporation (RTC). Although the regulatory environment was complicated, both FDIC and RTC adopted similar resolution methods under heavy political pressure and limited budget appropriations from Congress. These limitations determined the strategies used. Figure 7.2 breaks out by number of institutions the resolution methods used by the RTC. All methods involved either open auctions or bidding with high price determining success. Overall, the RTC in just two years resolved 747 failed S&Ls with over US$400 billion in assets. That's nearly two each day.

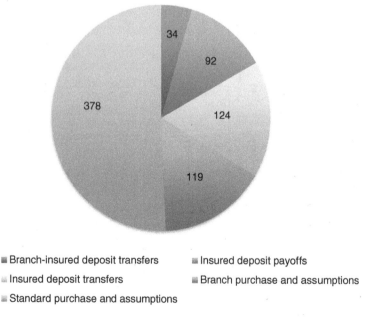

- Branch-insured deposit transfers
- Insured deposit payoffs
- Insured deposit transfers
- Branch purchase and assumptions
- Standard purchase and assumptions

Figure 7.2   Thrift resolution types by number of entities, 1980–1995.
Source: FDIC.

In a standard purchase and assumption transaction, a healthy finan-cial institution acquires the assets and liabilities of the failed thrift. Such trades accounted for US$318 billion of US$747 billion failed thrift assets. A second method, insured deposit transfers, involves a straightfor-ward transfer of deposits and some liabilities to a healthy institution while the regulator retains failed assets and other liabilities. A branch insured deposit transfer is similar, except it refers to insured deposits in specific branches. This compares to a simple payoff by the regulator of insured deposits. The third-most-used method was the outright sale of thrift branches. In this transaction, the bad assets of the failed thrift remained in a head-office book assumed by the RTC so that the branches were clean. In the end, nearly 74 percent were handled by outright pur-chase and acquisition.

By 1994 and the end of the crisis, the FDIC for its part had resolved 1,617 small banks with total assets of US$302 billion. The RTC over its term resolved 747 failed thrifts with total assets of US$403 billion. Total costs incurred by both came to US$124 billion or about 18 percent of total assets managed. Put the other way around, the two regulators recovered over 82 percent of the assets of failed banks and thrifts. The FDIC saw success quite differently; in concluding its study of the period it stated, ". . . the savings and loan crisis reflected a massive public policy failure."[4]

The Asia Financial Crisis and Chinese Bank Restructuring, 1997–2007

As was the case in 2008, the proximate cause of the internal crisis China faced in 1997 was external. In July 1997 Thailand unexpectedly deval-ued its fully convertible currency. Overexposed to foreign debt, the local economy verged on collapse as foreign lenders pulled out their funds. The crisis rippled across Asia to other countries that shared similar char-acteristics: a weak banking system, poor regulation and excessive foreign borrowing. China emerged from the crisis as a "pillar" of the region hav-ing refused to devalue its currency and lending US$1 billion to an IMF-led bailout of Thailand. For the first time, the international community did not view the country as a threat to the international order, but as a good citizen. But that didn't mean that China had no problems; it had escaped largely due to a very low exposure to foreign lenders and its closed financial system.

The party leadership, however, saw the weakness of its banking system clearly. In November 1997 the government organized a work conference on finance, and in early 1998 the premier presented an overall plan designed to reduce China's financial vulnerabilities. It was at this time that the central bank governor commented that 25 percent of bank loans had "disappeared like stones dropping into the sea."[5] In his report, the premier announced that money-losing state enterprises would be closed, sold, or merged. He also reorganized the central bank into regional, not provincial offices, stating ". . . the power of provincial governors and mayors to command local bank presidents is abolished as of 1998." He was referring to the centralization of the bank party secretaries under a committee led by the PBOC. He also announced a major program to restructure and recapitalize the four state banks. In sum, this program entailed the creation of a commercial banking and capital markets system similar to that in developed countries. The NPC formally approved his report and his plan. The effort lasted almost a decade. Needless to say this overall program marked a major change institutionally, economically as well as ideologically.

How did Beijing go about this change? For state enterprises, their closure or transfer to private ownership resulted in the loss of 25 million jobs. Accompanying this was a massive restructuring of the central government with the closure of many industrial ministries and commissions. On the financial side, its restructuring included closing 700 trust companies and shutting down bankrupt securities companies. In addition, urban and rural credit cooperatives were consolidated into new city and rural commercial banks. The state banks went through a major restructuring and recapitalization involving foreign partners and were successfully listed first on the Hong Kong exchange and later in Shanghai.

The total costs on an *ex post* basis for recapitalizations and write-offs is estimated to be over US$500 billion on a 1997 GDP of just over US$1 trillion and foreign reserves of around US$149 billion. Table 7.3 sums up the estimated costs associated with the closure of 700 trust companies, 11 securities companies, and many urban and rural cooperatives. There is no doubt that the reformers had spent significant political capital. As well, the scale of the program indicates the level of concern felt by the

Table 7.3 Estimated cost of recapitalization of Big Four state banks, 1998–2007.

RMB Bn	Amount	Purpose	Recap	Source	Disposal	Note
1997	16	Closure of trusts, urban and rural coops	–		16	
1998	270	Initial bank recap	270	Bonds issued to MOF	–	
1999	40	Capitalization of asset management companies (AMCs)	40	Bonds issued to MOF	–	
1999	858	AMCs issues bonds to respective banks	–	Bonds issued to banks	858	100% face value
2000	634	PBOC loans to AMCs for CCB/BOC bad loan acquisition	–	Loan from PBOC	634	100% face value
2002	10	Closure of 11 bankrupt securities firms			10	
2003	93	Capital writeoff at CCB/BOC	–		93	
2003	373	US$45 bn recap of CCB/BOC	373	Foreign reserves	–	
2004	279	PBOC auction of CCB, BOC NPLs	–	Other entities buy at discount	279	100% face value
2005	122	PBOC second-round loans to asset management companies	–		122	100% face value
2005	1	Capitalize Investor Protection Fund	–		1	
2005	620	PBOC finances ICBC bad loan disposal	–	PBOC loan	620	100% face value
2005	246	MOF IOU to Agricultural Bank of China (ABC)	–		246	
2006	118	US$15 bn to recap ICBC	118	Foreign reserves	–	
2007	139	US$19 bn for ABC recap	139	Foreign reserves	–	
2007	665	MOF IOU to ABC	–	MOF IOU	665	
Total	4,484	US	940		3,544	
US$ Totals	$541		$113		$428	

SOURCE: Carl Walter and Fraser Howie, *Red Capitalism*, 2nd ed., pp. 59–65, 73.

party and demonstrates just how rotten bank balance sheets had become under a command economy.

The financial engineering that went into the banks has been described in detail elsewhere.[6] The first step was a preliminary injection of new capital in the four banks by bond issuance to the MOF/national budget. Beijing then adopted a "good bank/bad bank" approach modeled after similar bank restructurings in Scandinavia and the United States. Each bank had its own "bad bank"; these are the national AMCs described elsewhere. Like the banks, each AMC issued a bond to the MOF for its seed capital. This was hardly enough to acquire the volume of problem assets from the banks, so the AMCs issued another set of bonds that were purchased by the banks, and the central bank also made loans to the AMCs. It was this money that was used by the AMCs to acquire US$170 billion of nonperforming loans (NPL) at *full face value, dollar-for-dollar basis* in the 2000 round of restructurings. This price-basis was used to prevent new losses by the banks (any discount would have to be written off) and so can be seen as the *de facto* addition of new capital. On the other hand, it saddled the AMCs from the start with assets that were hugely overvalued; it is likely that this first batch of accounting assets were like those "stones tossed into the sea," having no value at all. It is unclear whether losses were ever written off before the public listings of Cinda and Huarong, because they were surely not written off afterward!

The second step in 2003 addressed the need for new capital. It was originally believed that this would come from foreign "strategic" investors prior to bank IPOs. But the banks still had appreciable bad loans remaining, and potential foreign investors were leery of unknowns. At the time, of the four banks only CCB and BOC had sufficient earnings power and capital to absorb full write-offs with some capital remaining. But, having written them off, their bank capital would be far below regulatory minimum levels. The PBOC's solution was to tap the country's foreign reserves; this was approved by the party at the end of 2003. The banks each received US$22.5 billion in new capital, executing five-year currency swaps with PBOC to receive it in *renminbi*. The recapitalization was followed by a PBOC arranged auction for the remaining bad assets. The auction was *prearranged* so that there would be *recoveries* for the banks on the loans, further adding to bank capital.

What the happy auction winners did with these overvalued assets is unknown.

Unfortunately, all this proved to be too politically and financially expensive for some party leaders, and in 2005 the rest of the bank program was handed over to the MOF, which took a far more parsimonious approach: in both the ICBC and ABC cases no cash exchanged hands. The ministry issued five-year IOUs to both banks and took title to their bad loan portfolios again *at full book value*. The bad loans were placed in a so-called "co-managed account," for which the banks were responsible for achieving recoveries that were to be used to offset the IOUs. For the same purpose, the banks were also required to pay cash dividends to the MOF. In the end, the banks repaid the full value in cash for the MOF's simple piece of paper. It took over a decade for the banks to work down their debt.

The sum of all costs to the bank restructuring calculated at present value and then compared to 1997 GDP equaled around 41 percent, a high number due to the small size of banking assets in 1997 (see Table 7.1). It should be added that these results do not include all recoveries on bad debt by the AMCs. The general belief at the time was that 20 percent was, in fact, recovered. If this is the case, then on a fair value basis US$1.6 trillion can be subtracted from debt write-off expenses so that total costs to GDP become 24 percent and, of course, the more recoveries, the better the outcomes.

The US Mortgage Crisis, 2008–2015

It is impossible to describe the US mortgage crisis clearly in a short space and with the author's limited understanding, but it seems that in the United States the entire mortgage system had become rotten with so-called "subprime" mortgages. They were overpriced and then packaged with lesser-risk mortgages and sold by thinly capitalized special-purpose vehicles (SPV) to investors chasing a yield in a sustained low-interest-rate environment. The larger investment banks bought subprime mortgages from independent mortgage brokers and ultimately layered them with hundreds of other mortgages of varying degrees of risk in products called collateralized debt obligations (CDOs). Based on the theoretically low overall risk makeup of these securities, ratings agencies assigned overly positive investment grade ratings, thereby supporting their exaggerated valuations. In a low-interest-rate environment, demand for high-yielding investment-grade securities was near universal among financial institutions and funds, but some were greedier than others. They suffered the most.

Then interest rates began to increase. This had at least two effects; first the adjustable rate mortgages made to subprime borrowers got expensive, so they could no longer make their payments. Subprime defaults mounted and quickly undermined the value of this layer in CDOs. The second result was that SPVs could no longer borrow cheap funds arranged by their related banks to acquire mortgages to package and sell. When regulators ruled that SPVs were really not independent of their related banks, the banks were forced to bring the mortgages back on balance sheet. They then incurred losses that ate up huge chunks of bank capital.

Entities that had provided risk management products—that is, credit guarantees to help investors hedge risk—had also seriously miscalculated and simply failed outright. Savings and loans and mortgage brokers with subprime mortgages now stuck on their books faced severe liquidity problems. Everyone lost huge amounts of capital as the security sandwiches fell apart. The federal mortgage agencies Fannie Mae and Freddie Mac were stuffed with these things. Then in September 2008, the collapse of Lehmann Brothers created a liquidity crisis throughout the financial markets the world over. The crisis raised the question of whether Merrill Lynch was liquid and if not, how about Morgan Stanley and if not them, how about Goldman Sachs? This sudden lack of liquidity in the money markets nearly brought the entire system down.

As for the ensuing emergency bailout, the difficulties of America's major financial institutions grabbed headlines and possibly moved the Chinese Communist Party into an entirely different orbit. By far the biggest losses were incurred by the two Federal mortgage agencies, Fannie Mae and Freddie Mac. These agencies normally acquired qualified mortgages from banks, thereby freeing up bank capital. But prior to the crisis, the two agencies together had invested in over *US$5 trillion* in US mortgages including subprimes and were exposed to the bulk of the risk.[7] The Chinese held US$445 billion of these agency bonds. Who made that decision! This might explain why the premier demanded that the US government preserve his investment!

The bailout of the two agencies was made possible by an act of Congress in late 2008. Both Fannie Mae and Freddie Mac had been "sponsored" by the government, but supposedly privately owned; after 2008 the two moved clearly to government ownership and remain so today. The 2008 act authorized the US Treasury to acquire preferred shares in both with a combined value of up to US$445 billion. Their investment loss was calculated by the Congressional Budget Office to have a fair value of US$331 billion. On an *ex post* basis, however, adding up the realized differences between Treasury purchases of agency shares and dividends received suggests a *net profit* to the government of US$58 billion as of 2014. This is why some politicians have said that the government actually gained on its actions at least as far as the two agencies go. It all depends on how you count.

The second largest set of costs arose from the Federal Housing Administration (FHA), an agency authorized to make mortgages less expensive to what became called "subprime" borrowers by extending guarantees. The costs associated with the FHA's mortgage guarantee book and on newly originated mortgages during the crisis itself forced its bailout. These costs stemmed from three areas: (1) the 2008 Congressional act authorized up to US$100 billion in new guarantees that FHA actually made; (2) the Treasury absorbed losses on old mortgages booked before the crisis; and (3) the FHA guaranteed US$858 billion of risky mortgages at subsidized rates during the crisis itself. All told, on a fair-value basis calculated by the COB the FHA bailout cost US$60 billion as compared to an *ex post* basis of US$43 billion.

The famous Troubled Asset Relief Program (TARP) was created by an act of Congress in October 2008. The act gave Treasury the authority to purchase up to US$700 billion in troubled assets. Within two months, the Treasury had used US$248 billion extending loans to all major US banking institutions. This is what made the news. Funds were also extended to AIG, the guarantor of the bulk of derivative mortgage securities and to Chrysler and General Motors. Table 7.4 includes the value of TARP subsidies only to major US financial institutions. The COB in 2014 concluded that the fair value of these subsidies was US$64 billion. Later that year a Congressional panel estimated the number to lie between US$53–72 billion. In addition to the financial subsidies, a further US$100 billion was paid out to others including the

Table 7.4   TARP subsidies only to US financial entities; summary of fair value costs.

Institution	Capital Transferred	Fair Value	Institution	Cost US$ Bns
AIG	40	25.2	Fannie and Freddie	311
Bank of America	15	2.55	Federal Housing Administration	60
Citigroup	25	9.5	TARP	90
Citigroup	20	10.0	Small Business Lending	6
Goldman Sachs	10	2.5	Federal Reserve	21
JPMorgan Chase	25	4.38	FDIC	10
Morgan Stanley	10	4.25	**Total Fair Value**	**$498**
PNC	7.6	2.05		
US Bancorp	6.6	0.3		
Wells Fargo	25	1.75		
Total	**184.2**	**62.48**		

SOURCE: Lucas (2019), pp. 20 and 24.

auto companies and contingent liabilities of the Federal Reserve and FDIC. In total, then, the fair value associated with TARP is estimated at around US$90 billion.

The Federal Reserve also took on trillions of dollars of credit exposure during the height of the crisis. The COB calculated the fair value of these exposures as well and arrived at a "modest" estimate of US$21 billion, modest because much of the risk taken on was either collateralized, short term, or taken on as a result of auctions. In short, their net values were based on fair value calculations from the start. The FDIC acted to expand deposit insurance to stop possible bank runs, and extended loan guarantees for new bank debt. Lucas estimates a final bailout cost of US$10 billion.

The right side of Table 7.4 summarizes the various costs of the mortgage bailout arriving at US$498 billion—a huge number but again small as compared to GDP at 3.4 percent. On the other hand, it amounted to 33 percent of US$1.5 trillion in assets involved for a recovery rate of 67 percent. If the S&L crisis was a debacle, what was the mortgage crisis aside from being a global economic and political disaster?

China's Deleveraging Campaign from 2016 to 2019

It might be argued that China has yet to face a financial crisis, yet Beijing's actions suggest that the reverse is true. The Authoritative Person writing in 2016 knew very well that the country's financial system was close to, as he put it, tossing household savers' deposits into the soup, but that was 2016. Actions since then to rein in wealth management asset pools and find new bad-debt resolution methods are simply add-ons to the shadow banking and liberal accounting methods described in Chapters 4 and 5. The central government's effort since FY2015, the bailout start date, has been to strengthen the big state banks and let the smaller banks go, a version of the old "Grab the large and release the small (抓大放小)" SOE policy of the late 1990s.

Beijing takes all measures possible to protect the integrity of the major state banks or at least its appearance. Consequently, the cost of bailing out these huge banks is the incremental value of assets removed from their balance sheets since year-end 2015 up to the end of 2019 then discounted back to total bank assets as of year-end 2015; details of these costs are summarized in Table 4.2. On an ex post basis, simply adding up the subsidies results in a total of 26 trillion *yuan* or nearly US$4 trillion! Then there was the nearly US$500 billion of new capital sourced by selling each other bonds. But these are simply additions of numbers. Even on a fair value basis the result is shocking, costs total around US$4.4 trillion or 42 percent of GDP and 17 percent of average bank assets. Even assuming the standard (in China) level of recoveries (say 60 percent) only brings costs down to a level seen in the bank recapitalization period of 35 percent of GDP and 12 percent of total assets. Of course, a larger discount number would reduce fair value, as would more loan recoveries. But these numbers are huge because the cost of allowing the banks to grow into trees while retaining excellent performance metrics has also been huge: total banking assets in these years equaled three times GDP (see Figure 7.4 below). If the bailout date were set to 2010, when the party initiated its active support of state banks, the result would be far more shocking.

Figure 7.3 sheds light on the scale of Beijing's subsidies by showing their value versus actual charged-off loans and then comparing them to total bank risk assets. The regulator's official non-performing loan ratio

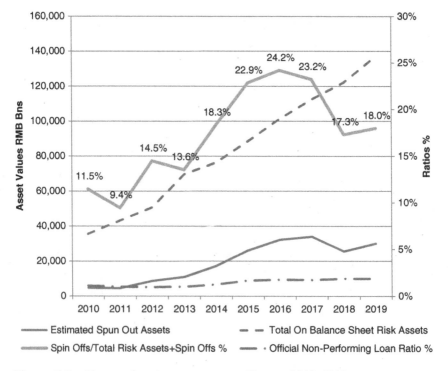

Figure 7.3   Non-performing versus spun-off assets, 2010–2019.
Source: See Table 4.5, CBIRC, author's calculations.

is the bottom line and, for the period reviewed, does not exceed 2 percent. To create a comparable ratio all spun-off assets are *added back* to the regulator's official risk-weighted asset number.[8] The resulting revised problem asset ratio begins at 11.5 percent in 2010 and peaks at nearly 24 percent in 2016, not that much different from the numbers in 1997 before bank restructuring began. After 2016, it seems that the deleveraging campaign had an impact, but, in general, as many suspect, the non-performing loans created by China's banking system are many multiples above what is officially stated or shown in bank audited financials; all such figures are at best illustrative.

Can this level of risk be resolved? The earlier bank restructurings left banks exposed to AMC bonds and MOF IOUs, but China's terrific economic growth after joining the WTO reduced these exposures to negligible figures before 2009.[9] The problem now is economic growth; the banks are huge today because there has been so little productive return on investment. To get more returns has required more and more capital, so balance sheets expand. On the other hand, restructuring the major banks, as was done earlier, is not an option; they are simply too large. Since 2016, regulators have worked to reduce risk exposures, primarily from WMPs, but the results remain wholly non-transparent. And it is less a WMP problem than a bank loan book problem: the loans may be current by accounting standards, but their maturities are too long, and the possibilities of full principal repayment are small. Loan books plus bond books need write-offs to arrive at a level that will fairly reflect their valuation. But with the party's policy of reining in the private sector plus antagonistic foreign policy, can real growth without stimulus resume?

The bigger problem may be that political leaders are not able to see just how big the problem has become; they may be fooled by the rosy appearance of bank income statements as reported to investors and Basel. Like leaders in the United States before the mortgage crisis broke out, the problem for China's leaders is grasping the sheer complexity of the financial system they have created or, better put, have allowed to evolve. In this system, all problems have been neatly squirreled away in the nooks and crannies of the state sector and, it must be said, in the investment portfolios of the Chinese people. One Authoritative Person who can see is a single light in a dark night. His voice is hardly enough in a huge bureaucracy whose members prefer to get on with other things.

Macro Comparisons and the Role of Central Banks

As Chapter 3 showed, the party has allowed China's state banks to metastasize over the decade-plus since 2009. Figure 7.4 compares the total assets of the United States and China banking systems against their respective GDPs. It shows why the cost outcomes of Chinese crises shown in Table 7.1 are as large as they are. Chinese banking assets even during the time they were being recapitalized had shot up to two times GDP—2.5 as of 2009 and then heading up 3.5 times in 2015. In contrast, US banks, even during the financial crisis, have held steady at one time US GDP. This comparison suggests that China has been using three dollars of bank assets to create one dollar of GDP as opposed to the one-for-one basis in the United States. Since 90 percent of state financial

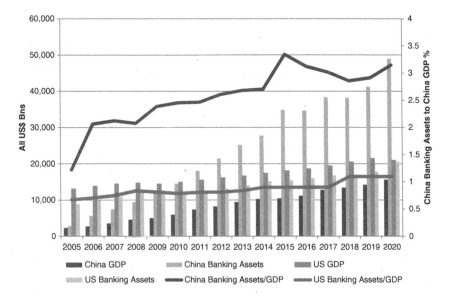

Figure 7.4   Total banking asset comparison, United States and China, 2005–2020.
SOURCE: China: *China Statistical Yearbook, China Banking Almanac*; the United States: Federal Reserve, YCharts, and World Bank.

resources are directed at the state sector itself, this simply points to the tremendous loss of capital involved in propping up the state system and the reason that real growth has been so difficult to achieve.

A further significant difference is the role played by their respective central banks. Reflecting its limited role, the asset side of the PBOC's balance sheet is extremely simple and made up primarily of foreign exchange reserves and bank deposit reserves and its liabilities of deposit reserves and currency in circulation. The Federal Reserve's balance sheet is far more complicated with assets consisting of US Treasury bonds and mortgage-backed securities (MBS) acquired during the financial crisis as part of its "quantitative easing" program. Its liabilities are currency in circulation and institutional deposits.[10] Figure 7.5 shows that the PBOC has decreased in size relative to GDP over the years 2007–2020. This is the result of a net decline in foreign reserves from 2015 and a slower growth in institutional deposits.

In contrast, the Fed's assets jumped by US$1.2 trillion in the two years from 2011 to 2013 when it bought illiquid mortgage securities to

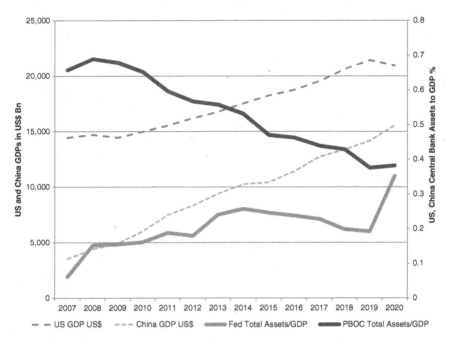

Figure 7.5 Comparison of China central bank assets to GDP.
SOURCE: *China Statistical Yearbook, China Banking Almanac and Bao et al. (2019).*

prop up the two mortgage agencies and extended loans to strengthen the major banks. Then, out of the range of the discussion here but still relevant, in 2019 the Fed injected massive amounts of liquidity into the banking system to counteract the effects of Covid-19. Over the years of China's response to the global crisis, the PBOC's assets have declined from nearly 70 percent of GDP in 2007 to just below 40 percent in 2020, while the US Federal Reserve has tripled its assets from 6 percent of GDP to 19 percent before Covid broke out.

The simple difference is that China uses its major banks the way the US government uses the Federal Reserve, to add liquidity into the economy. The consequences of this choice are the rub. The Fed buys securities held by financial institutions, but China's banks are making loans; they are buying loans as their assets. The Fed can sell the securities, perhaps taking an interest rate or market loss, but banks can lose both the principal and interest on their loans. On top of this, Chinese banks are publicly listed companies and, as discussed previously, must seek ways to present strong performance metrics. This also creates problems. The Fed has no such difficulties, since it is a government agency and is too complex to understand by the public and politicians alike.

There is another major difference: the Fed creates money out of nothing when it buys securities, In contrast, China's banks depend on deposits so under current conditions there must be a limit to their lending sometime. The PBOC itself does not create money as a matter of practice; it only creates RMB when it buys foreign currencies from China's exporter or foreign direct investors. Of course this could change. And this change would be a key indication of real financial difficulties.

Comparisons of State Net Worth

As shown in Table 7.5, no developed economy is comparable to the Chinese state; no Western or Asian government has tagging along with it the huge pile of state enterprise assets and financial entities that are found surrounding the Chinese state. China does not prepare a consolidated balance sheet of government finances, but in 2015 two PBOC analysts presented a paper at an IMF conference showing three versions of a Chinese state balance sheet based on the IMF format and definitions for the years 2010–2014.[11] Table 7.5 includes their work for 2014 as compared to IMF data for a few Western countries, Japan, and the author's version.

The table uses two IMF definitions of the state, "Broad" and "Public." The Broad case includes non-financial assets like land, real estate, and intellectual property; they are non-operating assets. The Public definition includes state enterprises. These IMF-prepared state balance sheets in the Public definition are also compared to the author's balance sheet presented in Table 6.1 and also in Appendix 2. As can be seen, other than Norway and its oil reserves, all other OECD states and, of course, the United States post negative net worth. Japan is in some ways the most comparable to China. In the Broad sense its assets in 2014 are very similar to China's totals; it is only in the huge scale of Japan's financial liabilities that there is a difference. Japan's case will be compared closely to that of China in Chapter 8.

Table 7.5   China government balance sheet versus developed
countries (2014) *(in US$).*

US$ bn	Financial Assets	Nonfinancial Assets	Liabilities	Net Worth	Of which Net Worth: State	Of which Minority Investors
Broad Definition						
Germany	1,091	0	2,449	−1,336		
Norway	8,885	0	1,058	7,830		
United Kingdom	593	0	2,030	−1,438		
United States	1,883	3,244	16,836	−11,709		
Japan	6,868	8,293	15,081	−8,213		
China, PBOC	6,731	14,428	5,330	15,829		
Public Definition						
China, PBOC	28,132	27,794	37,601	18,325	?	?
China, Author	27,607	13,676	34,259	7,024	2,894	4,135
China, PBOC adj.	28,132	13,366	32,271	9,227		

SOURCE: IMF; China: *China Banking Almanac,* Guihuan Zheng and Yue Dan; Appendix 2.

In the Broad case, China's non-financial assets bulge largely with real estate and land. There is no doubt that land in China is controlled by the state, but as discussed in Chapter 2, it is leased, not sold, to farmers and others. State enterprises may not even have valued the land their operations sit on. If land were to be sold at market values, state governments and enterprises would have to actually acquire land from their state parent and these new values would then be added to their balance sheets and this may already be the case. As one Chinese analyst notes,[12] it is the actual commercial development and sale of natural resources that makes it a state asset. The party, however, is not selling land outright as a commodity, and the probability of this happening is low. Therefore, the likelihood that this number provided by the PBOC report represents actual land values as somehow appraised or determined by the government can only be low. So, yes, land is the state's asset, it's just not an accounting asset. Any current commercial value of these potential assets or of such things as oil, gas, and mineral rights is already included in the market valuation of listed state enterprises based on their market capitalization, and this is already included in the balance sheet.[13]

Therefore, for 2014 if the "value" of land is assumed to be equal to non-financial assets in the *Broad* definition and is subtracted from the PBOC's calculation of the value of non-financial assets in the 2014 *Public* definition, it would leave, presumably, banks and state enterprises with a value of US$13.4 trillion. Adding this to financial assets gives a total adjusted value for Chinese state assets of US$41.5 trillion, as compared to US$32.3 trillion in liabilities (having subtracted the full value of Broad liabilities assumed as related to land) and a net worth of US$9.2 trillion and not US$18.3 trillion in the PBOC calculation.

The resulting balance sheet numbers are quite similar to those reached by the author for 2014. The net worth values differ from the author's only by the inclusion of a value for land that is wholly non-transparent.[14] The extremely rapid increases in financial assets and liabilities as opposed to non-financial assets from 2010 to 2018 in the Public definition for China are the point of making a deeper comparison with Japan. This trend suggests that the capital Beijing has pumped into China's economy during this period has not been put to uses that will drive growth in the future.

Comments

The characters of the two financial crises in China are very different. The costs of the bank restructuring efforts from 1997 were huge relative to GDP but created a financial system able to withstand the pressures of the global financial crisis. Moreover, the costs involved quickly became immaterial due to the rapid growth of the economy early in the century. In short, the money was well spent. Had the global crisis not occurred, financial reform in China would likely have continued and perhaps the country would have fit itself in as a member of the existing international financial order. But, as the opening scenes of this book suggest, the political balance inside the party in favor of capitalist reforms was delicate, even before the crisis. Once tipped reformers had to shift their political positions at once to avoid difficulties and they did so rapidly.

The second Chinese bailout, the deleveraging campaign, is quite different. It is an effort to restore order to the financial system now to prevent a future crisis from erupting. To date, its costs have proved to be huge since the scale of the financial system has outrun by multiples the economy itself. But this fact is obscured by the fine distribution of risk throughout China's vast geography. One of the party's pithy admonitions is "if the baby is yours, you take care of it (谁的孩子, 谁管)." This simply underlines the reality local governments face when dealing with financial challenges; what is the advantage in making your problems public? And if it's someone else's problem, Beijing need not pay attention, and it does not seem to view its huge state banks as major risks. Moreover, by including some proxy for land value in their state balance sheet, the central bank research team as well as those at the Chinese Academy of Social Sciences have shielded party leaders from any concern about the state's financial health. This makes a sustained and politically supported effort to reduce systemic leverage unlikely in the short term, meaning the problem gets bigger. Perhaps the coming demographic cliff will catalyze a response. What it might look like is a subject of Chapter 8, which compares Japan's experience with China's and seeks out possible policy paths that Beijing might consider.

Notes

1. These definitions and the approach are based on Deborah Lucas, "Measuring the Cost of Bailouts," unpublished paper prepared for *Annual Review of Financial Economics*, February 2019, https://gcfp.mit.edu/wp-ontent/uploads/2019/02/BailoutsV12.pdf.
2. This summary overview is based on Federal Deposit Insurance Corporation (FDIC), "Chapter 4, The Savings and Loan Crisis and Its Relationship to Banking," https://www.fdic.gov/bank/historical/history/167_188.pdf.
3. FDIC, *Managing the Crisis: The FDIC and RTC Experience*, Chapters 1–4, https://www.fdic.gov/bank/historical/managing/documents/history-consolidated.pdf.
4. FDIC, "Chapter 4 . . . ," p. 187.
5. As quoted in Nicholas R. Lardy, "China and the Asian Contagion," *Foreign Affairs*, July/August 1998, https://www.foreignaffairs.com/articles/asia/1998-07-01/china-and-asian-contagion?utm_source=google&utm_medium=cpc&utm_campaign=gap_ds&gclid=Cj0KCQiAw9qOBhC-ARIsAG-rdn538TAvAqjsTexygGkpf0OX085YmzB6xpudV7VYhjNciG8mgGKKdSgaAtBnEALw_wcB.

6. Carl Walter and Fraser Howie, *Red Capitalism*, 2nd ed., Chapter 3.
7. Much of the comparisons in both *ex post* and fair value definitions for this approach and calculation of US crisis costs is based on Lucas, "Measuring the Cost of Bailouts." See also Timothy Curry and Lynn Shibut, "The Cost of the Savings and Loan Crisis: Truth and Consequences," FDIC Division of Research, https://docplayer.net/175350006-By-timothy-curry-and-lynn-shibut.html.
8. This number includes both credit and market risk weighted assets divided into the total spun-off asset number. The latter number is valued as if all the assets were credit weighted (100 percent) since market risk assets cannot be separated out. Consequently it is somewhat overweighted.
9. A shoutout here to Paul Schulte!
10. For full details on the Fed's balance sheet see Celia Bao et al., "The Federal Reserve System's Weekly Balance Sheet since 1914," *Studies in Applied Economics*, Johns Hopkins Institute of Applied Economics and Center for Financial Stability, 2019.
11. See Yue Dan, Department of Statistics, PBOC, "The Compilation and Analysis of Chinese Government Balance Sheet," presented to the Eighth IFC Conference on "Statistical implications of the new financial landscape," Basel, September 8–9 2016.
12. Lou, Jiwei, *Rethinking Intergovernmental Fiscal Relations in China* (中国政府间财政关系再思考) (北京, 中国财经出版社, 2013), p. 12.
13. The market value of the shares of all listed companies equals the market capitalization of a stock market. This analysis assumes that this figure for the Shanghai and portions of the Hong Kong exchanges represents the value of all *profitable* state enterprises. All other state enterprises not included are from the viewpoint of this analysis of no value, e.g., the SOE Group parent. Depending on market trends the value of market capitalization and therefore the value of state enterprises will increase and decrease. On the balance sheet, this is shown by increases in the value of shares and the value of assets.
14. See Appendix 2 for a review of other state balance sheet calculations by Chinese analysts.

Chapter 8

Japanese Bubbles

Before long we'll probably find a body of a China donkey
under the cliff.

—*Reflecting on Aesop, a Chinese professor, October 2018*[1]

With so much leverage already built into the system, a growing fiscal deficit, and inflating the problem away a no-starter,
what policy choices does Beijing have? Given the attitude
evinced by the official quoted at the head of Chapter 9, there is no need
for choice at all; standing pat on the structure of the current system is
enough. And perhaps the Chinese professor quoted above is correct. To
shed a bit more light on this problem this chapter examines the case
of Japan in the 1990s. Japan went through eight years of serial banking
crises exacerbated by the bursting of a massive real estate asset bubble.
Although their economies are quite different, Japan's experience shares

some important similarities with China and might suggest ways China could adopt to resolve its own problems. Added to shared problems now are the rapidly aging populations in both countries. The costs of an aging population will add significant pressures to both fiscal systems and, in China, will create fiscal deficits that current budgetary arrangements will not be able to support. With growing deficits and declining household deposits something will have to change.

Bubbles and Japan's Banking Crisis of the 1990s

In Japan, a banking crisis came first, and then the bubble burst, making the crisis far worse. But what dragged the crisis out was a basic misunderstanding of the financial system. The Japanese regulatory system for banks was based on what was called the "convoy" system. Regulators restricted lending levels by any individual bank, so that all banks in the system, especially the larger banks, would grow at the same rate, hence the "convoy" metaphor. Financial institutions, all in the private sector, included large banks, including three long-term credit banks, regional banks, city banks, and urban cooperative banks. The crisis also affected housing loan corporations and securities companies. In place since the end of the war, the convoy system had created the strong belief within society and among regulators that large bank failures were impossible. Since regulators treated all banks as being equal, the public also did not differentiate among them; as in China moral hazard pervaded the financial system. But the system had been successful in channeling social savings into the manufacturing sector and helped drive Japan's recovery from the war. Its very success deepened confidence. Does this story sound familiar?

Financial deregulation came to this static system. Begun in the mid-1970s and hastened by pressure for reform from the United States in the early 1980s, reforms created change that ground up against the convoy system. As corporations became used to relying on capital markets rather than banks for funding, banks gradually lost their old profit engines, yet deposits grew. As a result, banks went down market to middle-market companies making loans secured with land, and they soon also began lending to real estate developers. And in a sustained low-interest-rate environment they lent aggressively. Bank credit risk became highly real estate oriented.

To this was added a large dollop of hubris. The mid-1980s were the years Japan broke out into the international economy. The country was booming and confidence in its continued growth created a kind of "euphoria" that took hold of all economic participants from corporations to the central bank itself.[2] All this combined to create asset inflation and what a Bubble! Real estate values quadrupled in the five years between 1985 and 1990! The Imperial Palace sat on land worth more than the entire state of California! Who can forget the images of Japanese corporate executives and government officials as they strode across the face of American business scooping up trophy assets? For a brief time it seemed as if Japan had won the war. Then the bubble burst, real estate lost 80 percent of its value by 1999, and Japanese business sold US properties at a loss.

With collateral rapidly decreasing in value, the next few years saw Japan's banking system crumble. As usual, problems began at the periphery and moved toward the center. And because of the success of the convoy approach there was no formal mechanism to stabilize failed institutions. Japan's Deposit Insurance Corporation (JDIC) had both limited funds and limited powers to manage such situations. For the first failed credit cooperatives in 1994 regulators had little choice but to use a collective approach that involved convincing similar cooperatives to chip in for the common good. This worked for only as long as the healthier institutions saw resolving the failed institutions as of more value than shoring up their own weaknesses, and these were growing quickly. Regulators soon understood that an entity was needed that could absorb failed banks. As a result, one of the early failed banks (TKB) was recapitalized to be used as a "bad bank."

Finally in 1995 the losses of seven failed housing loan companies went beyond what sponsoring banks could sustain, and funds from the government budget were tapped. This was the first case in Japan in which taxpayers' money was used directly to deal with financial instability. Public reaction was immediate and uniformly negative, and so strong that it became impossible for the government to use its funds again to address bank problems. The government's sensitivity to public disapproval is obviously a major difference with the Chinese case.

214 THE RED DREAM

In mid-1996 the government passed measures to create a stronger JDIC. These increased payout amounts, raised insurance premiums, transformed TKB into the Resolution and Collection Corporation (RCC) and gave it greater powers. But even at this point, the regulators' main thinking remained on resolving the small-fry credit cooperatives; they could not foresee failures of larger banks. But this was soon to change.

In the fall of 1997 the crisis moved to core parts of the banking system, including one of the three long-term lenders and a major regional bank. The first was temporarily resolved by a collective bailout, and the second merged with another regional bank. These Band-Aids didn't work, and both failed soon after. Now regulators and politicians could clearly see it: the old convoy system had to be replaced with a legal and institutional framework that could resolve large banks. But there would not be time. Before year-end 1997, a series of banks and a securities house collapsed.

The securities company, Sanyo Securities, caused the biggest problem. Sanyo was a borrower in the interbank market and had been ordered by courts to suspend its business. Consequently, it defaulted on an unsecured short-term loan. This was the first default ever in Japan's money markets and market participants panicked, creating a major liquidity crisis that forced the Bank of Japan (BOJ), the central bank, to flood the market with funds. In short, a small securities company default had paralyzed Japan's interbank market.

Almost the same time Yamaichi, a far larger securities house, collapsed. The cause of its problems was the revelation of huge off-balance-sheet liabilities. Instead of suspending its operations, as was the case with Sanyo, regulators allowed Yamaichi to wind down its business. This was to avoid legal-induced defaults like the Sanyo case. But where was the funding for this to come from? Although the new resolution framework had been put in place mid-year, the JDIC was as yet unfunded to the needed level. BOJ again picked up the bill.

When in November 1997 a large regional bank failed, the series of failures in a single month had a huge psychological impact on market participants, regulators, and the public. Rumors now flew about which bank or banks would be next. They would not wait long. In 1998 the Long Term Credit Bank of Japan (LTCB) collapsed, the largest one yet with assets of US$240 billion. The safety net put in place in 1997 was far too small to deal with such a large bank. LTCB's failure forced the government to build a workable resolution structure, and two new laws were passed. The first made possible the nationalization of troubled banks. LTCB was accordingly nationalized, its management replaced, and its balance sheet cleaned up. The "new" bank was put up for auction in early 2000 and sold to a US investment fund. This brought in new money and offset the costs borne by the Bank of Japan.

The second law created a powerful Financial Reconstruction Commission under the Prime Minister's office. With funding of 60 trillion yen of public money, the commission had the power and funding to address financial major problems. It moved quickly to recapitalize 15 major banks and it encouraged the consolidation of the industry.

From 1999 on, Japan's financial system stabilized and the banking crisis appeared over. From 1992 to early 2000, there were 110 deposit-taking institutions that had failed and been resolved at an *ex post* cost of 86 trillion *yen* (US$830 billion) or 17 percent of Japan's GDP; NPLs had peaked at 6–8 percent of GDP.[3] These costs were largely borne by public funds. In contrast, the savings and loan and the mortgage financial crises in the United States had both amounted to only 4 percent of GDP. The China bank restructuring was similar to the Japanese case in that it had extended over nearly a decade and costs had grown to a whopping 44 percent of GDP. One important lesson of the Japan and China banking cases was the length of time required to reach a resolution of problems.

Why Did Resolving Japan's Banking Crisis Take So Long?

Why did the Japan and China cases take so long to be resolved? It took Japan eight years to get its banking crisis under control. A regulator commented that "the magnitude of the bubble and thus the resulting size of non-performing loans were so enormous that they were far beyond anybody's expectations at the time."[4] But this is just admitting the failure to see the problem. There were a number of other factors that slowed regulatory and political actions. These included the following:

1. The persistence of the "convoy" paradigm slowed the ability to take appropriate earlier actions.
2. The central bank early on feared triggering a financial crisis by openly calling for improved safety structures.
3. A lack of appropriate bank provisioning and public disclosure of risks obscured the problem.
4. Bank capital ratios, therefore, overstated actual bank health; in a low-interest-rate environment, there was no cost to carrying bad loans. Moreover, the markets had closed to banks seeking to raise capital.

In China's case, major work had been done in the early 1990s to establish a market-based financial system. Basic legal structures had been put in place in 1993, including a Central Bank Law, Commercial Bank Law, and Provisional Regulations on Financial Institutions. Moreover, three policy banks were created to take over policy loans from what would become the new commercial banks. Most importantly in 1993 international accounting standards replaced the old-style Soviet fund accounting. But these laws had little effect at the time, and the policy banks refused to take over the policy loans. It is obvious that strong political forces opposed such an approach.

The 1997 Asia Financial Crisis opened the way for reformers to move forward. The default by GITIC, China's largest provincial trust company, and a professionally managed bankruptcy process that revealed assets worth only 12 cents to the dollar (sic) opened Beijing's eyes to banking risk. Political obstacles were suppressed, and in 1999 four "bad banks" were set up, one for each of the major state banks. But from the start it was unclear how losses would be paid for. Would funds in the budget be available? They were not, so other ways were created to manage bad assets. Of course, 20 years later this question still hangs fire as the China Huarong case shows. As one senior PBOC official in 1999 commented, ". . . it may be necessary for the central government to use public funds to make some compensation; while, at present, the central government does not have such arrangements."[5] Things have yet to change.

Even more challenging to old ways of thinking, two major alterations in the party administrative system were made. In the first, the reporting lines of party secretaries in bank branches were centralized in 1997 under a committee housed in the PBOC. The state was taking over the party! And second, the PBOC withdrew its provincial offices and established nine regional offices. Both changes were designed to reduce local party interference in bank and central bank operations, and both made it possible to start to create banks as real national institutions.

The party even formally confirmed these paradigm shifts in 2003. Its approval established the foundation of a market-based financial system with banks and regulators as institutions impervious to local government interference. A new banking regulator was added in 2003, the China Banking Regulatory Commission, a ministry-level agency (also set up regionally). These, then, were the institutional structures on which the bank restructurings moved forward and which would address any future bank failures.

It wasn't enough. All this effort over many years failed to change the party's fundamental operating paradigm: as soon as it was faced with a crisis in late 2008, the party reverted to command and control. In Japan, the public sees tax funds as belonging to it; in China the party sees the same funds as belonging to it and not to the market. This fundamental difference between Japan and China makes it difficult to draw clear lessons for China from the Japanese experience.

It is not surprising then that it took a further decade before a deposit insurance scheme was put into place, but its emergency powers were limited and dependent upon approvals by the State Council.[6] The gaps in institutional structure, the lack of clarity for how losses would be covered, allowing the bad banks to become conglomerates and a weak deposit insurance system means that the party will of course handle any banking failure no matter how large on an *ad hoc*, piecemeal basis. And this is exactly what has been happening in the cases of small- and medium-sized banks and the Ministry of Finance's own China Huarong.[7] And any closure, almost unthinkable, will be approved by the party and paid for and carried out by the PBOC.[8] But without having a law in place approved by the National People's Congress, the losses of a failed bank will continue to be paid for in non-transparent ways with the PBOC as a backstop, just as Citic is managing the Huarong mess.

More Points of Comparison, China versus Japan

So finding lessons in the Japanese experience for China is difficult. Japan is a democracy with a market economy and its banks are part of the private sector, whereas China's banks are an arm of the Chinese Communist Party and controlled by the party using the public's money. But even so, there are similarities in the experience of the two countries. As the case study of its banking crisis suggested, the crisis presented Japan with the need to make a major paradigm shift in the way it oversaw its banking system. But it took eight years of increasingly serious bank failures to destroy this old way of thinking.

In China, the party or some of its leading members appear to have conflated its political ideology with the need for Soviet-style command banking. This explains why the original bank restructurings took so long, why anti-market forces emerged so quickly after the start of the 2008 crisis, and why the party has lent massive amounts of capital almost entirely to the state sector. The party seems to believe that its control over all aspects of the country's governance and over all its resources allows it to ignore the basic laws of finance and economics. As is certainly clear at present, China's governing party has yet to put this kind of thinking aside. Judging by the Japanese experience, it will take a major domestic crisis to accomplish such a change; the Asian financial crisis and even global financial crisis were neither of them strong enough.

A second common feature is that government balance sheets of the two countries are the largest in the world among major economies. Figure 8.1 compares the distribution of government assets and liabilities of the two countries by sector. In 2017, the last year IMF data was available for Japan, its government's *gross* public assets and liabilities for the public sector totaled 533 percent of GDP. Not to be outshone, China in the same year showed state sector assets at 710 percent of GDP and 700 percent in liabilities. In Japan's case, public sector net worth is a negative 165 percent of GDP as liabilities created by near-continuous injections of capital have overwhelmed assets. The country is bankrupt, except that the government can continue to create money. For China, there is still a positive book net worth on a gross basis of 10 percent. But on a *consolidated* basis, the Chinese asset balance sheet still remains far larger than

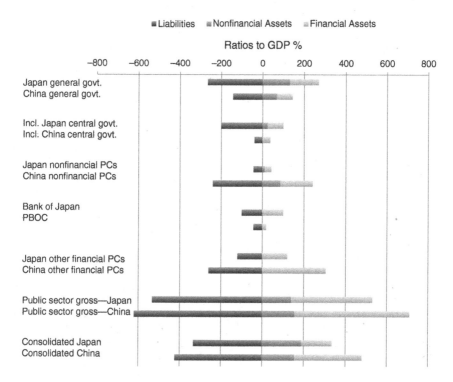

Figure 8.1 Public sector balance sheets, Japan, China, 2017.
SOURCE: Japan, Koshima (2019); China, author's calculations.
NOTE: PC indicates Public Corporations.

Japan's, at 455 percent vs. 333 percent of GDP, and its net worth is smaller at around 5 percent.

This figure illustrates the huge differences between the two state sectors and the two countries. The Chinese non-financial and financial sectors are far larger than those in Japan because the Chinese state owns them outright. This is where the Chinese Communist Party's governing paradigm crosses over into the real world; it owns the enterprises and banks because it thinks they strengthen party control.

It is hardly surprising that a third feature of both balance sheets is the predominance of cross-financing, where one entity of the public sector finances another and holds its debt. In Japan, even with consolidation such cross-holdings totaled 210 percent of GDP for 2017, of which public corporations—for example, Japan Post—held over half of government liabilities. In China the cross-holding level is 170 percent of GDP, of which banks hold state enterprise debt worth 50 percent of GDP; public corporations, including the central bank, insurance companies, and state banks, hold over 83 percent of central and local government debt. Mutual funds in China hold significant amounts of government debt.

It is not surprising, because the whole point of owning the banks is so the party can direct funds as it pleases to enterprises, projects, and other places. But is this a problem? In Japan the argument against cross-financing came down to two points. First, providing high levels of funding to other public corporations encourages inefficiencies and has resulted in across-the-board losses; and second, public corporations were acquiring government debt outside of the actual wholesale bond markets with internal amounts and interest rates set by the Ministry of Finance. In other words, there was a market used by non-government entities and one reserved only for the government. This lack of transparency ultimately led to unacceptably high levels of market volatility in the external bond markets.

Major structural reforms in 2000 broke down the wall between government and wholesale markets by cutting the links between government financing and public corporations. From that time on, the government transitioned to financing itself directly from the external market. This encouraged greater efficiencies, as higher market prices encouraged less borrowing. Public corporations including the post-office and social-security funds also became free to invest in non-government securities. These reforms merged the bond markets and led to the start of privatization of several public corporations including Japan Post.

China's debt market structure is similar to the old way in Japan. The central bank creates a managed yield curve and bonds are priced against it. This is just another way of saying the party sets the yield curve. There can be little trading, as discussed previously, meaning that the yield curve does not reflect market value. Government bonds, bank bonds, policy bank bonds, local government bonds, corporate bonds—none of these has a real market value. And since the government bond yield curve is indirectly the basis for pricing bank loans, interest rate reform, aimed at allowing a debt trading market to develop, threatens the value structure not just of all bonds but also all loans. This is where Japan's external market-priced debt market helped the transition. And this may suggest a possible solution for China. If it can gradually open certain parts of the bond market to market pricing, then it may open the way for a gradual transition toward real market-based prices.

Looking ahead, both Japan and China are faced with rapidly aging populations that will inevitably have a major impact on public finances. As populations age, expenditures on health and social security will increase as the tax base on a smaller working population shrinks. Japan's population peaked at 128 million in 2010; by 2060 it is projected to be only 87 million.[9] China's population is expected to peak at 1.45 billion in 2030 and in a recent study is projected to fall *by half* to 731 million by 2095.[10] This compares to a projection of 1.1 billion in 2100 made by the Population Division of the UN Department of Economic and Social Affairs.[11] Whichever projection is used, China is looking at losing somewhere between 335 and 714 million in population. These numbers are extremely hard to comprehend; the country as it has existed over the past 50 years will be changed in ways that cannot be imagined much less predicted.

Aging will cost a lot of public money. For Japan, the present value estimates made in 2014 of the costs associated with health and social security payments over the next 100 years total 654 percent of GDP. Of these costs, 436 percent will be covered by participants' contributions and 142 percent by budgetary transfers, with "other" contributing 76 percent.[12]

In China, the government has not established a centralized social security system;[13] the National Social Security Fund is designed only to offset deficiencies in local government funds. Calculation of the costs of medical and social security as has been done in Japan has either not been done or is not available for China. Ma Jun, the former Deutsche Bank China economist who joined PBOC in 2014, estimated fiscal expenditures using a bottom-up approach in 2011 for the years out to 2050, or halfway to the end of the demographic bulge.[14] His estimate of expenses to be paid by the national budget net of all medical insurance and social security contributions, calculated on a present value basis, was 27 percent of 2011 budgetary expenditures.

Although it may be true that Chinese standards of living are less than Japanese, this cost estimate feels seriously inadequate. It does not cover costs to be incurred after 2050 and its estimates of old age populations are low. Nonetheless, even at this level, the impact on the budget would make it extremely difficult for China to manage without massive changes to its current fiscal system designed to increase revenues dramatically or to shift expenditures away from some things. It may be that, at 24 percent of GDP, China's fiscal revenues have little more room to grow. And with GDP growth itself slowing, the problem looks even bigger. This is the major reason a rapid change of paradigm by Beijing is needed.

Comparative Cashflow Chains

While the 2000 reforms moved Japan's system of government finance toward a market basis, they did not change the country's deflationary economy. Although banks were stabilized, the country's long period of gradual deflation was just beginning.[15] The biggest macroeconomic problem in deflation is that the value of cash *increases* with the passage of time as the value of assets falls. This discourages companies from investing and households from spending. For consumers, it is better to wait now and purchase later when asset prices are lower. Moreover, by the late 1990s, Japanese corporations had begun to register financial surpluses, thus becoming net savers. If financing was needed, they could also access the domestic and international bond markets; banks were being disintermediated.

The government, hoping to kickstart economic growth in place of reluctant companies and consumers, began to issue huge amounts of government bonds (JGBs). These financed investment in public works and explain why the balance sheet in Figure 8.1 shows such a large general government sector for Japan, all those highways to nowhere. As for the banks they recorded strong growth in corporate and household deposits but had nowhere to lend; they had little choice but to invest in JGBs. In short, companies had surpluses, the government deficit grew, and banks invested in the deficit while consumers saved. This cash-flow chain runs entirely opposite to the 2000 public finance reforms that had been designed to promote economic growth. The past 30 years have seen the Bank of Japan trying to break this cash flow chain by ever greater lending; as the *Wall Street Journal* put it, Tokyo has become the "Frankenstein lab of quantitative easing."[16]

The Chinese situation was quite different. In China, the public sector relies on the liquidity created by the country's world-beating export economy dominated by private companies. Exports create foreign currency, which the central bank buys up, thereby boosting foreign reserves and money supply. Part of these export revenues go to household and corporate deposits, which the government channels to its own use. These include financing a huge state enterprise sector as well as both official and shadow budgetary spending in support of social services and infrastructure. Then, in late 2008, the party told the banks to lend, and they have been injecting cash into the economy ever since. The Chinese landscape was transformed in so many ways that it is unrecognizable. But as in Japan, all this money and massive infrastructure investment have begun to lead to deflation. In China, as shown in Figure 8.1, command lending has only led to a huge expansion of the state balance sheet, which in 2000 showed gross public debt of only 22 percent of GDP, and now 18 years later is a world-beating 710 percent. Assuming the export sector continues strong, new liquidity will be injected into the banking system making possible further balance-sheet expansion. But the party's intervention in the tech and real estate sectors combined with the evolving demographic problem have for now led to falling real estate prices and declining consumer spending while savings have increased.

How Might the Party Change Its Spots?

It is possible that the scale of the Chinese state sector and the failure of continued lending to ignite strong growth might prompt renewed pressures for financial reform. What would a Chinese reform look like? Figure 8.2 illustrates the major non-financial and financial parts of the Chinese state sector. The Ministry of Finance (MOF) through the China Investment Corporate (CIC) wholly owns Central Huijin, which is the principal aggregator and controlling shareholder of China's major state banks. The MOF does not, however, own outright China's major state enterprises. Rather, a non-government body, the State Administration for State Assets Commission (SASAC) was established to oversee their operations and, to a certain extent, appoint certain senior management, but it does not own the huge central enterprise groups either![17] In fact,

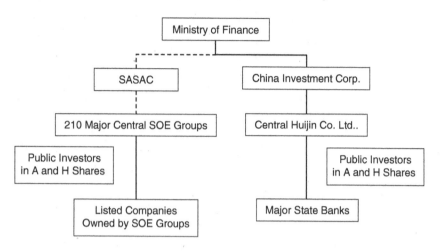

Figure 8.2   Nonfinancial and financial parts of China state sector.

there is no investment link between these groups and the state as represented by the sovereign, the Ministry of Finance. This link remains missing, although the banking reformers clearly understood its necessity by creating Central Huijin.

There are, however, cashflow links. The state banks pay dividends to their A and H share investors and to Central Huijin, which then channels the funds to CIC, and CIC then sends them to the MOF. But from the ownership angle, the major state enterprises present a far different story. The central SOE group companies are, in fact, the original state enterprises that existed prior to the corporatization reforms of the 1990s. These enterprises have never been incorporated and are not even systematically audited by professional accountants. Each enterprise group's realm includes dozens of related entities: police, courts, tourist bureaus, highways, bridges, uncountable automobiles and trucks and so on. Their scope reflects society as a whole, and so they are often known as a "small society" themselves. For obvious reasons, an entire group enterprise, unlikely to be at all profitable, cannot be listed on international stock markets (although such things have in later years been listed in Shanghai (整体上市).

If capital was to be raised on professional markets, collections of assets that could make up a profitable company had to be carved out of the group. After incorporation of these assets as a company limited by shares, the new entity's primary shareholder would inevitably be the related SOE company. When SASAC was established, it had not invested a single *fen* in any of the SOEs it was meant to oversee. When publicly listed and the enterprise paid dividends, SASAC got nothing; the dividends went to shareholders including the SOE Group parent. But neither did the MOF receive any dividend income! Early in the century, a struggle ensued. SOE Groups claimed that profits and dividends were compensation for the loss of critical assets, and moreover, they needed to support the countless state employees who had been left out. In short, the claim was that the group company was a social security scheme. But as Figure 8.3 shows, there is a good reason to fight. A large part of SOE profits, if paid into the national treasury, would offset the need to issue a significant part of new government debt. SOE profits would also fund a large part of government expenditures.

In this struggle for advantage, SASAC had no leg to stand on, because it was funded out of the national budget. However, the MOF certainly had a point, and so from 2011 the central SOE groups began to pay dividends, but these were tiny, in 2019 amounting to only 2.4 percent of

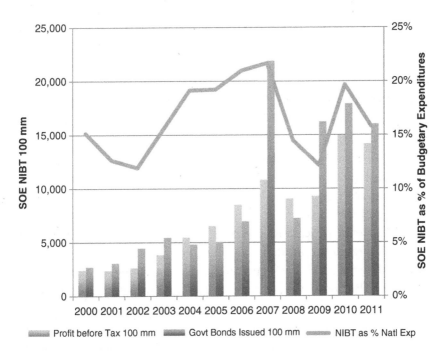

Figure 8.3   SOE profit before tax to government bonds issued, 2000–2011.
SOURCE: China Finance Almanac.

after-tax profits.[18] With a mounting budgetary deficit, which the IMF in 2018 set at more than 16 percent of GDP, growing is on for central SOEs to pay significantly more.

But the fight has already consumed over a decade at a huge forgone cost and resulted in a standstill; how can it be worth it? Even somewhat higher levels of dividends are not going to have a material effect on the state's massive debt. In contrast, letting most of these behemoths go would free up huge amounts of capital and would put an end to the political infighting between bureaucrats and enterprise managers. And it has been done before in the late 1990s when 25 million SOE retainers found themselves unemployed by the state. Why not consider keeping the major energy, railways, telecoms, and power companies and cut off the rest?

The Value of Chinese State Industrial Enterprise Assets

And why should Beijing hold onto all its central enterprises? Privatizing SOEs as a bloc would remove 200 percent of gross assets and liabilities, as well as 50 percent in bank lending, reducing China's state gross balance sheet to a mere 460 percent of GDP. Applying capital received from their sale could further reduce this figure or the capital could be used to top up social security funds. This section explores Beijing's collection of state enterprises to support this point.

It is well known that state enterprises are increasingly unimportant in driving China's economy forward. Estimations suggest that the share of state enterprises in China's GDP in 2018 was in the range of 23–39 percent, and their share in employment between 5 percent and 16 percent. State enterprises have become a minority player in their own country.[19] Figure 8.4 illustrates this decline in contribution to national industrial output.[20] The trend began to reverse itself slightly starting from 2009 amid the flood of loans channeled to and through state entities and, one suspects, private companies putting on "red hats." Even so, whether from contribution to output or to employment or to funding the state itself, state enterprises are not going to replace the non-state sector as the engine of China's economy.

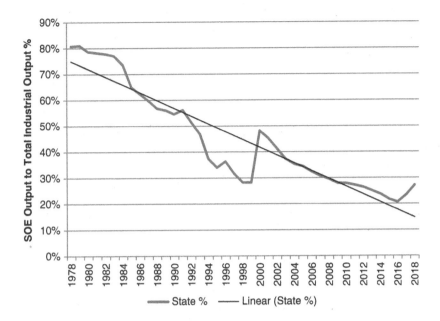

Figure 8.4   Trends in state enterprise contribution to industrial output, 1978–2018.
Source: *China Statistical Yearbook.*

In the early 1990s, state enterprises, even the larger ones, were extremely small; in a Western context they would have been considered middle market companies, defined as those with sales of US$1 million to US$1 billion. There were very few US$1 billion companies in China then. Beijing's experiment with raising capital on international stock exchanges from the late 1990s beginning with China Telecom in 1997 led to the creation of huge conglomerates, the "National Team," and the requisite bureaucratic structures.[21]

In 2006 certain central government agencies, such as the National Development and Reform Commission (NDRC), competed with SASAC to identify the critical sectors over which the state required "absolute controlling power." It was a fight for bureaucratic turf among agencies still deeply influenced by the Soviet paradigm of a modern economy. From these discussions arose the well-known "pillar industries" of the state; whether there are 7, 11, or 9 makes little difference. Table 8.1 lists the state's ownership in those industrial sectors that are consolidated in the MOF's almanac; the "pillar" industrial sectors are boldfaced.

Table 8.1 State contribution to industrial output, 2017.

	2017 State %
Tobacco manufacturing	99.4%
Extraction of oil and natural gas	*93.4%*
Production and supply of electric power and heat power	*91.5%*
Professional and support activities for mining	86.3%
Production and supply of water	72.8%
Mining and washing of coal	*66.9%*
Processing of oil and other fuels	*60.0%*
Production and supply of gas	*52.2%*
Mining and processing of nonferrous metals	49.5%
Manufacture of railway, ship, aerospace, and other transport equipment	*45.4%*
Mining and processing of ferrous metals	38.2%
Smelting and pressing of ferrous metals	37.0%
Smelting and pressing of nonferrous metals	*36.8%*
Manufacture of electrical machinery and apparatus	*36.5%*
National Average	**27.1%**
Manufacture of liquor, beverages and refined tea	22.8%
Manufacture of raw chemicals and chemical products	*21.1%*
Manufacture of automobiles	*16.9%*
Manufacture of chemical fibers	14.1%
Manufacture of general purpose machinery	11.8%
Manufacture of nonmetallic mineral products	11.8%
Manufacture of medicine	11.0%
Manufacture of computers, communication, and other electronic equipment	*10.3%*
Mining and processing of nonmetal ores	10.1%
Manufacture of measuring instruments and machinery	9.2%
Printing and reproduction of recording media	9.0%
Food manufacturing	7.1%
Manufacture of metal products	6.4%
Food processing from agricultural products	5.7%
Manufacture of rubber and plastics products	4.6%
Manufacture of paper and paper products	4.5%
Manufacture of articles for culture, education, arts and crafts, sports, and entertainment	4.2%
Manufacture of textiles	2.7%
Furniture manufacture	2.3%
Processing of timber, wood, bamboo, rattan, palm, and straw products	1.8%
Manufacture of textiles, clothing, and accessories	1.2%
Manufacture of leather, fur, feather, and related products and footwear	0.7%

SOURCE: *China Statistical Yearbook.*

Of these, only the oil, gas, coal, and electric power industries are majority owned and controlled by the state. Let the state keep these or whatever it feels key to state security.

Nicholas Lardy, in demonstrating the dominant position of the private sector, has done an excellent job of sorting out state and private assets and, therefore, the state assets.[22] The table does not seem to include the military or security sectors, at least directly. Nor does it include the infrastructure that has certainly facilitated GDP growth, but some of it may be included in the balance sheets of state enterprises. The aggregate value of military, security, and infrastructure assets, after subtracting related debt, may not change the state's balance sheet materially.

The European Chamber of Commerce in China in recent years has done two major reports on redundant industrial investment, the last one in 2015.[23] Industrial investment remains redundant because each provincial government wants to build up its own complete economy. Figure 8.5 shows the results for five major state industries for the years 2008, the first report, and 2014, the second. The data show that capacity utilization in two pillar industries, steel and refining, dropped by 10 percent or more and cement by 4 percent—this, during the six years that 100-story buildings were springing up in every provincial capital and the bullet trains were spreading everywhere! The report noted that the key factors to overcapacity included the fragmentation of industries driven by regional protectionism and a fiscal system that encourages local governments to attract excess investment. These conclusions are supported by the analysis in Chapter 2.

These tables and figures present a detailed snapshot of the state's industrial assets. They are, on the whole, a shrinking handful of oil companies, steel smelters, railways, telecoms networks, and coal mining operations. Compare these to the world-beating tech companies like Alibaba, TenCent, Didi Chuxing, TikTok, Meituan, and others that appeared from nowhere in the past 15 years. Notwithstanding the recent feats of the military and aerospace industries, state enterprises as a whole contribute a rapidly shrinking share to GDP growth, and their quality is declining. This is the party's contribution to China's economy.

Shrinking share, of course, leads to declining profitability. Finally, the nature of the Shanghai exchange itself may explain part of the reason that the value of state equity is depressed. Figure 8.6 shows the market's

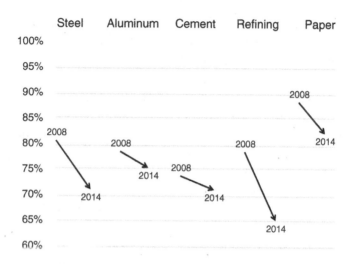

Figure 8.5   Trends in capacity utilization by industry.
SOURCE: European Chamber of Commerce in China, "Overcapacity in China," p. 3.

volatility meaning that share values can be exaggerated as well as under-valued without regard to the listed companies' profitability (or lack of it). Over the past 20 years there have been two major instances when the market has gone wild. The first over 2005 and 2006 was due to Beijing's deliberate policy of appreciating the *renminbi* against the US dollar, the second from 2013–2014 when margin trading was introduced. As the figure shows, the value of state shares and minority interest increased significantly during such periods. It is also unsurprising that there were so many IPOs of state enterprises during these times.

Figure 8.7 shows a similar picture by comparing the market value of state shares to the book value of state assets provided by the MOF. The figure shows the Ministry's book values always exceeding the market capitalization values, except in 2007 when *renminbi* appreciation against the dollar was expected by investors to go on forever. The book values of enterprises grew far more rapidly than the market recognized; this suggests that the market sees the state's investments as highly unattractive. But as market history has shown, markets can be manipulated and accounting values of state assets can, if desired, be brought into line with market values.

How should these state assets be sold? If the SOE is listed, then regulators should permit merger and acquisition transactions to take place; the stock markets have never been allowed to execute such

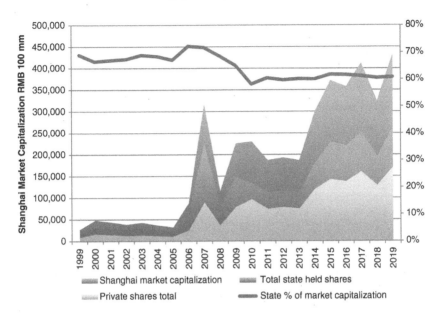

Figure 8.6   Shanghai market capitalization trends and share types,
1999–2019.
SOURCE: PBOC; author's calculations; post-2006 share reform numbers are based on assumption of
continued majority of shares held by state.

transactions in China. Second, regulators should permit the sale of
shares in listed SOEs at less than book price. Share prices at least provide a public valuation to the company through market capitalization.
If stock markets were allowed this role, it would generate huge enthusiasm and great levels of speculation, drive SOE values up, impact
global stock indexes, and maybe even catalyze a burst of economic
growth as happened in the early 1990s after Deng's remarks. If the
SOE is unlisted, then the asset exchanges that already exist throughout
China—with the principal one in Beijing—can handle ownership
transfer through public auction. China has the tools to make this work
and the signal it would send about China's intention to modernize its
economy and politics would be powerful.

   Who would buy state enterprises? If the bureaucracy stepped back,
there would be huge demand for all these assets. Whether insider, foreigner, or private sector boss, there would be plenty of interest because
buyers would see the economy opening up to all types of ownership.
A New China would emerge, still overseen by the party, but with a
booming industrial sector.

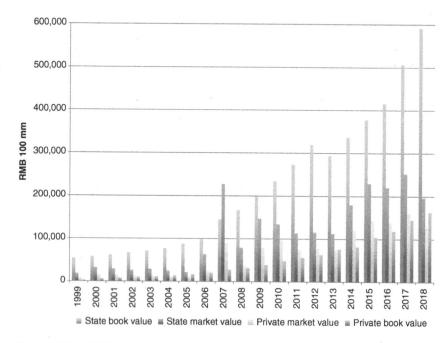

Figure 8.7   SOE book value versus market value, 1999–2019.
Source: MOF, PBOC.

Comments

If the comparisons with the United States and Japan demonstrate anything, it is that time is money. The reason why the original bank restructurings in China were so expensive was that it took a decade and costs
built up all along those years. Similarly for Japan, the eight long years
generated huge costs and led to an extraordinary period of deflation.
With a negative net worth of 165 percent of GDP in 2017, it is useless
to even calculate what deflation has cost Japan. The second thing these
cases suggest is the need to adapt to changing conditions. Japan took
eight years of pain to learn that its "convoy" paradigm was incorrect.

   As for China, the party took a decade to recapitalize its banks, after
recognizing their weakness was a threat. From 1989 to 2008 is 20 years.
These two decades saw the Chinese Communist Party abandon its her-
itage economic model for one that had been used by its supposed ene-
mies. But Deng Xiaoping was right. The success of the new model saved
the Chinese economy when the global financial crisis put a temporary
halt to its export-driven growth. How quickly party leaders chose to

ignore the lessons of even recent history! Now, with even more dogmatic leadership, China has recreated a bloated state sector and a shadow banking system that reeks of fossilized thinking but allows party leaders to gloat over the sound performance of its state banks. This paradigm is not a source of national security. Where is the off-ramp? It may only be found when the next crisis appears and forces a deep change that one hopes will be without too much damage.

Notes

1. *New York Times*, October 8, 2018, p. A12.
2. Shigenori Shiratsuka, "The Asset Price Bubble in Japan in the 1980s: Lessons for Financial and Macroeconomic Stability," paper prepared for IMF-BIS conference on Real Estate Indicators and Financial Stability, October 27–8 2003, *BIS Paper No. 21*, Bank of International Settlements, https://www.bis.org/publ/bppdf/bispap21e.pdf.
3. Hiroshi Nakaso, Chief, Monetary and Economic Department, Bank of Japan, "The Financial Crisis in Japan during the 1990s: How the Bank of Japan Responded and the Lessons Learned, October 2001," *BIS Paper No. 6*, p. 1. Nakaso provides a detailed picture of Japan's banking crisis.
4. Ibid., p. 17.
5. Xie Ping, "Bank Restructuring in China," Bank Restructuring in Practice, *BIS Policy Paper No. 6*, August 1999, p. 128. Xie was then head of the PBOC's Financial Stability Department.
6. Article 19.4, 中国存款保险条例 (China deposit insurance regulations), https://www.tspweb.com/key/存款保险条例施行细则.
7. Liu, Shiyu, "China's Experience in Small and Medium Financial Institution Resolution," October 31, 1999, *BIS Policy Paper No. 7*, pp. 298 ff, https://www.bis.org/publ/plcy07t.pdf. Liu was a vice-governor of the PBOC.
8. Zhu, Jun, "Closure of Financial Institutions in China," October 31, 1999, *BIS Policy Paper No. 7*, pp. 304 ff, https://www.bis.org/publ/plcy07.htm.
9. Noriko Tsuya, Keio University, "The Impact of Population Decline in Japan," Suntory Foundation Research Report, https://www.suntory.com/sfnd/jgc/forum/005/pdf/005_tsuya.pdf.
10. Stein E. Vollset et al., "Fertility, Mortality, Migration, and Population Scenarios for 195 Countries and Territories from 2017 to 2100," *The Lancet*, October 17, 2020, https://www.thelancet.com/journals/lancet/issue/vol396no10258/PIIS0140-6736(20)X0042-0. For a Chinese demographer's analysis that also suggests a 700 million decline in population see Wang, Feng, "The future of a demographic overachiever: long term implications of the demographic transition in China," Population and Development Review 37 (supplement), pp. 173–190 (2011).

11. Population Division, Department of Economic and Social Affairs of the UN Secretariat, "Probabilistic Projections Based on World Population Prospects 2019," August 2019, https://population.un.org/wpp/Download/Probabilistic/ Population/.
12. Yugo Koshima, "Japan's Public Sector Balance Sheet," IMF Working Paper, October 2019, p. 28. Koshima's paper is priceless and shows the policy implications of having a state sector balance sheet.
13. An excellent description of and commentary on China's medical and social security systems is China Labor Bulletin, "China's Social Security System," August 18, 2021, https://clb.org.hk/content/china%E2%80%99s-social-security-system.
14. Ma, Jun, *A Study of China's National Balance Sheet* (中国国际资产负债表研究) (北京, 社会科学文选, 2012), pp. 280–291.
15. This analysis is that of Haruhiko Kuroda, Governor, Bank of Japan, "The Battle against Deflation: The Evolution of Monetary Policy and Japan's Experience," speech at Columbia University, April 13, 2016, Bank of Japan, https://www .boj.or.jp/en/announcements/press/koen_2016/ko160414a.htm/.
16. Editorial, "Tokyo's Yield Curve Defense," *Wall Street Journal*, February 14, 2022, https://www.wsj.com/articles/tokyos-yield-curve-control-defense-bank-of-japan-interest-rates-11644866423. To gain an appreciation of what "quantitative easing" really does to an economy, see Christopher Leonard, *The Lords of Easy Money: How the Federal Reserve Broke the American Economy* (New York: Simon & Schuster, 2022).
17. For the history see Walter and Howie, *Red Capitalism* (2010), p. 143.
18. Yang, Zhiyang, *30 Years of China Fiscal Reforms* (中国财政制度改革30年), (上海, 上海人民出版社, 2008)), pp. 156 ff. Of course, SASAC's leadership tried to expand its role; see Wang Jun, "Company Profile: A New Manager for State Assets," *Beijing Review*, January 13, 2011, http://www.bjreview.com/print/txt/2011-01/10/content_323988.htm.
19. Chunlin Zhang, "How Much Do State-Owned Enterprises Contribute to China's GDP and Employment?" Working Paper, World Bank Group, July 15, 2019, https://openknowledge.worldbank.org/handle/10986/32306; Carsten A. Holz, "The Unfinished Business of State-Owned Enterprise Reform in the People's Republic of China," December 2, 1018, https://carstenholz.people.ust.hk/CarstenHolz-PRC-SOEreforms-2Dec2018.pdf.
20. Lardy provides a detailed explanation of the data behind this chart. See Nicholas Lardy, *Markets before Mao: The Rise of Private Business in China* (Washington, DC: Petersen Institute for International Economics, 2014), pp. 72–76.
21. For background on this, see Walter and Howie, *Red Capitalism*, Chapter 7.
22. Lardy, *Markets before Mao*, pp. 54 ff and 75 ff. See also Lardy, The State Strikes Back, pp. 133 ff. for his comments on state assets and their value.
23. European Chamber of Commerce in China, "Overcapacity in China," 2016, p. 3, https://www.europeanchamber.com.cn/en/press-releases/2423/european_chamber_releases_new_major_report_on_overcapacity_in_china.

Chapter 9

Chinese Balloons

The system is built so that it cannot fail.

—*Chinese official, September 2013*

It's been a long road to this point and it may help to go back to see just how it led here. The original question that catalyzed these pages was about the Chinese fiscal system. It was not about new or old taxes, but about how money flowed within the state. This quickly led to local governments, how they financed themselves and where they got their funding. Local governments mean not just the local administration, but also all the enterprises and financial institutions in their jurisdictions, state or not. Beijing deliberately underfunds their budgets, encouraging their continued self-reliance. When property development became a big thing 20 years ago, financing it also became big business; it was not just Evergrande or Country Garden that borrowed, local governments did too. And so did all their suppliers, trucking companies, and so on. It was a big combined and coordinated operation that contributed, according to some analysts, almost 30 percent of China's GDP.

So where did the money come from? In China there can only be one place: ultimately it comes from banks. So where did the banks get the funding to make more and more loans as their balance sheets grew up to Heaven? They got it because the party opened the country to foreign investment and the country's economic model became export oriented. More exports equals more corporate and household deposits. Then the party responded to the global financial crisis by telling the banks to lend it all and liquidity poured out mostly into the government sector. All state entities worked hard to put this money to use, and China's appearance changed. And the banks, by any measure, grew huge: in 2020 nearly 3.5 times the country's GDP. And they grew fast.

How could their performance metrics looks so strong? There can be only one answer to that: they spun off unwanted assets. The party in Beijing worked with regulators to develop channels and products that would take the assets away. Asset management companies were not enough. This shadow banking system grew very large, but it was also not enough. So clever ways were developed to manipulate accounting principles to manage down bank "risk-weighted assets." These banks are, after all, Global Systemically Important Banks.

How did all this liquidity and investment activity impact the government sector? The only way to tell would be if the government produced a consolidated balance sheet including local governments, banks, and enterprises, and lending to the private sector. Despite a lot of research by the PBOC and other Chinese analysts around 2014, the government apparently chose not to publicly present such a balance sheet. But the IMF does for other countries and it gives guidance on how a balance sheet should be put together. So a rough one for China showing the decades between 1978 and 2018 was created using official numbers. Its scale after 2008 became huge, but still felt more or less accurate. The picture it paints is of the party's profligate use of other people's capital.

Comparisons between how China and the United States managed two financial crises were made to confirm the overall scale of waste. For the United States, the costs of the savings and loan crisis of the 1980s and the mortgage crisis from 2008 were compared. From a purely cost perspective, United States management surprisingly proved quite efficient; in both cases, costs came in at around 4 percent of GDP. The Congressional Office of the Budget provided these cost figures so they should be accurate as far as they go. For China—using figures shown elsewhere in this book—the costs of the bank restructuring from 1997 and the deleveraging campaign from 2016 were also quite similar, but they were very high, over 40 percent of GDP. This again suggests poor management and supports conclusions about the state balance sheet's scale.

What can China do to substantially reduce the financial risk it has built up? Would the Japanese experience of a banking crisis combined with the collapse of an asset bubble provide suggestions? The two economies are very different, one state-owned and the other based on markets, but there are suggestions that come out of a brief examination. The first relates to how the Japanese government's eyes were blinded by an outdated regulatory system. They believed that an old system protected Japan's big banks from collapse. It took eight years of increasingly large bank defaults to demolish this belief and compel effective action. In Japan, waste of time, as bureaucrats and politicians argued, led to the expansion of the crisis. This sounds similar to many aspects of the Chinese experience.

This is the lesson that is perhaps the most important for China: old ways of thinking need to be responsive to the times. The recapitalization of its main banks required the party to reject Soviet-style economic arrangements that the Soviet Union's collapse had fully discredited anyway. And they *did reject* this past history and ideology as they proceeded to build out their own version of capitalist markets. This is what enabled the party to respond effectively to the 2008 financial crisis, saving the country enormous difficulties. But then they almost immediately disavowed that experience and the work of 20 years and took China back to a command-style economy.

Almost equally important is that both Japan and China are facing huge demographic challenges as their populations begin to rapidly age. The Japanese government has prepared for the associated costs by building adequate social security funds, but it again took many years to arrive at a realistic estimate. China has not done enough. Demographic projections suggest that by 2100 its population will be reduced from between 330 and 760 million people. The costs will be huge. How will the party address the medical and living needs for these people when the only way it responds now is by city-wide lockdowns? Above all, the party needs to recognize that pay-as-you-go will not work. China's budgetary revenue is insufficient even now and it will soon no longer be able to count on banks to lend endlessly: their deposits will be shrinking. The party must throw away old fossilized thinking once and for all. Then it must find the assets that throw off enough cash to support Chinese parents and grandparents as they age. Can the party respond to this challenge?

The Party's Ruling Paradigm

All of this raises many more questions than might be addressed here. But what if the state sold most of its enterprises? If the state makes investments in enterprises only to provide employment and social security, then Zhu Rongji has already demonstrated that this is unnecessary by closing down or selling state enterprises in the late 1990s. That left 25 million looking for jobs, but their children found them in the private sector. The small SOEs Zhu turned over to the workers (民营化) quickly turned into the export dynamos of today on the east coast of China. If the party is afraid of social instability, there was none in the 1990s; consider what might happen later on as the aging process gathers way.

The private sector has long since proven it can employ more and pay more plus make a profit as well. Why then does the party cling to its enterprises? Does the party think it makes the nation or the party itself stronger? Does the very idea of "amalgamation" of the state with the private economy make any sense? The time for Soviet-style industrialization is long gone, replaced by the service sector and technology. Or is it a matter of power or history—Lenin did it; so should we? If it is simply power, then control of the disciplinary commission and police provides plenty of coercion, but a stronger economy with an effort to fund social security will provide far greater political support. As for Lenin, does he matter? Well, it turns out that he does because his is the very paradigm the party lives by: a "socialist market economy" overseen and controlled by the party. Lenin has to go.

It can be argued that the party owns whatever it says it owns, *viz.* Ant Financial, Didi Chuxing, and all the private data it and other tech companies have accumulated. It has always been difficult to actually identify the boundaries between the state and non-state sectors, particularly *non-state* because as events have shown there is no truly private sector in China. The Emperor decides exactly what he owns when he wants to. However, the Emperor's own assets are out of fashion, polluting, and uncompetitive. And the world-beating innovators that he is seizing, he is in the process of destroying. So cut these old assets away and support, not take over with ill-trained party cadres, the new ones!

Can the state make use of all the data the tech companies are passing on? There is a reason why workers in fintech want to "lie down (摊平)," their work is not easy. Are there staff in the PBOC or in the banks willing to work as hard to integrate the different systems of Alibaba, Tencent, Ant and others? Can state institutions pay the salaries and benefits required by other staff that can do such work? Different kinds of staff. Consider the result had the party oriented the economy toward technology and less toward real estate and traditional industry far sooner than it has done. How many Foxconns and Taiwan Semiconductor Manufacturing Companies (TSMCs)—global leaders built up by one small *province*!—would there have been then? And would the value of the country's social welfare funds be so opaque and inadequate?

Chinese Balloons

Chinese officials have spoken with great certainty about their system's strength (at least in public), as if they really believe that the party can control all risk. Other officials have explained how this system was designed to work using a metaphor about balloons. The party controls the system, which is, it seems, like a giant balloon. Not my metaphor. This large balloon must never be allowed to explode; if it does, the party is lost and, so it believes, the country is lost along with it. Consequently, the party has arranged things so that the large balloon contains many, many small balloons. If some of these pop, the party can rush in and easily extinguish risks so that the stability of the large balloon itself will not be seriously impacted. This is the party's version of Japan's convoy system.

This metaphor of balloons accurately describes events in 2021. The failure of small banks on the periphery of China's financial system mirrors the start of Japan's banking crisis. As in Japan, China handled each of the failed entities with custom solutions by introducing a managing bank or new shareholders. Then a major crisis at the very core of the system broke out when China Huarong, a universal financial institution with nearly US$300 billion in total assets, was unable to submit its audited financials to the Hong Kong Stock Exchange. This was an institution majority owned and presumably controlled by China's Ministry of Finance! Huarong was semi-sovereign.

The resolution of the Huarong problem was not simple; the MOF could not just write a check to cover Huarong's problems. Aside from the recapitalizations of three of the four state banks, public funds in China have not been used to resolve financial crises. This would require the not-so-rubberstamp National People's Congress to approve. And the party appears not to want to expand any discussions about the financial system's vulnerability. Even putting in place an institutional framework, as has Japan, would seem unthinkable and, anyway, the AMCs already show that this approach is not reliable. How then can banks assemble a resolution plan? It would call the party's ability to control events into question. Because of all this, the bureaucratic struggle over who would resolve Huarong took months until finally someone was found to take its problems on. Public funds were not used at all. This doesn't mean that Huarong's problems have been resolved, far from it! It simply means that the MOF is no longer primarily responsible and the work-out can be handled with no public scrutiny. No matter, the costs associated with Huarong's resolution will add to the state's overall debt and, kicked down the road as it will be, the costs will multiply.

The party is obviously aware that such problems will crop up in future, but seeks to keep them small and isolated by moving fast and with full strength when one breaks out. This kind of strategy is easy to see in Beijing's handling of the series of small bank failures in 2020. It can also be seen in its "zero tolerance Covid" policy of today. By spreading out and pushing financial assets down deep into the system, Beijing has increased the number of smaller asset holders. At the same time it has done everything possible to strengthen the major state banks. Let the small local banks fail; just protect the core of the system. Japan did not find this approach to be effective. As China's state debt continues to grow, will the balloon system work when it is called upon?

What might be indicators of systemic distress in China? The lack of new liquidity would bring the big balloon under stress. Now exports, the private sector's profitability, the people's savings and the PBOC's slow feeding of deposit reserves into banks are the factors that keep the balloon inflated. But things change. Ill-considered foreign alliances might impact exports, old people will draw down their savings, and the end of deposit reserves is in sight, then what? The balloon would begin to sag. Could foreign reserves be used to keep it firm? Will the People's Bank begin real quantitative easing by buying up troubled securities out there in the system? Will the party begin to privatize its state enterprises or sell its banks? These are some of the indicators of trouble. But the history of Chinese crisis management suggests that any solution will be long in arriving and weigh heavily on the national economy.

Convergence Revisited

Now, three decades have passed since Deng's Southern Excursion in 1992. They have witnessed the Chinese Communist Party adopt two starkly different approaches to the modernization of China. The first was itself a reversal of the policies and experience of the years since 1957; the old ideas were tossed out but too slowly. In the 1980s it entailed the party and its state bureaucracy tinkering with the old system; in June 1989, if nothing else, society reached the conclusion that such an approach simply did not work. From the time of Deng's trip south to the bankruptcy of Lehman Brothers in September 2008 the party eliminated much of the old Soviet-inspired bureaucracy and embarked on economic modernization at the hands of markets it loosely supervised. As for the party itself, it had been gradually stepping back from direct engagement with social and economic life since the mid-1990s. China's entrance into the WTO sped up these trends and the country prospered perhaps as it never had before. This was economic modernization by excluding politics and the bureaucracy, and it had splendid results.

Even a rough balance sheet of the state sector shows that during those years Beijing continued to channel the vast bulk of the country's resources to state enterprises and other agencies. Highly self-reliant local governments sustained social stability by scrabbling up money from all possible sources to fill budgetary gaps and build out infrastructure. These actions by the party never produced efficient financial results, but profitability has never been its objective. The National Champions that have been created by Wall Street and listed on international stock exchanges may show good performance metrics, but these champions are just a part of larger groups that, if consolidated group financial statements were made, would show their true nature as simply poorly performing SOEs. The publicly listed profitable parts simply support the part hidden in the state's shadows.

At the local levels, self-reliance rules as party officials seek out financial resources so they can fill budgetary gaps and build roads, airports, and new cities. Their ultimate objective is a strong GDP number created by any kind of economic activity that employs the populace so there is no social unrest. Banks, trust companies, state and private enterprises organized by local party committees work together as a team to achieve these goals. If, once completed, the airports, trains, roads, and new cities briefly enhance economic value, this is an unexpected plus. The far more likely outcome is that these assets all too soon won't be needed while they have been contributed to the state's overall debt and on balance not a *fen* to its net worth.

This story is repeated at the central level driven by a party that cannot hold itself accountable. When China joined the WTO, the floodgates of international capital opened and the eastern coastal provinces prospered as never before in Chinese history. This prosperity was by design channeled into banking deposits that funded China's leap from a has-been country to the second strongest in the world. Its banks and enterprises dominate the heights of the *Fortune* 500.

The sources of China's growth have now become clear. These include a financial system saturated with dubious assets at every level, vastly underfunded healthcare and pension systems, a real estate sector with 64 million empty apartments, a bullet train system that cannot cease laying track and an overly leveraged state balance sheet that exposes the country, the party, and the world to credit and market risks that the state itself cannot absorb. All the while the political sphere is fragmented by a personal crusade to establish one-man control in the guise of a campaign to eliminate corruption in the party. This is modernization by the Mao Zedong School of political campaigns.

China's coastal provinces became modern with bustling economies and a middle class of well over 300 million people because the party and its bureaucracy stepped back two steps and opened the country up to the world. And the world over has now become dependent on the manufacturing prowess of the country's private sector. But a revivified traditional bureaucracy and party organization, driven by fear of the almighty Disciplinary Commission, on the one hand, and a virus on the other has closed the country off, damaged the most advanced parts of the private sector, destroyed Hong Kong, and allowed financial risks in the system to build.

Political campaigns amid excess financial leverage, mispriced financial assets, and a growing lack of liquidity due to the inevitability of demography surely make it difficult for China's central government leaders to see the risks, just as it was for leaders in the United States and Japan, but for far different reasons. The anti-corruption campaign has blinded and paralyzed the bureaucracy and the majority of the party from identifying problems and taking action. The one man who clearly saw the problems in financial "trees" has even been forced to make a self-criticism.

China may have the tools and the political capacity to manage the state's massive leverage, but the party must resolutely break the bonds of its deeply embedded political beliefs so it can recognize constraints. It cannot continue to do all things at once; some actions will have to be forgone. Can the party really afford to cushion the real estate sector's contraction? Is the Belt and Road strategy with its huge expenditures in developing countries supportable? Is the country's military buildup sustainable? And how to ease off from the "limitless" friendship with Russia? As for the majority of local governments located deep inside China, their bankrupt condition and the reluctance of Beijing to take decisive action suggests that their "independent kingdoms" will continue to be littered with unfinished housing and vanity projects for a long time to come; these local governments are on their own. And the party has not even started to think seriously about the costs of its looming demographic crisis. With the clearest of vision shared by few, the picture of China's financial landscape seen in 2016 by the "Authorized Person" is hardly the China Dream presented to the country and the world in 2012, it is the Red Dream.

Appendices

Appendix 1: Estimated China Government–Only Debt Obligations, 2009, 2015–2019

Note	RMB bn	FY09A	FY15A	FY16A	FY17A	2018A	2019A
	GDP	33,535	67,671	74,412	82,712	86,989	98,140
	Central obligations to GDP	40.9%	39.8%	40.8%	40.6%	42.4%	41.6%
	Local obligations to GDP	28.9%	30.5%	35.9%	62.3%	66.2%	73.8%
	LGFP/Gov't Guided Funds to GDP	2.7%	18.9%	30.0%	36.9%	42.2%	43.3%
	NPL to GDP	8.9%	14.9%	17.4%	20.5%	21.2%	19.6%
	Total	**79%**	**85%**	**94%**	**123%**	**130%**	**135%**
	A) Central Government Obligations						
1	a.Central Government bonds including savings bonds	5,541	10,150	11,468	12,901	14,361	16,105

Note	*RMB bn*	FY09A	FY15A	FY16A	FY17A	2018A	2019A
2	b. MOF special bonds, receivables and AMC bonds	808	700	796	791	786	802
3	c. MOF assumed local government debt	200	0	0	0	0	0
4	d. CIC MOF 1998 + 2007 Special Bonds	1,820	1,820	1,820	1,820	1,820	1,820
5	e. Policy Bank bonds	4,450	10,996	12,395	13,454	14,517	15,725
6	h. Ministry of Railways/Huijin	396	1,233	1,341	1,480	1,615	1,673
7	i. Big 4 Bank bonds	486	2,009	2,522	3,143	3,806	4,696
	Sub-total: Central Obligations	**13,701**	**26,908**	**30,345**	**33,589**	**36,905**	**40,821**
	B) Local Government Obligations						
8	a. Outstanding local debt less bonds	7,800	10,301	5,993	3,754	1,283	1,703
9	b. Net out 50% CDB policy bank bond o/s	−1,600	−3,300	−3,541	−3,770	−4,074	−4,352
10	c. Local government bonds	−200	4,456	9,363	12,756	15,327	21,118
11	d. LGFP/Gov't Guided Funds	NA	12,771	22,320	30,557	36,750	42,502
12	d. Local contingent obligations = 50% of total debt	3,900	7,379	7,678	8,255	8,305	11,411
13	e. MOF assumes local debt	−200	0	0	0	0	0
	Sub-Total: Local Obligations	**9,700**	**31,607**	**41,813**	**51,552**	**57,591**	**72,382**
	Sub-Total: Local + Central Obligations	**23,401**	**47,534**	**57,049**	**85,141**	**94,496**	**1,13,203**
	C) Non -performing Assets						
14	a. Central asset management companies' obligations	90	2,016	3,475	4,652	4,869	4,954

Note	RMB bn	FY09A	FY15A	FY16A	FY17A	2018A	2019A
15	b. 7% NPL rate on non-local corporate loans	2,406	4,814	5,213	5,671	6,232	6,767
16	c. Existing bank NPLs	504	1,274	1,515	1,697	2,032	2,414
17	d. Total non-standard wealth management products	0	3,713	5,084	4,786	5,081	5,081
18	e. Asset-backed securities times 15%	0	80	86	131	222	296
	Sub-Total: NPLs	**3,000**	**10,060**	**12,951**	**16,937**	**18,436**	**19,216**
	Total Public Debt Obligations	**26,401**	**57,594**	**70,000**	**1,02,078**	**1,12,932**	**1,32,419**
	Public Debt to GDP	**79%**	**85%**	**94%**	**123%**	**130%**	**135%**

SOURCES: (1) China Bond; (2) state bank audited financial statements; (3) assumption; (4) Red Capitalism pp. 148 ff; (5–7) China Bond; (8) Table 5.3; (9) assumes CDB finances local projects; (10) China Bond; (11) IMF estimates in PRC Article IV Consultation, various years; (12) assumption; (13) assumption; (14) Huarong, Cinda audit statements times two; (15) assumption; (16) CBIRC; (17) China Wealth Management Report, various; (18) China Bond, assumption.

Appendix 2: The State Sector Balance Sheet

In 2015 PBOC analysts led by Yue Dan presented an excellent though too brief paper at an IMF conference providing three versions of a consolidated Chinese state balance sheet for the years 2010–2014. Their work provided pictures of all three IMF-based definitions, narrow, broad and public. Table A2.2 includes their work compared to similar IMF data for a few Western countries and Japan. The author's versions are also included for comparison. The IMF Countries are shown only in the "broad" definition mentioned earlier, as is China in 2010 and 2014. In the Broad definition, all government enterprises and banks were excluded while the Public definition includes them.

Two other works have also explored China's state balance sheet. Li Yang and others at the Chinese Academy of Social Sciences have provided two works in this regard. It is unfortunate that they have not provided a consolidated state balance sheet, instead showing central and local government balance sheets separately. Presented this way, it is impossible to create a single government balance sheet using their data (which is largely unsourced) given the large amount of intragovernment transactions that must first be canceled out in any consolidation. This approach is not helpful in any analysis of the state's overall financial condition that seeks to arrive at policy suggestions.

Ma Jun, a very sophisticated economist, formerly Deutsche Bank's specialist for China, and now at the PBOC, has taken a similar approach. These books were all written during the 2011–2014 period, the same time as the two PBOC authors presented their IMF paper. It is to be hoped that this complex project has not been dropped.

The author collected data only from almanacs and printed materials. For materials from Chinese government databases such as ChinaBond,

Table A2.1   Summary balance sheet of the Chinese state sector, 1978–2018.

RMB 100 mm	1978	1990	2000	2008	2010	2018
Financial Assets	4,729	28,930	175,095	485,414	831,799	1,930,225
Non-financial Assets	4,794	18,738	100,639	740,938	774,595	2,024,629
including:						
Fixed Assets adjusted for market	3,364	12,917	74,664	272,253	468,397	828,054
Inventory	1,430	5,821	22,275	57,788	106,325	415,854
Non-productive Assets	0	0	3,700	410,897	199,873	780,721
Total Assets	**9,523**	**47,793**	**275,734**	**1,226,352**	**1,606,394**	**3,954,854**
Financial Liabilities	5,731	37,932	215,499	1,047,728	1,263,414	3,501,780
Total Liabilities	**5,731**	**37,932**	**215,499**	**1,047,728**	**1,263,414**	**3,501,780**
Net Worth	**3,792**	**9,861**	**60,234**	**178,624**	**342,979**	**453,074**
of which:						
Minority Interest	0	0	28,231	99,715	209,322	256,967
State Net Worth	3,792	9,861	32,003	78,909	133,657	196,107
Note:						
Net Financial Assets (Liabilities)	-1,002	-9,002	-40,404	-562,314	-431,615	-1,571,555

NOTE: The 39.5 trillion *yuan* figure for total 2018 assets compares favorably to the 47.4 trillion *yuan* figure published by *Caixin* in 2018. See "China Reports $67 Trillion in State Assets," October 24, 2019, https://www.caixinglobal.com/2019-10-24/china-reports-67-trillion-book-of-state-assets-101474684.html. The *Caixin* figure, quoted from a report made by the State Council to the National People's Congress, may include military and other assets the information for which is not publicly available. The author's balance sheet also does not separately include land or mineral rights since they are not commercially sold and so cannot be valued. To the extent they are valued these values are included in the assets of state enterprises.

SOURCES: 1: *China Banking Almanac;* 2: 1949–2005 China Financial Statistics; 2010-2018, PBOC, Sources and Uses of Credit funds; 3: *China Finance Almanac;* 4: PBOC, *Financial Stability Report;* 5: State Administration of Foreign Exchange; 6: China Securities Central Depository Corp. Author's summary and judgments.

Table A2.2   Comparative government sector balance sheets.

US$ bn	Financial Assets	Non-financial Assets	Liabilities	Net Worth	Of which Net Worth: State	Of which Minority Investors
Broad Definition						
Germany 2014	1,091	0	2,449	-1,336		
Norway 2014	8,885	0	1,058	7,830		
United Kingdom 2014	593	0	2,030	-1,438		
United States 2014	1,883	3,244	16,836	-11,709		
Japan 2010	6,060	9,709	15,158	-9,098		
Japan 2014	6,868	8,293	15,081	-8,213		
Japan 2016	7,261	8,142	15,695	-8,435		
2010 China – PBOC	3,818	10,136	2,939	11,015		
2014 China – PBOC	6,731	14,428	5,330	15,829		
Public Definition						
2010 China – PBOC	14,621	15,985	18,061	12,545	?	?
2010 China – Walter	12,603	11,736	19,142	5,197	2,026	3,172
2014 China – PBOC	28,132	27,794	37,601	18,325	?	?
2014 China – Walter	27,607	13,676	34,259	7,024	2,894	4,135
2018 China – Walter	47,150	22,774	62,956	6,968	3,012	3,947

SOURCE: IMF for OECD countries, Japan and the US; BIS for China PBOC paper, and author.

249

PBOC, CBIRC, SAFE and similar government agencies the pages used were saved or printed out. The concern is that online Chinese data can be easily changed. For these reasons, it was difficult to gather all more recent data that would have made a 2019 or later balance sheet possible. A full explanation of how the author assembled the balance sheets is available on request.

Selected Bibliography

Websites

Bank for International Settlements, www.bis.org
Caixin, www.caixin.com.cn
China Banking and Insurance Regulatory Commission, www.cbirc.com.cn
China Bond, www.chinabond.com.cn
China Investment Fund Association, www.amac.org.cn
China Wealth Management Association, www.chinawealth.com.con
Federal Reserve Bank, www.federalreserve.com
China Trustee Association, www.xtxh.net
Home of Internet Lending, www.wdzj.com
Hong Kong Stock Exchange, www.hkex.com.hk
International Monetary Fund, www.imf.org
Ministry of Finance, www.mof.gov.cn
People's Bank of China, www.pbc.gov.cn
State Administration for Foreign Exchange, www.safe.gov.cn
The Wire, www.thewirechina.com
Wind, www.wind.com.cn

Publications

Almanacs

China Ministry of Land and Resources, China Land and Resources Almanac (中国国土资源年间), annual (Beijing, Dida Caiyin Co., Ltd.).

International Monetary Fund, "People's Republic of China Article IV Consultation, annual, imf.org.

Ministry of Finance, China Finance Almanac (中国财政年鉴), annual (Beijing: Finance and Economics Press).

Treasury Department, Ministry of Finance, Local finance statistical materials (地方财政统计资料) annual (Beijing: Finance and Economics Press).

People's Bank of China, China Banking Almanac (中国金融年鉴), annual (Beijing: China Banking Press).

People's Bank of China, Financial Stability Report (中国金融稳定报告), annual, www.pbc.gov.cn.

Shanghai Finance and Economics University, China Fiscal Development Report (中国财政发展报告), annual (Shanghai: Shanghai Finance and Economics Press).

State Statistical Bureau, China Statistical Yearbook (中国统计年鉴), annual (Beijing: China Statistics Press).

Su Ning, Chief Editor, 1949-2005 China Financial Statistics (1949–2005 中国金融统计), two volumes (Beijing: China Banking Press, 2007).

Books, Articles, and Monographs

Bao, Celia et al., "The Federal Reserve System's weekly balance sheet since 1914," Studies in Applied Economics, Johns Hopkins Institute of Applied Economics and Center for Financial Stability, 2019.

Chen, Weidong and Yuan, Xiaohui, "Financial inclusion in China: an overview," *Frontiers of Business Research in China*, no. 4 (2021), https://doi.org/10.1186/s11782-021-00098-6.

Chen, Yuantung, "Current problems and reforms of China's financial system," *US-China Business Review* 2, no. 1 (2001).

Chong, En-bai et al., "The long shadow of fiscal expansion," Working Paper 22801, National Bureau of Economic Research, http://www.nber.org/papers/w22801.

Chung, Jae Ho, "Beijing confronting the provinces," *China Information* 9, nos. 2/3 (Winter 1995).

Country Analyst Unit, "Shadow banking in China: expanding scale, evolving structure," Asia Focus, Federal Reserve Bank of San Fransisco, April 2013.

Dikotter, Frank, *The Age of Openness* (Berkeley: the University of California Press, 2008).

Donnithorne, Audrey, "China's cellular economy," *China Quarterly*, no. 52 (October–December 1972).

Faure, David, *China and Capitalism: A History of Business Enterprise in Modern China* (Hong Kong: Hong Kong University Press, 2006).

Federal Deposit Insurance Corporation, "Chapter 4, The Savings and loan crisis and its relationship to banking," https://www.fdic.gov/bank/historical/history/167_188.pdf.

Federal Deposit Insurance Corporation, "Managing the Crisis: the FDIC and RTC Experience," Chapters 1–4, https://www.fdic.gov/bank/historical/managing/documents/history-consolidated.pdf.

Feuerwerker, Albert, "The Chinese Economy, 1912–1949" (Ann Arbor: Michigan Papers in China Studies, No. 1, 1968).

He, Qing and Li, Xiaoyang, "The failure of Chinese peer-to-peer lending platforms: finance and politics," *Journal of Corporate Finance* 66 (February 2021).

Holz, Carsten A., "The Unfinished Business of State-owned Enterprise Reform in the People's Republic of China," *Journal of Economic Literature* (December 2, 2018).

Holz, Carsten A., "Economic reforms and state sector bankruptcy in China," *China Quarterly*, June 2001, pp. 342–367.

Huang, Ray, *Taxation and Government Finance in Sixteenth Century Ming China* (London: Cambridge University Press, 1974)

Huang, Tianlei, "Tracking China's debt-to-equity program," Peterson Institute, June 2019, https://www.piie.com/blogs/china-economic-watch/tracking-chinas-debt-equity-swap-program-great-cry-and-little-wool.

IMF, Government Finance Statistics Manual (2014), https://www.imf.org/external/Pubs/FT/GFS/Manual/2014/gfsfinal.pdf.

Jin, Jing and Zou, Heng-fu, "Soft-budget constraints on local government in China," World Bank Papers, http://www1.worldbank.org/publicsector/decentralization/cd/china.pdf.

Koshima, Yugo, "Japan's public sector balance sheet," IMF Working Paper, October 2019.

Kuroda, Haruhiko, Governor, Bank of Japan, "The battle against deflation: the evolution of monetary policy and Japan's experience," speech at Columbia University, April 13, 2016, Bank of Japan, https://www.boj.or.jp/en/announcements/press/koen_2016/ko160414a.htm.

Lam, Raphael and Wang, Jingsen, "China's local government bond market," International Monetary Fund Working Paper, WP/18/219.

Lardy, Nicholas R., *Markets before Mao: the rise of private business in China* (Washington DC: Petersen Institute for International Economics, 2014).

Lardy, Nicholas R., The State Strikes Back: the end of economic reform in China? (Washington, DC: Petersen Institute for International Economics, 2019).

Lardy, Nicholas R., "China and the Asian Contagion," *Foreign Affairs*, July/August 1998, https://www.foreignaffairs.com/articles/asia/1998-07-01/china-and-asian-contagion?utm_source=google&utm_medium=cpc&utm_campaign=gap_ds&gclid=Cj0KCQiAw9qOBhC-ARIsAG-rdn538TAvAqjsTexygGkpf0OX085YmzB6xpudV7VYhjNciG8mgGKKdSgaAtBnEALw_wcB.

Leonard, Christopher, *The Lords of Easy Money: How the Federal Reserve Broke the American Economy* (New York: Simon & Schuster, 2022).

Li, Yang et al., 2013 China's National Balance Sheet (2013 中国国家资产负债表) (北京, 中国社会科学唇舌, 2013).

Liu, Defu et al., The complete volumes on party secretary work in the banking system under a vertical leadership structure (垂直领导体制下金融系统党委书记工作全书), two volumes (Beijing: Dangdai Zhongguo Press, 1999).

Liu, Shiyu, "China's experience in small and medium financial institution resolution," *BIS Policy Paper No. 7*, October 31, 1999, https://www.bis.org/publ/plcy07.htm.

Lou, Jiwei, "Rethinking intergovernmental fiscal relations in China" (中国政府间财政关系再思考) (北京, 中国财经出版社, 2013).

Lucas, Deborah, "Measuring the cost of bailouts," unpublished paper prepared for *Annual Review of Financial Economics*, February 2019, https://gcfp.mit.edu/wp-content/uploads/2019/02/BailoutsV12.pdf.

Ma, Jack, "Bund speech," https://interconnected.blog/jack-ma-bund-finance-summit-speech.

Ma Jun, *A Study of China's National Balance Sheet* (中国国际资产负债表研究) (北京, 社会科学文选, 2012).

Mann, Jim, *Beijing Jeep: The Short, Unhappy Romance of American Business in China* (New York: Simon & Schuster, 1989).

McGregor, Richard, *The Party: The Secret World of China's Communist Rulers* (New York: Harper Perennial, 2012).

Nakaso, Hiroshi, "The financial crisis in Japan during the 1990s: how the Bank of Japan responded and the lessons learned, October 2001," *BIS Paper No. 6*.

Paulson, Jr., Henry M., *Dealing with China* (New York: Hachette Books, 2015).

Rogoff, Kenneth, and Yang, Yuanchen, "Has China's housing production peaked?" *China and the World Economy* 21, no. 1 (2021): 1–31, https://scholar.harvard.edu/rogoff/publications/peak-china-housing.

Sanderson, Henry, and Forsythe, Michael, *China's Superbank* (Singapore: Bloomberg Press, 2013).

Segal, Gerald, "Does China matter?," *Foreign Affairs*, September–October 1999.

Shiratsuka, Shigenori, "The asset price bubble in Japan in the 1980s: lessons for financial and macroeconomic stability," paper prepared for IMF-BIS conference on Real Estate Indicators and Financial Stability, October 27–28, 2003, *BIS Paper No. 21*, *Bank of International Settlements*, https://www.bis.org/publ/bppdf/bispap21e.pdf.

Stigum, Marcia, *The Money Market* (New York: Dow Jones-Irwin, 1983).

Tsuya, Noriko, "The impact of population decline in Japan," Suntory Foundation Research Report, ttps://www.suntory.com/sfnd/jgc/forum/005/pdf/005_tsuya.pdf.

Vollset, Stein E. et al., "Fertility, mortality, migration, and population scenarios for 195 countries and territories from 2017 to 2100," *The Lancet*, October 17, 2020, https://www.thelancet.com/journals/lancet/issue/vol396no10258/PIIS0140-6736(20)X0042-0.

Walter, Carl, "Convergence and Reversion," *Journal of Applied Corporate Finance* 32, no. 4.

Walter, Carl, "Was Deng Xiaping right? An overview of China's equity markets," *Journal of Applied Corporate Finance, University of Rochester Simon Business School* 26, no. 3 (Summer 2014).

Walter, Carl, and Howie, Fraser, *Privatizing China* (Singapore: John Wiley & Sons, 2005).

Walter, Carl, and Howie, Fraser, *Red Capitalism*, 2nd ed., (Singapore: John Wiley & Sons, 2010).

Wang, Feng, "The future of a demographic overachiever" long-term implications of the demographic transition in China, Population and Development Review 37 (supplement) 2011: pp. 173–190.

Wang, Shaoguang, "The rise of the regions: fiscal reform and the decline of central state capacity in China," in Andrew G. Walder, ed., *The Waning of the Communist State* (Berkeley: University of California Press, 1995).

Wong, Christine P.W., "Rebuilding government for the 21st century: can China incrementally reform the public sector?," *China Quarterly*, no. 200 (December 2009).

Wong, Christine, "The fiscal stimulus program and public governance issues in China," *OECD Journal on Budgeting*, vol. 11/3, 2011, http://dx.doi.org/10.1787/budget-11-5kg3nhljqrjl.

Wong, Christine, "China: public investment under reform and decentralization," World Bank Country Case Study, 2014.

Wong, Christine, "Plus ça change: three decades of fiscal policy and central-local relations in China," Working Paper WP22CW1, National University of Singapore, Lincoln Land Institute, June 2021.

Wright, Logan, and Rosen, Daniel, "Credit and Credibility: risks to China's economic resilience," Center for Strategic and International Studies, October 2018.

Xie Ping, "Bank restructuring in China," Bank Restructuring in Practice, *BIS Policy Paper No. 6*, August 1999.

Yang, Zhiyang, 30 years of China Fiscal Reforms (中国财政制度改革30年), (上海, 上海人民出版社, 2008).

Yue Dan, Department of Statistics, PBOC, "The compilation and analysis of Chinese government balance sheet," presented to the Eight IFC Conference on "Statistical implications of the new financial landscape," Basel, Switzerland, September 8–9, 2016.

Zhang, Chunlin, 2019, "How Much Do State-Owned Enterprises Contribute to China's GDP and Employment?," World Bank, Washington, DC. © World Bank. https://openknowledge.worldbank.org/handle/10986/32306 License: CC BY 3.0 IGO.

Zhang, Le-Yin, "Chinese central-provincial fiscal relationships, budgetary decline and the impact of the 1994 fiscal reform: an evaluation," *China Quarterly,* March 1, 1999.

Zhang, Longmei et al., "China's high savings: drivers, prospects and policies," IMF Working Paper, WP/18/277, December 2018.

Zhang, Yuanyan Sophia, and Barnett, Steven, "Fiscal vulnerabilities and risks from local government finance in China," IMF Working Paper, WP14/4, January 2014.

Zhu Jun, "Closure of financial institutions in China," October 31, 1999, *BIS Policy Paper No.* 7, pp. 304 ff, https://www.bis.org/publ/plcy07.htm.

Index

260 INDEX